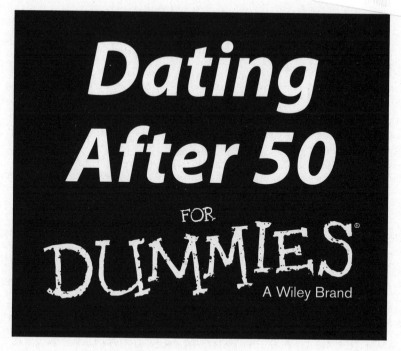

Dating
After 50
FOR
DUMMIES®
A Wiley Brand

by Pepper Schwartz, PhD

Dating After 50 For Dummies®

Published by: **John Wiley & Sons, Inc.,** 111 River Street, Hoboken, NJ 07030-5774, www.wiley.com

For general information on our other products and services, please contact our Customer Care Department within the U.S. at 877-762-2974, outside the U.S. at 317-572-3993, or fax 317-572-4002. For technical support, please visit www.wiley.com/techsupport.

Wiley publishes in a variety of print and electronic formats and by print-on-demand. Some material included with standard print versions of this book may not be included in e-books or in print-on-demand. If this book refers to media such as a CD or DVD that is not included in the version you purchased, you may download this material at http://booksupport.wiley.com. For more information about Wiley products, visit www.wiley.com.

This and other AARP books are available in print and e-formats at AARP's online bookstore, www.aarp.org/bookstore, and through local and online bookstores.

Library of Congress Control Number: 2013952428

ISBN 978-1-118-44132-9 (pbk); ISBN 978-1-118-46094-8 (ebk); ISBN 978-1-118-46095-5 (ebk)

Manufactured in the United States of America

10 9 8 7 6 5 4 3 2 1

Contents at a Gl

Table of Contents

· ·

Introduction

· ·

Some things about dating never change, no matter how old you are: You have to figure out who to look for, where to look, and how to recognize this person when you meet him or her. You have to protect yourself and listen to your inner warning bells if they go off. And you may have to navigate the tricky territory of a sexual relationship.

But dating after age 50 brings its own unique challenges and benefits. The dating world and the ways to find a soul mate have changed since you last tested the waters. For example, you need to think about who you want now as opposed to who you needed or desired when you were younger. The days of bars and dances are pretty far behind you, so you're left to find new ways and new places to look for dates — through friends, acquaintances, singles clubs, new hobbies, or online. And finally, sex is really important in a relationship no matter what age you are because pleasure and intimacy always make a relationship more intimate emotionally and physically. But if you haven't been sexual in a long time, you need to know what expectations are like these days when dating. For example, you may be unsure of how to talk about important topics such as sexually transmitted diseases, physical disabilities, performance issues, and monogamy.

Put simply, now that you're past 50, dating is a different experience than it was when you were in your 20s or even your 30s. You've changed, the culture has changed, and who you're looking for is likely to be quite different as well. The important thing to remember is that you can be successful. You can have many great experiences along the way to finding someone wonderful. Try not to be intimidated in the beginning, even though it's perfectly understandable to feel that way. It may seem overwhelming when you first go online, join a singles group, or get fixed up, but you'll soon rediscover old skills or learn new ones. Think of it as an adventure and you may be surprised to find out that you like the journey as well as the destination.

Sure, you may face some setbacks along the way, and you may have to revise your approach to dating a few times. But if you keep at it, you'll learn new things, grow as a person, and be likely to find not only a date but a precious and passionate love. I'm not exaggerating at all. If you think that passion and deep love are things of the past, think again. Countless people express with delight how falling in love again has been no less wonderful or intense than it ever was. Get ready for a great payoff for the energy, time, and good attitude that you bring to this new phase of your life.

About This Book

Dating After 50 For Dummies is written expressly for mature adults who are either reentering the dating world after a long absence or have been doing it for a while, unsuccessfully.

This book is a guide to dating over age 50; it's full of information about how to find a date, begin a date, secure someone's affections, and create a successful dating relationship. Though I wrote this book with people over 50 in mind, it contains information that applies to people far younger. But the book takes note of the special conditions of being a baby boomer — or beyond. For example:

- ✔ The possibility of having been in a long-term marriage or relationship until recently
- ✔ The possibility that you haven't dated in 20 to 50 years
- ✔ The challenges of coming to dating with adult children and a complex family network from a previous relationship
- ✔ Fears about safety, especially with the new Internet technology for dating
- ✔ Issues about changes in health and appearance

You may have experienced significant changes in your life that have brought you back into the dating game, such as the loss of a beloved spouse, the breakup of a long term marriage or cohabitation, a change in looks or health since the last time you were "on the market," or simply a loss of confidence since the last time you practiced flirting. You may have married young, changed sexual orientation, or been through a series of relationships that never quite made it to commitment. This book aims to change your insecurities to confidence and your almosts to solid, happy relationships. Five insecurities that I address and help you overcome are:

- ✔ You're too old.
- ✔ You aren't attractive enough.
- ✔ You'll never find someone really first-rate out there.
- ✔ You don't know how to choose someone great.
- ✔ You'll fail because you'll say or do the wrong thing.

These aren't unreasonable insecurities; you're a mature individual and you've been informed by a lot of past experience. But the past is the past, and you should always face the future with optimism, especially because you'll have new information and a guide to help you along the way this time.

Though the whole book is useful, each chapter stands alone and doesn't need the previous or following ones to be understood or used. Think of *Dating After 50 For Dummies* as a reference book that you can dip into when you have specific questions about getting started or are entering a new phase of a relationship and want to know a bit more about something that didn't concern you up to that point. You're not required to have any sort of cumulative memory (this is especially reassuring to those whose memory is increasingly challenging!).

I've included the occasional sidebar, which may have a story about dating that illustrates a specific discussion or some additional information you may or may not be interested in. Sidebars are considered to be optional reading, so don't feel compelled to read every one of them unless you just can't help but devour each and every word in this book!

Within this book, you may note that some web addresses break across two lines of text. If you're reading this book in print and want to visit one of these web pages, simply key in the web address exactly as it's noted in the text, pretending as though the line break doesn't exist. If you're reading this as an e-book, you have it easy — just click the web address to be taken directly to the web page.

Foolish Assumptions

Some people who reenter the dating market have had some discouraging experiences early on. They feel like they're sinking in a sea of misunderstandings, awkward introductions, and incredible mismatches. Just the fear of these kinds of experiences happening can paralyze people and stop them from pursuing dates. So sometimes for some people, dating comes to a screeching halt before anything even happens.

In writing this book, I made the following general assumptions about who might be reading it. If any of these statements ring true for you, you're in the right place:

- ✔ You feel like you're floundering in the dating marketplace or you're too nervous to even begin.

- ✔ You've tried dating, met the wrong people, and got depressed or frightened, or you were ignored by the people you approached.

    ✔ You feel you don't know how to present yourself, much less manage a date.

    ✔ You were once a successful dater, but that was 30 years ago or more, and to say you're just feeling rusty would be a vast understatement.

The discussions in this book pertain to everyone, but not everyone reading them will come from the same emotional place or personal history. Using too much diversity in terms bogs down a book, so I use some shorthand terms. Because most people who read this book have been married, I use *marriage* as a convenient term for any long-term, committed relationship — a loving partnership that has intertwined finances, living spaces, future plans, health-care, taxes, and so on. I recognize, however, that people can make a deep commitment outside of matrimony.

Also, I use male and female pronouns for most of the discussion, but I think almost everything in the book is applicable regardless of whether you're in a couple that's heterosexual or same-sex. Chapter 16 discusses issues that may only or more greatly affect gays and lesbians who are living together or are married.

Icons Used in This Book

Although I think every word of this book is as valuable as the one before, some information is especially important. Because I don't want you to miss this information, it's marked with an icon.

This icon notes something you can do to activate an important goal of dating. This is usually a very concrete suggestion to help you take action.

Information marked with this icon underscores something about dating that you always need to keep in mind.

This icon indicates safety-related information or a caution about certain kinds of people or behavior. Though dating is generally safe, there are some odd or unbalanced people in the world, and you want to know how to avoid them or, having met them, how not to put yourself in a dangerous or embarrassing situation.

Beyond the Book

In addition to all the advice and anecdotes you can find in the book you're reading right now, this product also comes with some access-anywhere goodies on the web. Check out the eCheat Sheet at www.dummies.com/cheatsheet/datingafter50 for helpful insights and pointers on writing a stellar online dating profile, planning affordable but still enjoyable dates, and your first sexual experience together. You can also discover ten ways to feel sexier at www.dummies.com/extras/datingafter50.

Where to Go from Here

You have to get started! No more foot dragging or hand wringing — there's no time like the present for beginning this new phase of your life. Yes, dating after 50 isn't all that easy, but most worthwhile ventures take some energy, heart, and a learning curve to get where you want to go. If you can make a commitment to at least start reading the chapters that interest you most, you've entered into a new state of consciousness about yourself and your future. You don't have to do everything at once. You can start reading, stop, and wait — but by all means, eventually pick up the book again and put it into practice. After you feel more confident about yourself, what to do, and where to go, you may surprise yourself and find that dating after 50 is a whole lot more fun than dating was when you were younger!

If you're looking for a good place to start, I recommend the chapters in Part I for a little self-reflection and to prepare yourself for the adventure ahead. If your head's in the game but you don't know where to turn to meet people, dive into Part II. For sensitive matters like sex and money (though not together!), Part III is the place to be.

Part I
Getting Started with Dating After 50

In this part...

✔ Find out how to get psychologically prepared for dating. Your success depends on how motivated and self-confident you are, but most people don't get there automatically. Examine your fears and hopes, and brush up on some skills.

✔ Make sure that you're over your ex, even if parting was painful. Whether you are a widow or a divorcé or ended a long-term relationship, you need to have your mind open and ready for someone new.

✔ Identify your core requirements for deep and permanent love as well as optional criteria for people you're interested in dating. You can't reach a destination unless you've picked one out, and you can't meet the man or woman of your dreams if you don't know what could make them so.

✔ Separate the person you used to be from the person you are now by letting go of assumptions and dating criteria that you settled on when you were 25.

✔ Take a long look at yourself and be honest about updates that you can make to your appearance to bring your best self to the dating world. You may need to work out, shop for new clothes, or try an updated haircut. It's amazing how much better you feel and how much more attractively you come across as a human being when you feel good about yourself.

Chapter 1

Jumping (Back) into the Dating Pool

- -

In This Chapter

▶ Evaluating the state of your mind and body

▶ Knowing the best places to find dates

▶ Keeping safety in mind

▶ Saying and doing the right things in a relationship's early stages

▶ Talking about sex and money

*W*hen you haven't dated for a long time, dating again may seem so daunting that you don't want to approach the subject, much less start the process. But sooner or later, you feel a change in the way you think about various activities and daily life, and you know you'd like companionship or maybe a life partner. You also know that just waiting for the right person to show up hasn't been a successful strategy. At some point you realize that you need to tackle what it means to date again, and you start thinking about who you're looking for, where to look for potential dates, and what you have to do to prep yourself for dating.

Dating takes some rethinking of how you use your time and how you want to present yourself. Quite frankly, if you haven't dated recently, the rules of the road have changed, and you need some time to learn what they are. This book is meant to be a guide to dating — from renovating your dating skills and intuition to figuring out online dating to meeting people in new places. I also cover safety, which was probably not so important when you were in high school but is terribly important when you start meeting new people at this stage of your life.

Dating can be a lot of fun, and it's definitely a growth experience. Yes, it has its down moments and frustrations, but the upside is terrific. You can have a great romance, meet interesting people, learn a lot about yourself, and widen your horizons. Dating after age 50 (or at any age!) is worth the effort.

Getting Real: How Do You Feel about Yourself?

As you take on dating after some time out of the game, you need to evaluate your state of mind and body. I suggest that you work through some checklists to evaluate the emotional and physical state you're in now. This is ground zero because if you don't feel good about yourself, you'll transmit that feeling to everyone you meet, and it will undermine the possibilities that may have been there if you had come across as a self-confident person who is living a fulfilled life. You need to make sure that you can feel good about yourself before you even get fixed up, go online, or join a singles group.

Your psychological checklist

Chapter 2 contains some tools to help you review your state of mind, but in general, you have to attend to the following main aspects of your emotions:

- ✔ **Let go of past failures or frustrations and assume you can do better.** You also need to let go of the hold on your soul that people you've loved or lived with still have. Your past relationship may have left you with shrapnel in your heart or a beloved spouse may have died and left you sad and lonely. Life deals people grave losses and traumas, and no one, least of all this author, minimizes these losses. The challenge is to put them in a place that allows you to approach someone new full of optimism and energy for exploring a relationship. If you're not in emotional shape to do that, you have to work on your emotions until you're ready to open up to someone new.

- ✔ **Get to a good place regarding your feelings about yourself.** You're older now and no longer have the face or shape of a 25-year-old. Of course, you know that rationally, but you have to find a way to feel good about who you are now. If you don't like the way you look, you can either do something about it (exercise, lose weight, and so on) or accept the belief that you're worth knowing — and desiring — just the way you are.

- ✔ **Surround yourself with people who are supportive of your new quest for love.** If your children are unsupportive, tell them to get over their qualms and think about your needs as an individual. Hang out with friends who are happy for you and who send you back into the search for love if you start to back off. Everyone needs support, and you need to be willing to look for it and avoid naysayers.

- ✔ **Think about who you're looking for and why.** You have much to consider now that you're not building a family with someone or just starting out in life. Chapter 3 has a list of core characteristics that are important to consider for potential dates, but you need to take into account some differences at this stage of life. You may want to think more out of the box now that you aren't picking the father or mother of your children. The person who was right for you in your 20s or 30s may not be a good fit in your 50s. On the other hand, you may still need someone who shares your values and fits into the culture of your family and friends. The bottom line is, before you go out again looking for love, you may want to revisit your romantic criteria.

Your physical checklist

You may be "camera ready" — or not. It's easy to get sloppy about your looks if no one is admiring you. Sometimes it's the little things people forget about (like clean nails!) that no one brings to their attention; others may look at those seemingly small imperfections, though, and make assumptions. Going out again requires giving yourself an honest once-over — or asking a supportive friend to do it for you. For example:

- ✔ **Hairstyle:** Has yours been the same for the last 20 years? Maybe that's not a good thing. Even men sometimes need a more stylish cut. Hair should look clean, neatly kept, and at the very least, not immediately aversive. And guys, most women find those comb-overs to hide bald or thinly covered areas unattractive. Consider an alternative.

- ✔ **Clothes:** Clothes need to be clean and unrumpled. Wear something that doesn't look like you slept in it or used it for a tablecloth. If you look like a mess when you meet someone, the person may never take the time to find out you can generally put yourself together very well.

- ✔ **Hygiene:** Examine your fingernails, your breath, your body odor, and whether your hair looks dirty or greasy. It may be the end of the day, but you still need to look and smell fresh when you're meeting a date. For some people, something as seemingly trivial as dirty nails can be a deal breaker.

- ✔ **Weight:** Let's face it: It's a weight-conscious world. That doesn't mean that no one will want you if you're heavy, but it does mean that getting dates is easier if your weight reflects overall good health. Dating is a good motivator for setting up a healthy eating and exercise plan, which is invigorating, helps boost self-respect, and has health benefits. But don't hesitate to begin dating just because you're not at your best weight. Lots of people are in the same boat you're in, looking for someone to love, and many will accept you just the way you are.

It's not all about looks in the dating world, but your first interaction with someone is heavily influenced by appearances, so you need to pay attention to what you wear and your physical presence.

Looking in All the Right Places: Where to Find People

Dating for people over 50 used to be difficult. After you asked everyone you knew to fix you up, you still didn't have a clear path. These days, however, because of longer and healthier lives, cultural shifts, and online dating, meeting people isn't so difficult (although meeting the right person always takes a bit of time and resilience!). Chapter 5 gives you some clear directions about places that offer good possibilities to meet good people, but it all comes down to the five options I discuss in the following sections.

Events targeted at single people

Most cities have events that are specifically organized for single people. The nice part of these events or outings is that you're going to something you'd enjoy anyhow. It may be a bicycle trip, a wine tasting, a white-water rafting trip, or a series on foreign films, but the idea is that everyone who attends has a common interest, so you'll have something to talk about when you meet someone who interests you. At the very worst, you'll make new friends.

Public places

As you go about your day, you're constantly thrown together with new people, and some will be single and interesting. The hard part is getting to meet them because the only thing you have in common, to begin with, is being in the same place at the same time. That's why when you're at a grocery store or post office, or at the train station or an airport, you have to keep your eyes peeled. Consider all these places an opportunity, but you have to look for it and seize the moment by being inquisitive, friendly, and approachable (or approaching!).

Online dating

Online dating isn't for everyone, but it's where the people are. Millions of them, in fact. And the fastest-growing group among them is people over 50. That's why Chapter 6 is full of specifics about how to date online, because honestly, the choices are vast, and the chances of meeting someone you'd never meet any other way are high. Furthermore, online dating is the only way you can preselect a large pool of possible dates according to age, interests, and values. It's also the best place to go in terms of selecting people who are obviously interested in dating and available for a relationship (apart from the occasional jerk who's really married, but those people are the exception to the rule).

In Chapter 6 I go into detail about how to write profiles, select quality people, and learn the art of 20-minute coffee introductions. I don't call them *dates;* instead, these are really *auditions,* so you need to treat them as a kind of speed-dating experience, not real dating. Still, superficial as these first meetings may be, they eventually put two people who should be in front of each other together, and then real dating commences.

Parties

Younger people have parties all the time, but after 50, not so much. Still, parties, whether they're fundraisers, political get-togethers, or large office celebrations, are a good time to meet people you don't know. It takes a bit of guts to introduce yourself to someone you don't know at these large gatherings, and a naked fourth finger on the left hand doesn't always tell you whether someone is single. Still, it's worth going to these kinds of events because there are likely to be people there you don't already know.

Hobby-related activities

One of the best ways to meet people who share some of your passions is to meet them while you're engaging in said activity. That may mean skiing, going to an art opening, or taking an evening class on film, history, or anything else that you love. This way of meeting people is a long shot because there may not be any single people there besides yourself — or no single people who attract you — but if you do meet someone, it's a great way to begin a relationship.

Try as many ways to meet people as you can. You never know which approach is going to pay off.

Making Your Safety a Priority

Unless you fall in love with the boy or girl next door, your coworker, or someone you've known for a long time, dating, almost by definition, is going out with someone you don't know. That means you need to be cautious about how you meet people, where you meet them, and what information you give them.

I talk more about safety in Chapter 8, but in a nutshell, here are the five core aspects of safe dating:

- ✔ **Never give out your address until you've thoroughly checked someone out and are sure he's a safe person.**

- ✔ **Never give out your home phone number until you're sure this is an emotionally stable person.** A rejected person who's unstable could start harassing you over the phone, and you may have to cancel your number, which is a pain in the neck.

- ✔ **Always do due diligence on the information your date gives you.** You should be able to use the web to find out whether he has a criminal record, works where he says he works, is married, and so on.

- ✔ **Never let someone you've met for coffee or just a few dates walk you to your car.** The chances of meeting someone who would push you into the car and kidnap you are extremely low, but not impossible.

- ✔ **Pay attention to early jealous behavior or compulsive calling or visiting.** If it occurs, back away from the relationship immediately (but do it in a kind manner; you don't want to stir up feelings of anger if you can help it).

Navigating First Dates and Beyond

In the early part of a relationship, you need to watch out for a number of pitfalls. I cover them in Chapter 7 and in other chapters in this book. The following sections outline some of the highlights.

Polishing your conversation skills

Starting a conversation with someone you barely know is always a bit awkward. It's hard to know what will lead to mutual interest. There are some graceful ways to get conversation flowing; here are some ideas:

- ✔ **Talk about things that interest your date.** You really need to know how to talk to someone. If you've talked or read a profile already, bring up subjects you know this person is interested in. Make sure you get to cover something meaty.

- ✔ **Talk about a variety of subjects.** Not all your sentences should start with "I," and not all your stories should be about yourself. Pull out some subjects that contain both of your interests; for example, if your date is a chess player, and you are too, start talking about chess.

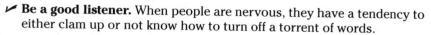

✔ **Be a good listener.** When people are nervous, they have a tendency to either clam up or not know how to turn off a torrent of words.

One way to know you're listening is to ask the other person questions about herself.

✔ **Don't forget to use a little chemistry — after all, this is an interview for a date, not for a job.** If you're attracted, show it, albeit in a subtle way. Hold eye contact, smile, and lean forward. Show you have emotions and sexuality.

It's one thing to show that you're attracted; it's another to come across as a lech or someone desperately trying to be a femme fatale. Avoid the extremes and just flirt a little, not a lot.

✔ **Avoid being controversial on this first meeting.** You may have political differences, but there's no reason to take them on immediately — unless that's an extremely important aspect of how you choose someone to be in your life. Even then, you can find out someone's opinion and state your own without getting into anything inflammatory. Raising the temperature at the table is exhausting and unnecessary. You also don't want to close something down before you get a chance to know who this person is in other important realms of your life.

✔ **Whatever you do, leave your ex out of this.** Talking about the person who deserted you, or whom you left, or who was the light of your life, is never a good idea.

It's easy to start talking about an ex even if you don't want to because your date may bring up her terrible divorce or breakup. Best thought: Nip it in the bud and change the topic. You'll be doing both of you a favor.

✔ **Save the bad news for later.** No one needs to know your hospital record or your job problems when you're just getting to know each other.

This first date is still an interview, and you may not get another chance to talk to this person if it doesn't go well. So try to be your most interesting, warm, and compelling version of yourself. Have fun!

Being resilient

Probably the single most valuable characteristic you can have in dating is resilience. Sometimes you meet a lot of people, and none of them is right for you. You have to develop a nice way to tell people that they're not "the one" without being impolite or cruel. Harder is accepting that speech from someone else when you're really interested. But what can you do? Taste doesn't always match up. It's great when it does, and upsetting when you don't see why this person doesn't feel the same way you do, but the fact is, if he doesn't, then you have to move on.

Holding on to a "keeper"

The best part of a relationship happens when you're interested, the other person is interested, and you start to date. The stakes get higher, so you need to consider each escalation of the relationship so you don't do something that undermines this new connection. You need to do things to make this person value you and slowly ease into each other's lives (see Chapters 9 and 10 for more on this).

✓ **Create great dates.** This is a time to be imaginative, to create fun or moving experiences that make you memorable. You should also open yourself up to new experiences because your date likely has something in her life that you haven't tried yet or don't know much about. Possibilities include a new sport or a class together that takes teamwork (tennis, cooking, and so on). Or perhaps you want to go exploring or even do something charitable that shows your date's depth as well as your own. (Chapters 9 and 19 give you additional ideas.)

Most cities have a city magazine or bulletin that lists special activities for the week. Look them over for great ideas.

✓ **Introduce your date to impressive and warm friends.** You learn a lot about people from meeting and getting to know their close friends. Meeting your friends can make you seem all the more wonderful, and it also helps you see how your date would fit into your life if the relationship were to deepen.

✓ **Meet your date's friends and family . . . and win them over.** Granted, it's not like meeting the family when you were 25, and the parents were the grown-ups. Now this entails your date's adult children and her friends who've lasted a lifetime. But these people have real influence and clout, which may or may not have been true in your youth. If you want this relationship to last, you want these people to like and trust you. (See Chapter 10 on how to make the first introductions successful.)

Don't introduce friends or meet family too soon. Get the relationship strong and grounded before you let in all these other opinions!

Moving into Tricky Territory: Sex and Intimacy

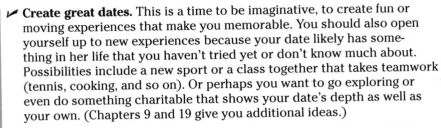

After you realize you have chemistry with someone, sexual contact usually isn't far behind. These days, given that you've probably been married (maybe even several times) or in a series of serious cohabitations, the expectation is that a serious relationship will include passion and sexuality. But people may have very different ideas about what sentiments should be in place before sex occurs. The following sections consider the usual themes that come up at this point (see Chapters 11 and 12 for more on sex and dating).

How long do we wait?

How long you wait before having sex is a personal issue. For some people, a few dates and a strong attraction is reason enough. In fact, many people have sexual intercourse or some kind of advanced sexual contact on the first real date.

Other people want to wait until they know what kind of relationship they're in and whether it's serious enough to qualify for sexual intimacy. More often than not, some kind of conversation about the relationship precedes sexual intercourse, but it's a great understatement to say that there's generally incomplete communication about sex and what it means.

How do we talk about it?

Obviously, if talking about when to have sex and what it means were easy, everyone would do it — and that's not the case by a long shot. Chapter 11 takes on this problem in some detail, but suffice it to say that you *can* have the conversation, and it can make you a better, more intimate couple. Talking about sex doesn't make it less passionate when it happens, but not talking about it may cause at least one partner enough worry and insecurity to impede sexual pleasure, create inhibitions, and obstruct emotional comfort.

So how do you begin? By being frank and direct. Literally say, "Before we have sex, I want to talk about issues that are important to me and also tell you things about myself that you need to know." Some dates greatly appreciate this because they have issues to talk about too, and they don't want to shock you or disappoint you. For example, a man who has had prostate cancer and has a pump in his penis so that he can have erections needs to tell his dates that he has to pump up his penis to have intercourse. He can assure her that the experience will still be pleasurable for both of them. If he conveys this information in an unembarrassed and enthusiastic way, his date is likely to feel unembarrassed and enthusiastic, too.

If you need to have this kind of intimate conversation about your body before having sex, do it at dinner or over a coffee or drink and not in bed. Your partner may not want to have sex, and navigating the situation in bed is way more difficult than making an agreement in a restaurant not to go forward.

What does sex say about the relationship?

Sex means different things to different people, and that's the problem. Some people think having sex means two things: that it's at least a serious dating relationship, and that it will now mean a monogamous commitment. This is a common understanding but hardly universally shared. If you think sex of any sort is a big deal, you definitely want to discuss what your entry-level standards are for creating a sexual connection. If you don't care what sex means (or don't care enough to have any difficult conversations), remember that it may mean something different to your partner and that the consequences of misunderstanding your date's expectations may be more than you want to handle.

What about monogamy?

One misunderstanding people have is about whether having sex with one person means not having sex with anyone else. To be clear, not everyone thinks that having sex is a promise of fidelity from then on. If you really care about monogamy — either from a health or an emotional perspective, or both — then have the conversation about the meaning of sex before you do it. Maybe sex won't happen then or ever, or maybe it will just happen later in the relationship, when you're both on the same page about what it means or entails. But at least there will be no regrets or accusations of feelings of betrayal.

What kinds of safety precautions are necessary?

Ideally, no act of sexual intercourse or oral sex should happen without a conversation about safe sex and the eventual use of a condom. Public health educators even recommend *dental dams* (thin pieces of latex that can cover the vaginal opening) because genital herpes can be transmitted by oral contact, and — rarely but possibly — the HPV virus that produces tooth decay can be transmitted.

Common practice, however, is much less ideal. Studies have shown that really low percentages of heterosexual men and women use condoms (gay men do much better). Chapter 12 talks more about this problem.

Talking about embarrassing issues

Other issues may be involved with sexual contact besides what it means about the relationship and whether it signals the beginning of monogamy. Older individuals can be painfully aware of how their bodies have changed and perhaps how they negotiate having disabilities caused by life-threatening illnesses such as cancer, heart problems, or diabetes, all of which can influence how their bodies look or whether they're orgasmic or able to have a full or automatic erection.

Bringing up such issues may actually be less awkward than you imagine. Most partners are sympathetic about these kinds of problems, and there are always ways to work around them that are easier if you broach the topic ahead of time (see Chapter 12). Many adults change their expectations of what a partner can and can't do as the decades pass by, and very few people expect their 50-plus partner to be a sexual athlete. Some are, but not the majority, and most people are ready to make all sorts of accommodations — and still enjoy each other tremendously!

Money These Days

Which is more awkward to talk about, sex or money? It's a tough call. Dating has changed (and continues to change), and it's never safe to assume what dating etiquette is when it comes to who pays for dating costs. Chapter 13 covers dating and money matters in depth.

Sharing costs

Though some men are traditional and would be offended to have a woman pay for a date, other men now want a 50-50 split. Traditional women are offended at the new deal, but feminism has reached men, and many believe that if women want to be equal partners, they need to be equal payers as well. If you're a woman who likes to pay your own way, this newer philosophy will be comfortable for you. If you're a woman who's used to male generosity, and you don't want to change the tradition, you have to look for a man with more traditional values.

A 2013 study showed that the majority of men now want women to pick up the check at least occasionally.

Weighing the considerations of a fixed income versus a working income

One newer issue about money is between people who are still working full time and people who've retired. Retirement can bring new economic necessities that working people may not understand. The difference between partners' incomes may not appear great in some cases, but it makes a big difference in how discretionary income is allotted.

You may find yourself in a situation where you like someone very much, but because one of you is working and the other isn't, certain kinds of vacations or expenses may not be possible unless one of you subsidizes the other. This level of largess requires rethinking gender roles. Even today, many women aren't used to being the one who pays for many luxuries or even just day-to-day expenses because men have traditionally had this role. But many of today's men are tired of paying the lion's share of expenses or simply can't do that anymore because they're on a fixed income.

You have to decide what new accommodations you're willing to make to put a lifestyle together with someone who's not at the stage of work or retirement that you're in. You can take income or budgetary constraints into account when choosing your dates, but if that seems too coldblooded, at least make sure you check out the fundamentals early on, such as whether your date is retired or is earning a living that would work with your lifestyle. If money is an issue for you, it doesn't pay to ignore it when you're falling in love with someone.

Special Dating Strategies for Gays, Lesbians, and Bisexuals over 50

Much of what you read in this book applies to all daters, whether straight or gay. But some topics and differences are unique to people who are looking for a partner of the same sex. Chapter 16 looks at some of the issues that gay men and lesbians have to take into account. They include:

- **Finding people of your own age:** All daters tend to want someone slightly or a lot younger than themselves. This seems to be true among gay men and lesbians, and it means that finding places that have people interested in their own age group is very important.

- **Finding people in places beyond bars or gay community centers:** Bars seem to be great meeting places for younger gays or lesbians, but they don't work so well for older people. Also, gay men and women who congregate only or mainly in gay places are different from the ones who prefer mixed groups. Online dating has helped a lot of people 50 and older find age-mates, and in Chapter 16 I explore other places that may work well for gays and lesbians searching for a partner, including gay and lesbian sites on the Internet.

Political elections and affinity groups (like fellow mountain climbers) are great places to find partners if they're open and affirming about sexuality in general. If an election ballot has measures that affect gay people, you'll find many gay people working on the issue.

✔ **Negotiating monogamy:** Unlike heterosexuals, the majority of gay men make no assumption that monogamy begins when sexually intimate dating begins. Though many gay men want monogamy (both for emotional and health reasons), a sizable number of men think that the core nature of male sexuality is non-monogamous. Gay sex expert and columnist Dan Savage has advised gay partners to be "monogamish," which seems to mean that it's good not to run around all the time, but on the other hand, you'll probably be less disappointed in your partner or less frustrated yourself if you construct a relationship that allows for occasional outside sex.

✔ **Negotiating safe sex:** Safe sex is incredibly important for gay men. AIDS is deadly and infectious, although it may respond well to treatments, when available. Gay men are very much at risk, so using a condom is critically important. Some men don't want to use them; if that's the case, the couple shouldn't have penetrative oral or anal sex.

✔ **Overcoming your credibility problem if you're a female bisexual:** "Straight by graduation" is a saying about young women who have romances with other women in college, meaning that women seem to have affairs in college with other women but drop the connection when they graduate and go into the real world. As a result of bisexuals having the "option" to go to their nonstigmatized heterosexual identity when it's compelling to do so, lesbians tend to distrust self-described bisexuals. They don't want to be dumped by a lover who suddenly or gradually begins to swing closer to the more "respectable" idea of being more centrally heterosexual.

Maintaining the Rest of Your Life while Dating

It's easy to lose track of your life when you're dating. It's so exciting to meet new people, and dating one or several people can start to take up all your discretionary time. But don't let that happen, even when you're overcome with passion and have a real crush on someone. You need your friends and family in the long run for advice and friendship, and that means sharing a date with them early on. In Chapter 10 I go over timing a first introduction to someone you're steadily dating. You want to make sure it's not too early or too late. It's too early if you don't know how you feel about this person, and therefore, you don't know how to introduce the person to your friends or family. It's too late if your date is a mystery to everyone who knows you, and the people who are close to you start to feel left out of an important part of your life.

Another advantage to an earlier rather than later introduction is that you'll learn a lot about how your date fits in and also get early input from your friends and family. You want to be careful and not get over-influenced by either positive reinforcement ("Don't let this one get away!") or negative reaction ("Isn't she a little short for you?"). You want advice but not a cacophony of opinions and directives. This means you have to look at your friends somewhat differently and decide whose advice really matters.

Most of all, you want to test the waters to see whether you can fit your date into your life (and whether you can fit into her weekly routine). Practicalities are important. There's love, and then there's "fit," and you want to make sure you have both!

Chapter 2

Determining Whether You're Ready for a Relationship

In This Chapter

▶ Doing some self-reflection to see whether you're ready to start dating

▶ Navigating the reactions of friends and family

▶ Starting to date after the death of a spouse

*M*any people who think they're ready to date are not. A number of things that they think, do, or hold on to can torpedo dating success. Doing some self-reflection and focusing on the issues covered in this chapter are crucial for reentry into the dating market.

Going Through the "Ready for Dating" Checklist

Working on your attitude and expectations is a critical part of getting ready for dating and being able to have a new relationship. When I talk to people one-on-one, I often see so much obvious defensive behavior and negativity that I wonder why anyone would want to be this person's friend, much less her lover. This is particularly true as people age. Life is hard enough without surrounding yourself with people who are downers. It's not necessary! Many people have been through so much but still project a happy, grateful, open approach to the world. Research shows that people are drawn to this kind of person — and of course, I want them to be drawn to you. When people meet you, you want them to feel like some warmth, charm, and happiness have just walked into their life. I know this sounds a bit flowery, and you may be smirking right now, but I'm asking you to portray the person you can be when you feel good about your life and the world.

Dating after 50 carries some special challenges. This section guides you through some reflections that are key to preparing you for dating and new relationships. In addition to advice on improving yourself, I also touch on challenges you may encounter with your children, other family members, and friends.

Developing an optimistic point of view

You've lived for a considerable while now and gone through many experiences, and that's both a blessing and a hardship. The blessing: You've become wiser, you know the ropes, and you've had many experiences to learn from. The hardship: You've taken some lumps — perhaps some major ones — along the way, and those experiences have soured your perspective. For example, perhaps you married the wrong person, were in an emotionally or physically abusive relationship, or just haven't had a satisfying relationship in your life. Naturally, these circumstances could taint your approach to dating; you're looking at dating from the basement rather than from a penthouse! I don't blame you, but those feelings will keep you from getting what you really want — a great companion or a perfect match.

People who have a pessimistic point of view broadcast it more than they know. The lines of their face point down instead of up. They automatically bring up all the old clichés about dating when you're older:

"There are no good men."

"Women just want you for your money."

"Men just want someone to be their nurse."

"Women come with too much baggage."

I've heard these stereotypes about men and women over 50, and I'm here to tell you that they don't represent the truth. Like all generalizations, they describe *someone,* but they don't describe *everyone.* They don't describe the majority. What's more, they display a viewpoint that isn't helpful. If you approach dating from its problems — its "what ifs," its "hopelessness," even its "dangers" — you're defeating yourself before you begin. I'm not going to tell you that dating is a piece of cake, but if you follow the advice in this book and work on your issues, you can find someone to love.

 Look at your face in the morning when you leave, at least once during the day, and when you come home at night. Is your face relaxed? Is it friendly? If not, soften your eyes and mouth and relax your expression. Work on looking pleasant and happy as a natural state of being.

Here are a couple of things you can do to work on your approach to the world:

- ✔ **Think of all you have to be grateful for.** Start with the basics. Can you hear and see? Do you have the body parts you need? All you have to do is see how physically challenged some people are to know that being able to move around and take in your world helps a lot.

- ✔ **Consider the good things about where you live.** If you live in a place where you can vote, live without fear of daily attack, and have fresh water, good food, and the right and ability to work, you have more to be grateful for than many of the world's inhabitants.

- ✔ **Realize that you have some financial capability.** You were able to afford this book. If you have any financial cushion at all, you're way more advantaged than most people in the world.

- ✔ **Remember who has loved you — even for a while, and especially for a lifetime.** Do you have siblings you're close to or friends who support you? Every person in your life who gives you affection or respect is someone you should treasure.

Bottom line: You have a lot going for you that you don't always let yourself treasure, and you should. Let that awareness support your mood and your perception of a possible romantic future.

If you tend to get depressed when things don't work out right away, put a list of things to be grateful for on your bathroom mirror or your refrigerator door. Make sure you remind yourself of all the good things in your life.

Letting go of a past relationship

To date again — and do it successfully — you have to get rid of lingering attachments to your ex, the one that got away, or your past, and let yourself get on with your future.

- ✔ **Stop magical thinking.** In the back of your mind, you not so secretly think that somehow the person who left you will return, suddenly realize how wonderful you are, turn your platonic friendship into something passionate, divorce the person he left you for, and come back to you. Have these things ever happened? Yes, and so has winning the lottery. The odds are heavily against you. Why would you bet on something that's truly unlikely to happen and that stops you from loving someone else?

- ✔ **Stop remembering only the good parts.** Yes, there was that romantic beginning and the terrific trip to Belize. But don't stop remembering there. Remember also the inability to communicate, your former partner's flash anger, or his depressive withdrawal. Remember his lack of loyalty or inability to give you compliments. Remember the tough stuff that not only broke you up but also made you unhappy many times during the relationship. As time goes by, people tend to gloss over the bad stuff and think only about the happy times. Doing so has its good points; it helps you get over painful memories. But it's a fantasy that keeps you attached when you really have to move on.

✔ **Stop wanting something just because you can't have it.** Being dumped is sometimes a powerful aphrodisiac. You may have felt ambivalent when you were together, but when your partner pulled the plug, he became irresistible. Try and tease apart "losing" from love. Think about how this relationship would have played out over the long run and see why ending it may have been a good idea — no matter who did it.

✔ **Stop extrapolating that relationship to all relationships.** If your ex wooed you well and then treated you badly, it's sad and regrettable, but not necessarily repeatable. People aren't clones of one another, and though there may be some reason you've had more than one destructive relationship, that doesn't prove that no good relationships are out there. You may need to reexamine your part in why relationships end and perhaps get some counseling. But don't think the problem lies in the idea that everyone else is defective — they're not.

Being open and willing to change

You may think you're ready to date but you really aren't, because even though you want a relationship with another person, you want that person to conform to everything you're doing, and you're not going to change at all.

Relationships don't really work well that way. You're going to meet someone who probably lives quite differently from you, and if you insist that your life is going to stay exactly the same, the person may just decide that getting to know you isn't worth it.

I'm not saying you have to up and move in with someone or change cities; such changes are far down the road of dating. But you may have to do some of the following:

✔ Learn a new hobby.

✔ Do less of your usual hobby.

✔ Get up earlier, go out later, or just change your routine.

✔ Hang out with a new crowd sometimes.

✔ Be more punctual, or less.

✔ Exercise more or differently.

✔ Spend money in different ways.

That's just a beginning, but you get the idea. You may have routines you don't even recognize as routines, and now you have to examine them and maybe change them so that your day or weekend is much different from what it used to be. If it's too different from what you want, then this isn't the relationship for you. But if any difference turns you off or upsets you, then you may not be ready to date yet.

Checking your self-esteem and feeling worthy of love

You must be able to think of yourself as a worthwhile, highly datable person before you actually start dating. Some people have an overinflated idea of themselves as a gift to the dating marketplace, but more people suffer from the opposite problem — insecurity about who would want them. This is particularly true among older people who haven't dated since they were awkward high school dweebs or heartthrobs (if they ever were). If you never thought of yourself as popular or self-assured with the opposite sex (or with the same sex, if you're gay), you may never have gotten over that image, even if you subsequently had a great relationship. So wouldn't you say it's high time to shuck that image?

The self-confidence of many attractive, intelligent, amusing, and interesting people dissolves when they think of entering the romance market. But you have to get over these feelings of inferiority. You should be realistic — perhaps George Clooney or Angelina Jolie wouldn't be blown away by you — but there's a lot of latitude outside of that rarefied air. If you really don't think you're all that great for anyone, get some counseling to help you realize your strengths and help you approach or be approached by someone worthy of who you are and what you have to contribute.

You may not need a counselor, though; you may just need some myth removal. The following sections discuss some myths that many people believe but that simply aren't true.

You have to be thin

If you look around you, you'll see that most people aren't thin. And yet they have a partner. True, some people met when they were slimmer and then gained weight, but many of them met when they were packing more than a few extra pounds. Believe it or not, some people aren't that body-conscious, and your body fitness isn't their gateway requirement. Yes, you'll do better on the dating market if you're fit, but being fit isn't the absolute key to the kingdom. Women in particular aren't as demanding as men in this arena — many of them figure they can fix the guy afterward! Men are more likely to prefer a woman who isn't obese, but not all men want a woman to have zero body fat. Remember, you're older now, and though many people like a fit person and certainly look for signs of health and self-care, the lessons of life prove that weight is only one consideration, not *the* consideration.

You have to be under 50 to be datable

You may have heard that the biggest growth in online dating is people over 50. It's true. People over 50 have a harder time finding other single people in everyday life, so they've come to the Internet for convenience in locating potential partners. Most of the people they're looking for are within a ten-year range of their own age, and the vast majority, men and women, would be happy with someone their own age.

Granted, most people think they're "younger" than everyone else their age, but they still act on what they see in the person they meet, not what year they see on a birth certificate. Sure, some 60-year-old men date 40-year-old women, but they're the exception, not the rule. In general, younger partners aren't cruising around looking for much older ones.

You have to be wealthy

Most people aren't wealthy. Many people are on a budget — sometimes a strict budget — but they still find someone. Money is alluring, no doubt about it. But most older people aren't entering the dating market because they're looking for someone who will make them rich. Of course, that's most people — you do need to worry about the scary minority who are looking for a sugar daddy or sugar momma and who will say anything you need to hear, and certainly try and get in your pants, if they think it will help them get into your pockets.

If you see a personal ad or online profile that advertises a beautiful woman or attractive younger man looking for someone "generous," stay away. A lot of these people are professional scammers or sex workers.

You can't have children at home

Some people love children, even other people's children. And because you're not going to get rid of your own, you probably have to look for someone who thinks kids are a plus, not a minus. Sure, some people are finished with parenting and just don't want to face renewed family obligations. But many people want someone who loves children and will be a welcome presence with their own children. Many parents who've dated women or men without kids have found that it's a big problem when someone they love doesn't understand the priority that one's own children have in life. They often realize that it's usually a better match when two parents find each other.

In online dating, people have a chance to decide whether they can deal with a partner who has kids at home. If you enter your deal breakers and must-haves, you'll only meet people who are open — or not open — to dating someone who's still parenting her kids daily.

You have to be good looking

Few people are as good looking over 50 as they were under that age. But they've gotten used to it! Changing the way you look also changes the way you see others. Though some people can't change their idea of who they think is attractive and still want someone who they would have wanted when they were young, most people aren't that constrained. That isn't to say that people aren't attracted to handsome men or beautiful women — just that they generally change that definition to be age-appropriate.

You can increase your attractiveness by how you act, smile, and focus on other people. Clean, high-quality clothes and good personal hygiene go a long way to creating some chemistry.

Dealing with unsupportive children

Children vary in their response to a parent dating. Some children, particularly adult children, are delighted that their parent is dating again. They want you to be happy. Others are nervous. They aren't sure you know what to do or will make wise choices. Finally, there are the ones who are outraged. You're too old, they say — it's ridiculous. They actually intercede and threaten you, saying that you'll ruin their life if you start dating again. You have a few options about how to handle this:

✔ Call a meeting and include the kids who are upset as well as any who aren't. Have an open discussion about any or all of their fears. Argue the case that, although you enjoy their company, it's not the same as having someone you care about romantically.

If you don't have a child who's on your side of this issue, ask a supportive friend to be there with you. If this person has standing with your children, he or she may be able to influence them. The friend may also turn down the heat on — and add some light to — the conversation.

✔ Talk to your upset family and react to their specific fears.

- If they're worried about legal and estate complications, tell them you're not going to do anything with legal implications, but if you do, you'll involve them to make sure their rights are protected.

- If they're worried about your safety, let them participate in guarding it. Tell them that if they're worried about the person you're dating, they can meet him and look into his background.

- If they feel you're too old to be in love or to date, show them some data. Recommend they visit `www.aarp.org/home-family/dating` and see how many older people are looking for love.

Some children will bully or guilt-trip you on this. You need to resist. Remember, they wouldn't allow you to meddle this much in their lives! Draw some boundaries here; they're not allowed to insult you.

Fielding advice from friends or family

Your family and friends are going to be very interested in the fact that you're dating. Out of goodwill, and perhaps general nosiness, they'll want to know who you're seeing and what you're doing. If your family and friends are like most people, they'll all feel compelled to give you advice.

Whether that advice is good is a judgment you have to make. But here are some issues to ponder:

✔ Are they projecting their needs and values onto you?

✔ Are they making you feel stronger and better (good) or more worried and insecure (bad if it's not justified)?

✔ Do they generally have better insights than you do about situations?

✔ Are they giving you advice about things that are none of their business?

The special case of single parents

Children who've been raised in a single-parent household may be understandably upset at what they perceive as the dilution of a special relationship. If you were previously in a relationship with their mom or dad, they may also be protective of your ex's place in your life, even if it hasn't been an altogether participatory one.

If they're younger and living at home, they could be disruptive or cold to anyone you're seeing. You need to take extra care to reassure them, talk to them about your needs, and ensure they don't feel invaded or forgotten.

If you feel that their advice is useful and helping you move forward, by all means take it. But if their advice isn't welcome or useful, this is another time to draw boundaries. Thank them politely, and move on. If that would be offensive to them, then just say you're reading up on the topic and getting lots of information and advice, and you need to digest it. You can tell them that later on (by which you mean much later on, maybe never), you'll ask for their advice.

Preparing Yourself to Date Again as a Widow or Widower

Each kind of loss has its own special impact. Perhaps surprisingly, widows and widowers who've lost a partner with whom they've had a wonderful relationship are often more motivated than others to date again. And perhaps it goes without saying that if the relationship was awful, the loss of that partner may feel like the end of a prison sentence, and the desire to pair again is fraught with anxiety.

Still, even for the motivated widow or widower, there's a good chance that reentering the dating market may feel like infidelity, or even betrayal. A deceased spouse may have even given specific permission and encouragement for her partner to love again after she's gone, and yet doing so still feels wrong to the surviving spouse. So many things can complicate adjustment: feelings of guilt over being the survivor, difficulty imagining being in love again, fear that you *would* fall in love again, and perhaps most difficult to control, the feeling of being robbed, of a partner taken before her time.

Healing with the help of grief counseling

Though no one can tell someone how long to grieve, when grief continues unabated, it takes a toll on an individual's health and is emotionally taxing on everyone around the person. If you've lost too much weight, aren't getting proper sleep, or are suffering other deep and prolonged symptoms of grief, you may need to get outside help.

Some professionals specialize in grief counseling. If you want to get over your loss and can't, then it's time to ask for help. Friends and family can only do so much. At some point they'll no longer want to hear you go over and over the same emotional territory, and even if they want to be there for you, they'll feel bad because they won't know how to help you.

Grief counselors can help you come to terms with your loss. They'll meet with you as long as it takes and find ways for you to grieve much less. The meeting can be one-on-one or in group sessions, which boast a lower cost and have the added benefit of seeing other people struggle with and triumph over their sadness, which can be a model and an inspiration.

To find a grief counselor, check out the Association for Death Education and Counseling (www.adec.org), GriefNet (www.griefnet.org), www.therapists.psychologytoday.com, and local bereavement groups.

Facing criticism from grieving children, family, or friends

When someone well-loved dies, children, family, and friends may guard the person's memory and position in the family with fearsome intensity. The missing mother or father can become an icon, a saint, or at least a position in the family that can't (and according to some people, shouldn't) be replaced. Even if you've healed enough to want to fall in love again, it may not be clear whether the people who were closest to your partner are in the same emotional place as you. They may see a date, much less a new partner, as proof of your superficiality — or even worse, your lack of real love for their mother, father, sister, or brother.

The best way to deal with this issue is to face it head on and announce your intention to date way before someone is actually in the picture. Schedule one-on-one meetings with children, family members, and friends and tell them that you aren't forgetting the person you mutually loved but that you want companionship and love. You may receive compassion and support, but you may not. In fact, you may be stunned at how angry and irrational some people's responses are.

If you face horrified reactions to your announcement, try as best as you can to be understanding. The reactions are usually because the people closest to your deceased partner are still hurting, and they see your new life as eclipsing their loved one's memory — which, of course, is all they have left. Their feelings may also have less noble reasons; they may just resent the fact that you're starting a new life when their loved one can't be in it. But as understandable as their raw emotion may be, you have to be firm and not cave into their pressure, if they bring it to bear on you. You can venerate a loved one's place in your life without dedicating the rest of your life to a monastic existence.

Getting over over-idealization

Dating is hard work. Odds are you won't go on one date, fall in love, and live happily ever after. Idealized romance stories usually start with a sudden look, and both parties are gobsmacked and immediately drawn into each other's life. But it may be quite the opposite. Maybe it will be the slow but sure appreciation you have of someone you work with or come into contact with in a store. No matter how it starts, you'll encounter situations that aren't what you hoped for and people you have to know for a while to understand — and perhaps get interested in.

Don't set yourself up for failure by imagining that dating will immediately provide you with an abundance of great possibilities. People run the full range, from completely out to lunch to amazingly wonderful. You'll be on your game some nights and say the wrong things on a different occasion. If you accept these imperfections now and just try and do your best, you'll do well over the long run. If you don't over-idealize the process or the people but instead are open to meeting imperfect people (like you, and everyone), you'll be much more likely to ultimately meet someone unexpected but exciting. In the meantime, you need resiliency. You'll be on a steep learning curve in the beginning, and not all experiences will be pleasant. But if you stick around and gain knowledge about dating and about yourself, you'll eventually find someone who's smitten with you and who will become very important to you — possibly for the rest of your life.

There isn't necessarily a "right" time to start dating after a loss, but it will probably help soothe others' feelings if you wait a year. It generally takes a few years for people's emotions to soften. If you wait long enough, your children and extended family may even urge you to start dating again.

Chapter 3

Figuring Out Who You're Looking For

In This Chapter

▶ Rethinking who is right for you

▶ Finding a match in temperament, personality, and values

▶ Steering clear of certain manipulative types

*W*hen you're contemplating dating again, sooner or later (preferably sooner), you'll spend some time thinking about the specific characteristics of the person you're looking for. This is a critical moment of getting ready for dating because it affects who you approach, how you "interview" someone, and even where you look for potential mates. If you never dated much or haven't dated recently because you were in a long-term relationship or marriage, the idea of who you want to be with may be so confusing that you haven't really thought about it in depth.

One easy mistake to make is to think the person you want now is the same as the person you've always wanted or a near duplication of the person you once loved. Life experience, time, new circumstances, and new horizons may make you want to rethink that proposition.

The issues discussed in this chapter may help you come to new conclusions about who you want by expanding the categories you're willing to consider — or at the very least, by giving you better information that helps you confirm your original thoughts. I also give you some realistic facts about how to keep your expectations in line with who you're likely to meet in this post-50 dating world.

Updating Your Dating Criteria

Dating after 50 requires a change of perspective. When you were in middle school, your eyes may have drifted to anyone with freckles. When you were in high school, perhaps you had a secret crush on the captain of the football team, the homecoming queen or king, or someone you acted or sang with. After high school, you may have been brought to your knees with lust and adoration toward your study partner or someone in your group of friends. If you were like a lot of other young people, your hormones usually influenced your decision — perhaps not entirely, but with intensity.

When you felt it was time to make a commitment, you may have had a specific list of characteristics this person had to have, and it may have included whether the person was going to be successful in life (money, career), what kind of mother or father the person would make, how much you liked the person's looks, how deeply you wanted to be with the person, and whether your parents approved of your choice. If you married or made a commitment before your mid-30s, you probably had all kinds of fantasies about who your mate would be and what your mate would do in life; you probably met or exceeded some of these expectations, but some were woefully off-course. But however it ended up, it was all based on visions of the future; you didn't have enough of a track record to know how it would all work out over the next couple of decades.

Things have changed, and you need to take those changes into account in terms of who you look for and how good a fit this person is for this part of your life.

Recognizing that people change over time

Though people try to beat age as much as they can, the facts are the facts. Even if you look like you're 35, you're not. All those years have taught you a lot, and chances are they've brought other people a lot of insight and maturation as well. This means that people are often a much better version of themselves than they were 25 years ago, so if you run across an old high school or college chum, you shouldn't jump to the conclusion that the person is the same. Sure, there's something to the old saying that "a leopard doesn't change its spots," but then again, people aren't leopards. People change through personal crises, career ups and downs, job changes, parenthood, the loss of those dear to them, bouts with alcoholism and other addictions, overeating, medical difficulties, and more. Don't jump to conclusions when you see an old acquaintance on Facebook or at a reunion and the person is interested in getting to know you again.

Quite a few people do find a partner at reunions, on Facebook, or by chance encounters with old friends or even past dates. Don't rule them out.

Looking beyond a potential parent for your children

When you're young, marriage or commitment often includes an assessment of your partner as a potential parent. Men may have chosen someone whose ambition was to be a great mother or someone who was willing to put her career away or on hold for the child-raising years. Women may have focused on a man's desire for kids, his desire to be involved in their daily life, and his capacity to make the kind of money that they'd like their family to enjoy. A couple may have made many sacrifices, no matter what kind of couple it was (cohabiting, same sex, and so on), in order for the children to be well taken care of.

However, you may have kids who are grown up or almost grown up, out of the house, pursuing their own careers, and raising their own families. If you do have kids at home, then a partner's willingness to be involved in their life and his ability to relate to children matters a lot. In fact, how a partner relates to even adult children is important to most parents.

But relating to your children and raising them are two different issues. The criteria for picking a parenting partner are different from those for thinking about the next stage of life. You're not signing up a partner to support your children or create a compatible parenting style. You don't need to worry about discipline or education. You don't need to pick people based on how they would do these jobs. You can even differ on parenting philosophy because you're not going to be practicing it together.

Letting go of the need to please your parents and friends

If you were close to your parents when you were young, you probably wanted them to admire and accept your partner. You wanted their approval. Maybe now, however, it's time to give that up. If it was ever your own life to live, it certainly is now. And this time around, if you hanker for a cowboy, why not go for it? If the racial, religious, or class boundaries you observed so carefully no longer matter to you, don't continue along those old paths. A lot of the world opens up to you if you take all those tight strictures off and allow yourself to meet and enjoy different kinds of people.

Updating your economic considerations

If you've done well and are quite secure in your future ability to live the kind of life you want, you may be able to disregard how economically independent your date is. If you think your date is great but not high earning or even economically stable, it may not matter to you. You can afford to fall in love with an unpublished writer or poet or someone who lives on a rather meager fixed income. If you find other amazing things about the person, why let money stop you?

On the other hand, if you have a tentative hold on your economic future, you may need to think about the fiscal as well as the physical attractiveness of your partner. As you face the future with retirement or less earning capacity in mind, money becomes a different kind of consideration in how you choose people to date and how you think of them as serious partners. You may need to be careful about preserving your assets, and you need to date people who can help carry the expense and be serious about people who won't erode your economic lifeline. These aren't romantic thoughts, of course, but they're necessary ones.

Thinking about health

Youth and optimism go together. When you were young, you may not have experienced disabling disabilities or had to cope with a partner's significant health problems. But as people turn the corner at 50, many more health issues surface, and some of them are quite serious. If you have serious medical issues, you need to disclose them at some point, and so should the person you're dating. Health becomes something that you can't take for granted. As age progresses, some people radiate health and vitality and many don't.

Think about how much you're willing to love someone who may need some caretaking or who has the emotional depth and character to be there for you with whatever health issues you're facing or will face. For more on the convergence of dating and medical issues, turn to Chapter 14.

Selecting Dates: Which Qualities Are Core? Which Are Optional?

There are many things that you'd want from a date if you could design your date the way you can design a house. You could pick out style and substance, hobbies and values, appearances and temperament. It would definitely be a made-to-order product.

But that's not the way it works in real life. Someone may walk in with the deep blue eyes you're looking for but not the luxuriant hair you find so fetching. A person may have a great sense of humor but a strangely harsh and unattractive voice. Your potential partner may be brilliant but emotionally unpredictable. No package is ever perfect — however perfect it seems to be on first meeting.

Prioritizing with the rule of five

If you create a list of 20 or more perfect, must-have qualities you absolutely insist on someone having before you'll even go out on a date with her, my guess is you won't go out very often (perhaps not at all). When you require a lot from your potential dates, your chances of being lonely and dissatisfied with life go up a lot.

Because the point of this book is to get you dates, help you have great experiences, and eventually lead you to find someone to love and be loved by, I offer the *rule of five*. You can pick five major qualities as "must haves," and then you have to start being flexible. Take a look at the qualities in the following list and rank them, starting with the most important quality at number 1. Then cut off everything above number 5 and see whether you can live with the idea of being with someone who has the first five qualities but not some of the other ones. If you can, you're on your way to having an active and interesting dating life.

_____ High income

_____ Great looks

_____ Economically secure

_____ Wealthy

_____ Prestigious profession

_____ Very intelligent

_____ Great sense of humor

_____ Great body

_____ Gregarious (loves people, gets along with many)

_____ Wise

_____ Romantic

_____ Calm and thoughtful

_____ Loves your children

_____ Loves animals

_____ Loves food and wine

_____ Athletic

_____ Wonderful lover

_____ Loves travel

_____ Loves books

_____ Shares your political party and philosophy

_____ Loves to stay at home and cook or garden; loves domesticity

_____ Great family background

_____ Great dancer

_____ Loves music and musical events

_____ Loves cultural events like opera, theater, and art movies

Friends can satisfy some of these qualities, so some qualities don't have to be your partner's strong suit. Sometimes you can help your partner learn to like your hobbies or lifestyle. Also, if you insist on all your interests or habits being shared, you don't open yourself up to new experiences.

Holding firm on your deal breakers

It's one thing to specify what you want; it's another to specify what you _don't_ want. Rank the following qualities, starting with the most important deal breaker at number 1, and add your own if you don't see your own deal breaker. If you find that your top 5 becomes top 6, 7, 8, or more, be aware that your long list of requirements may exclude a very large number of people.

There's a difference between deal breakers and things you don't like but could tolerate if a person has enough other things going for him. Don't put down something as a deal breaker unless it really would be insufferable.

Things I can't live with:

_____ A smoker

_____ A liberal

_____ A conservative

_____ Someone who drinks a lot

_____ Someone very religious

_____ Someone non-religious

_____ Someone who doesn't like being around children

_____ Someone who doesn't like being around animals

_____ Someone who needs to live with animals

_____ Someone who wants me to change where I live

_____ Someone who wants to move to a different state

_____ Someone who doesn't work

_____ Someone whose work is extremely time consuming and important to him

_____ Someone who doesn't want a regular sexual life

_____ Someone who isn't slim or fit

_____ Someone who talks a lot

_____ Someone who's very quiet

_____ Someone who's extremely athletic

_____ Someone who isn't at all athletic

_____ Someone who's not very interested in spectator sports (football, basketball, tennis, soccer, and so on)

_____ Someone who's not seriously into at least one of the following: movies, theater, art, dance, or opera

_____ Someone with grave health issues

If you have children at home, you may have a different list

If you have kids at home, obviously your number-one priority has to be that your date likes kids and has the capacity to love your children. Here are a few other things to think about prioritizing:

✔ Someone who understands that children's needs sometimes take precedence over adult needs

✔ Someone who doesn't resent private family time

✔ Someone who can fit into your family time and enjoy it

✔ Someone who has children and so understands how to relate to them

Selecting substance: The five C's

Appearance, hobbies, values, goals, and lifestyle choices are all important, but I've found that the characteristics of temperament and behavior are most important for the long run. These would be important at any age, but they're especially important as you face the future when you're older. If you find these five C's in a potential partner, how can you not have a great relationship?

Character

Sometimes, people are so entranced by someone's intelligence, looks, or charm that they forget to look at character. Big mistake. Character includes integrity, honor, loyalty, and conscience. If a person has character, she does the right thing, even if it's costly. She sticks by her vows, works hard to earn not only your respect but her own respect, and doesn't steal, flee, or treat people badly. She's a person of substance who earns your admiration and the admiration of others. That doesn't mean she always acts as you would have her act; she adheres to principles, which may mean that even if you want her to cut corners or look the other way, she won't. You know who she is, what she's made of, and how she'll act in a crisis. She has your back, and that's an awfully important attribute. If you believe a person has strong character, you may want to make other allowances in your list of "must haves."

Communication

It's not easy when you have a difference of opinion, values, or goals, but that happens over time, even between people who are very much alike. There can be struggles over something that happened or what one of you wants to happen and the other does not, even early on in a relationship. The difference between a successful relationship and a floundering one is often how well two people can talk to each other, work to see each other's point of view, and discuss things in a way that doesn't insult the other person or raise the temperature in the room so high that no real understanding or negotiation can take place. If you can talk your way through issues and come to an understanding that you both feel good about, you have something worth pursuing further.

Caring

You need a person with the capacity for caring. As people get older, they need someone with a good heart and the ability to express it, even more, perhaps, than they did when they were younger. Sooner or later, they need someone who has compassion for the challenges they have over this life stage — things that were mostly theoretical in the first 50 years and now are quite real. It could be the loss of dear friends or family, health issues, complications in the lives of their adult children or grandchildren, or reverses in their careers or livelihood. A partner can be great fun, love your hobbies, and be intelligent and charismatic, but none of that matters if your partner doesn't have a big enough heart to love and care during times of stress and need.

Chemistry

You may be surprised that I list chemistry as one of the five core characteristics, but chemistry is more than just sexual chemistry. Chemistry is looking at each other and liking what you see. It's enjoying the way the other person smiles or the look in his eyes when he looks at you. It's important that you like the way a person touches you. Some people are even sensitive to the way their partner smells; it's critical for them that they're pleased by their partner's scent.

No one knows exactly why one person's expressions are so pleasing and others leave them cold, but the fact is they do. You ignore a lack of chemistry at your peril because if you stop being pleased by your partner's physical presence, it takes a toll on a relationship. Granted, people change shape and looks over time, and sexual interaction may be less intense over time, but the essence of chemistry sticks around.

Compatibility

A good indicator of compatibility is that the two of you get along easily. You like to do a lot of the same things or you're delighted with adopting some of the new things that the other person brings into the relationship. You seem to have similar amounts of energy, and you like each other's children and friends. If you've started spending a lot of time together, you find that you're developing patterns that you both like. People who have this experience often are amazed at how comfortable they are with each other and how easy it is to get along.

This is a very good sign. Habits and lifestyle do matter. You can date people of good character who are good communicators, have good hearts, and are attractive to you but whose life doesn't seem to mesh with your own. It's nobody's fault, but they have solidly different habits than you do, and they want to live an essentially different life than you do. This lack of fit can be heartbreaking, especially after you admire or even love this person's fine qualities. Compatibility is experiencing a good fit that works for both of you.

Considering personal values and practices

Spirituality and religion, sexuality, passionate pastimes, family participation, lifestyle, and money — these are all usually important, but you may put some higher on the list than others. In any case, it's important to think about them in advance so that you can discuss them when you're interested enough in someone to think about future dates and perhaps a bigger future.

Spirituality and religion

Spirituality is the cornerstone of some people's lives. Their religious practices are a trellis upon which all other aspects of their life are hung. They're observant daily and go to the temple, mosque, or church of their choice regularly. Of course, there are extraordinary variations on this theme. Some very religious people don't attend services regularly but subscribe to the principles and practices of their chosen or inherited religion, and others are casual about their religion's traditions and practices but still have an emotional attachment to their faith. Sometimes, people who are more casual toward their religious traditions or dictates may be mistaken as unattached to their religion. But the culture of religion runs deep, and they may have strong feelings of attachment, even if they disregard religious communities and never go to formal places of worship.

Then, of course, there are people who don't like religion, don't practice it, and would find themselves upset to be with someone who did. Many of these people feel that religion is either irrelevant or the cause of much of the world's violence and vengeance. They see religion as a practice that happened because people needed an explanation for the mysteries of life or a set of rules and ethics for people to follow rather than the wisdom and direction of God.

Somewhere in this mix are people who describe themselves as "spiritual but not religious." They find themselves moved by a higher power, but they have their own unique explanations for what that power is and how they evoke it. They may believe it comes from nature or from exploring one's own humanity. Spirituality is important to them, but they reject traditional religious institutions and either create their own or just privately have their own spiritual path.

There's room for all kinds of common cause or all kinds of conflict when people are in different categories of spiritual or religious practice or belief in God. Some couples who differ greatly on religion do find a way to practice their own beliefs without disrupting the relationship. In the child-raising years, this is hard to do, and a differing vision of a child's religious path can be a deal breaker. If the child-raising part of the life cycle is over, however, there may be more room for a "live and let live" position of religion and religiosity. Nonetheless, some people feel so strongly about religion that they can't date, much less live with, someone who doesn't share their practices and beliefs.

Sexuality

People can strongly differ about both sexual practices and the centrality of sex in a relationship. Though you could argue that young hormones have died down some and lost their desperate urgency after you pass age 50, some people feel no different from the way they used to and don't want to sacrifice these years to a becalmed sexual life.

In the beginning of a relationship, there's usually a heightened sexual interest, but how that is expressed over time is yet to be seen. You can get an idea of how important sexuality and sensuality are to people, however, from their body language, their approach to you, and, as the relationship develops, what they say and do. You can glean much from the compatibility of each other's kisses — failure to like the way your partner kisses is a deal breaker for many people!

To figure out how important sex is to your date, you need to have some deep discussions. Passion subsides over time, but the question is, how important is it to each of you to hold on to that passion and connect sexually and sensually on a regular basis? Many relationships have soured — or broken up — because the partners had vastly different needs for sex and different ideas or practices about monogamy. If you don't like sex all that much, you'd be best served by finding someone who feels the same way you do. If sex is a core need and pleasure in your life, you have to be sure that it has the same priority in your date's life. Of course, the issue of sexual loyalty is tricky because few people state that they need an open sexual lifestyle — even if that's what they intend to do.

Don't presume monogamy, even while dating. You have to ask when the time is appropriate. If you worry about a person's capacity for sexual loyalty, ask her what she thinks about non-monogamy in general. If she thinks it's not a big deal or that it's expected over the life cycle, you have a pretty good idea of how she may act if she were tempted.

Passionate pastimes

On first blush, it may not seem like differences in hobbies and entertainments would matter a whole lot. But picture this: You love golf and play every chance you can get. Your partner not only doesn't like golf but also really wants to take that time and see the world. You're finally retired and can spend time doing what you want to do, and the two of you are deeply attracted to opposite passions. At this point, it's no laughing matter. The only way you can both enjoy your passions is to engage in them separately — but that means spending a lot of time alone. That's why what people like to do with their discretionary time is so important! When people share at least some central passions, it bonds them, whether it's showing dogs, playing tennis, traveling, or tracing ancestry. It doesn't seem to matter what it is; just an element of compatibility is what's important.

Having different passions doesn't doom a relationship, as long as you keep an open mind. People can go to resorts where one person goes golfing and the other goes exploring. Also, when there are other, deeply compelling qualities that move the relationship forward, often one or both partners will take at least some interest in the other's passionate hobby or sport. People have taken up golf for love and then continued it because they find that they enjoy it.

Family values and participation

Even though child-raising may be over, family ties remain strong. Most parents care deeply about how their date relates to their children. Many people over 50 are in the "sandwich generation" where they have duties for both children and parents. Duties are one issue — pleasure is another. Your date may be deeply embedded in his extended family and want you to be involved too. Or you may have a family that you see often and need for your partner to accept these frequent family visits — or better yet, enjoy them.

Some people, however, are alienated from their families (or certain members of their families) and may not interact much with relatives, parents, or even adult children living at home. Family systems are complicated, and they're sometimes only lovable (or even sufferable) to the person who has grown up in them. You may need to share similar values about family time and family obligations or your differing perspective could be a significant wedge between you and become a deal breaker.

Don't wait too long to introduce your potential partner to your family members if they're an integral part of your life. If your date doesn't want to be in this kind of family system, better to know it sooner than later.

Money

Calculations about money may not be very romantic, but they're an essential feature of compatibility. How much you have, how much your partner has, what you share and don't share, and how you split dating expenses are prickly questions and rarely a fun discussion. If you both earn equal amounts of money, then at least you can limit the discussion to whether you'll be egalitarian (you split everything) or traditional (the man pays for everything, or everything but the occasional treat the woman offers, like tickets or a special dinner). If your incomes are significantly different, and the man doesn't want to pay for everything, there's no clear answer. In fact, a woman who has a higher income may not want the man to pay for everything because that would mean the couple can only afford to do what he can afford to pay for — and that would significantly limit their options.

The rules about money and dating are in flux, but they seem to be going in a less traditional direction, even among older adults. Women who grew up in a world where men paid for everything may be shocked when, after a few dates, the guy says that he thinks they should alternate paying for dinner or that he'll pay for dinner but she should pay for the game tickets. Likewise, a man who's prepared to pay the bill may find it uncomfortable when his date insists on paying her share.

Compatibility quiz

What kind of personality do you prefer? Choose one or the other! Your choices may make you think about qualities that you haven't considered before, and they should reveal what — and who — you want.

Risk-taking	versus	Risk-averse
Calm and controlled	versus	Passionate and excited
Methodical	versus	Innovative
Laid back	versus	High energy
Humble	versus	Very self-confident
Embraces favorites	versus	Explores new things
Dominant	versus	Happy to follow
Seeks consensus	versus	Opinionated
Serious	versus	Lighthearted or teasing
Introvert	versus	Extrovert

You need to have a conversation to parse out how the two of you will handle money. If you disagree about who should do what or if your date insists on you paying your share when his resources are much greater than yours, this may be a source of serious incompatibility. However, if you have enough goodwill and interest, you have plenty of room to compromise based on practicalities (who has more money) and evolving gender roles (what is fair, not what is traditional). Philosophies about money and fiscal habits and values only get more important as a relationship progresses. If you don't like the other person's attitudes about money or his behavior with money and can't come to a comfortable compromise, then it's unlikely you'll put together a compatible relationship.

Guarding Yourself against Dates in the Danger Zone

If you've been out of the dating market for a long time, you may not recognize some of the pitfalls that certain types of people present. This section isn't intended to scare you, but being aware of a few red flags can help you save time and energy so that you can move on to more promising dates. I don't want you to jump to conclusions about anyone, but if you recognize any of these kinds of people on a date, you may want to back off.

Most people are what they seem to be, so don't be so wary that you don't give people a fair chance. Dating success requires a combination of having an open mind and an open heart but not sacrificing your good judgment in the process.

Narcissists

Everybody can be selfish — that's only human. But narcissists are *always* selfish. It's all about them, 24/7. Narcissists are only nice to get what they want, and they have no larger principles of fairness or responsibility. That means their promises mean nothing; they only make such promises if they think you need to hear them. And they only make good on those promises if doing so helps them get what they want.

Narcissists are extremely charming. The clever ones mirror you and tell you exactly what you want to hear. Others talk only about themselves, and at the end of the date, they probably don't know one thing more about you than they started with. They make a lot of "I" statements and even tell you about you — before you do. They think they know more about everything than you do. They break dates carelessly or court you with passion and then disappear mysteriously. They change plans on you without taking your needs or expectations into consideration. If you've had enough of this kind of treatment (and the hope is you *will* get fed up), then you may want to end the relationship and look for someone who has the capacity to love someone besides herself.

A note of caution here: Narcissists often have a very fragile ego (which is one of the reasons they protect it all the time), so you want to break up with one carefully. You don't want this person in a rage because you've punctured her egocentric bubble. If you can, use one of the following statements; even though they're cowardly and untrue, you're better off using them if you feel this person could be dangerous if crossed:

> "It's not about you. You're amazing, so I know I'll regret this someday. But I just can't commit to anyone right now."

> "You're too good for me. I'll never feel worthy. I need something much lower key."

> "There's something wrong with me. I just can't sustain a relationship. But thank you for all the good times we've had."

People with borderline personality disorder

People with *borderline personality disorder* are completely self-absorbed — to the degree that it's a clinical diagnosis. These people have such deep needs for attention that they can't stand anyone else getting it. They may fly into a rage if their ego is threatened, and they never, ever feel responsible for anything that goes wrong. Someone else is always at fault.

People with this disorder define "high maintenance." They'll have you walking on eggshells, apologizing, trying not to get them angry, and catering to their every need. How did they get you to this place? It didn't happen suddenly — they were charming in the beginning, perhaps smart, and maybe very handsome, successful, or beautiful. But as time goes on, you notice that they're manipulative. They may play you against someone else and make you insecure and jealous. It only gets worse, so if this description starts to sound familiar, date elsewhere.

If your date talks often about past lovers and partners and starts comparing you unfavorably to them, this may be a sign that you're with someone who is at the very least a narcissist and possibly has borderline personality disorder.

Players (ludic lovers)

If you're dating just to date and not looking for a partner, then by all means date what psychologist John Lee has called "ludic lovers" and what others often refer to as "players." Whatever you call them, these people adore the challenge of falling in love and winning over someone's heart before losing interest. They like the "game" of love, not the deeper processes of commitment and attachment.

Some players are obviously manipulative, but not all of them know what they're doing. In their mind, they're unlucky in love and have just never found the right person who can hold their attention. Sooner or later (usually sooner), they find fault with everyone they've ever been with or loved because some trait emerged that "destroyed" the relationship. They have many hopeful beginnings, but somehow, nothing is ever quite right.

Recognizing players isn't always easy because your relationship with them begins in the way your dream first date would begin. They're totally taken with you. They come on strong, and they're amazed at how perfect you are and what a great fit the two of you are. Average players may use lines that turn you off — you know them when you hear them. But if you encounter players who believe in their own infatuation, call it love, and indulge in it without remembering that they always feel this way in the beginning (and forgetting the rapid falling-out-of-love sequence not far ahead), they may give off no danger signals. Your only cue may be how quickly and deeply they fall for you. So be cautious and follow the old adage about something being too good to be true.

If you meet someone you suspect is a player, delicately find out how long he has been on the dating circuit, how many relationships he has had in the last few years, and how long the relationships lasted. It's easy to ask whether he was ever married and for how long. In general (though not always), you can predict the future from the past.

Money scammers

Who wants to have to buy someone's affections? Don't kid yourself about someone who asks you for money or gifts or manipulates you so that you offer these things. For such a person, the money is the most important thing about you.

Men and women who want access to your bank account can be difficult to recognize right away. They know that you may be sensitive about such things, so they probably won't come right out and ask you your net worth. But they will ask you questions designed to find out how well you live. They may hint at things they'd love you to buy them or have a story (perhaps true) of an economic hardship, hoping you'll jump in and help them out. You have to decide whether you like being a sugar daddy or momma. If your generous nature overcomes your caution, remember that this person's love for you may only go pocket-deep.

Chapter 4

Bringing Your Best Self to the Dating World

The most successful daters believe they're going to succeed and prepare to be successful. Assuming this confident attitude may seem difficult when you look in the mirror and see less-than-supple skin and a few (or more) gray hairs. But don't be so hard on yourself. Many people over 50 think they're too old to date, but unless your ambitions include people 20 years younger than you, chances are that many people will find you appealing. Granted, you may have let a few things slip over the years (that weren't due to gravity), and you may need a little spiffing up to be ready for prime time, but that's easier than you think, and it has the benefit of making you more self-confident and healthier. After all, if you find someone to love, you want to be mentally and physically healthy enough to stick around a long time.

Without being disrespectful, my assumption is that most people who haven't dated in a long time could use a bit of a makeover in some area of their appearance. No one is hopeless; everyone has a better version of himself just waiting to be uncovered. This chapter offers a review of possible areas of your personal presentation that need renovation. Some suggestions follow about how to be the best version of yourself, starting with your state of mind and mental obstacles that you can overcome to feel more confident.

Research shows that most people reach an opinion about another person's attractiveness within seconds of meeting. That's why it's so important to take care in how you look, meet, and greet someone in those first few moments of connection.

Pushing Past Mental Blocks That Leave You Feeling Insecure

Sometimes all that stands between you and love is how you feel about yourself. Most people are unnecessarily hard on themselves, thinking things like "No one would ever want me" or "I'm just not what I used to be, and it's too late for me to find someone."

Banish these deflating and disabling pronouncements from your thoughts and your speech and replace them with positive ones. If you have a high opinion of yourself, you're going to do well in the dating market. It's that simple.

The following sections touch on some of the mental blocks you may encounter and explain how to push them out of your way so you can get back on the road to love.

Getting over the feeling of being too old

You're never too old for love. That's a fact. Lovers can be no less compatible or inseparable in managed care facilities than they were in high school or college. Since when was an age limit put on love, or for that matter on sex?

Deciding that being older disqualifies you in the dating market is self-defeating. Many people say, "I'm done with all that dating business," but that defensive attitude closes down options prematurely and may just be a reaction to feeling too old or uncompetitive in the romance market.

Age is truly not a barrier. Many love stories happen for people in their 70s, 80s, and even 90s. You can be positively youthful in your 50s and 60s these days — unless you decide otherwise. You have a lot of time in front of you, and so what used to be a downward slope at midlife is truly just a long plateau. Health difficulties can take a toll on you, but you're not the only one with those issues. You may find a person with some of the same issues who's open to being with someone who can be empathetic about life with physical challenges. Even if your walk is creaky, your heart is still functioning. Age isn't a barrier unless you let it become one.

Do you find people your age attractive? Think of some of them and then think about whether they have wrinkles or other signs of age. They probably do, and you still find them attractive. Looking at things from this angle may help you believe that other people will look at you and think you're good looking too.

My pineapple theory

Some people don't start dating again because they've tried it before and were rejected by someone they liked or didn't get any suitable dates for quite a while. These kinds of experiences can really puncture an ego, and the natural reaction is to veer away from any further rejections. But you can view meeting someone you like who isn't interested in you another way and turn the experience into just another educational moment that helps further refine who you like — and who will like you.

I call it my *pineapple theory*. Here's how it works: I don't like pineapple. I pick it off my plate if it happens to find its way there. But pineapple is some people's favorite fruit. They look for pineapple on a menu or in a supermarket and stock up. It's the same pineapple whether I don't like it or someone else does. It's just a matter of taste.

So that's a way to think about yourself. You aren't attracted to everyone you meet, so why should you expect the person you're interested in to always be attracted to you? Taste is so arbitrary; it really doesn't say anything about people, and it only means that, for whatever reason, one of you doesn't think the two of you are a match. When you both do, and things "click," you have time to find out whether the two of you are still a match when you share more things and know more about each other. But it takes that click to begin, and in order to date, you can't be hypersensitive about the fact that the other person may not share your enthusiasm. This isn't to say it isn't disappointing when that happens. It hurts when someone interesting doesn't call back or refuses a second date. But you need perspective: This is a road you're traveling, and it may take a while to get to your destination. Have patience and have faith in yourself. A match will happen even if it doesn't happen the first time you're drawn to someone.

Concentrating on your current strengths

Some people are insecure about dating because they focus on the qualities they used to have. Maybe you just aren't as strong, athletic, handsome, beautiful, muscular, or thin as you used to be. You can concentrate on those changes and get depressed or you can focus on your current strengths — strengths that you may not have had when you were younger and that can do a lot for your attractiveness in today's dating market.

The best ego builder is to make a list of your strengths. You'll be surprised at how long that list is! Then review your list and think about people who would appreciate those strengths. Here's the list of a woman who hasn't worked in a long time outside the home but has been a community activist:

- ✔ I build strong and lasting friendships.
- ✔ I have the respect of people I've worked for and of people who've worked for me.
- ✔ I've raised children I can be proud of.

✔ I think I'm wickedly funny. I usually crack people up.

✔ I play the piano extremely well, and I know a lot about music.

✔ I'm flexible, low maintenance, and easy to get along with.

✔ I'm a strong swimmer.

✔ I plan great vacations.

✔ I can make a dollar go far.

✔ I'm a charitable, compassionate person.

Doesn't this sound like someone quite a few people would respect and like to know? Make your list of current strengths and you'll probably impress yourself! You'll surely feel better about putting yourself into dating mode, and the list will also give you even more direction about what kind of person is likely to appreciate these strengths and want to know you better.

After age 50, you have new things to brag about. Qualities you took for granted are in scarce supply and are suddenly nominated for your strengths list. Being economically solvent may be attractive, even if you aren't rich. General health or a good job may not be flashy, but they're still things people are attracted to. And it really is a strength to have good eyesight as you age. Even that your children are financially independent or that your extended family has no drama may qualify as something worth pursuing if someone has come out of a situation where family drama killed the relationship. See how many of these apply to you:

✔ I drive well and safely, day or night.

✔ I have a good retirement plan and take care of myself financially.

✔ I have good friends and an active social life.

✔ I'm in good health.

✔ I participate in active sports.

✔ I can have intercourse (even if I need lubricant or an erectile drug).

✔ I have the ability, money, and desire to travel.

✔ I have a nice place to live.

✔ I have children who aren't in trouble and are nice, supportive people.

✔ I don't have extensive debts.

✔ I've had a happy life and have an optimistic attitude.

Before you reject someone quickly, make a list of her strengths. This exercise may stop you from making too hasty a decision.

Moving on from a previous rejection that really hurt

Everybody has long memories when it comes to pain. And heartbreak is one of the losses that hurts the most. Being older, the chances of having had some heartbreak in your life are pretty high. Depending on how difficult the rejection was, the mending period may seem endless — and in some cases, it just doesn't go away.

If you were ever totally, madly in love and someone (a spouse, a fiancé, or a lover) left you, you may be haunted by the loss. That goes double if you thought he was the love of your life. Being rejected can shake your sense of self-confidence and desirability, but you have to heal for several reasons:

- ✔ **Feeling hurt creates toxic chemicals.** Your cortisol levels remain high because you're stressed. You need to conquer that sadness or it will literally make you sick by depressing your immune system.

- ✔ **Staying in pain over someone gives him far more power than he should have in your life.** Isn't it enough that he hurt you once? You owe yourself some happiness, and you need to deny the person who hurt you any continuing power over your right to feel good about yourself.

- ✔ **No one person is that special.** There are plenty of good people in the world who offer great things. You may think this person is irreplaceable, but it just isn't true.

- ✔ **No one person's opinion should matter that much.** Yes, this person didn't want you, but that hardly makes you worthless. Fabulously beautiful and handsome movie stars and models have been dumped and cheated on. It wasn't because they weren't attractive or interesting enough that somebody left them. It was because they weren't a match or the other person fell deeply in love with someone else.

- ✔ **Look at all the wonderful friends you know who were left or cheated on or had to divorce.** You know some great people who weren't loved enough by people they were clearly superior to in the first place! You understand that they deserved better; can't you say the same for yourself? Of course you can — and you will.

If you have a picture of the person who rejected you on display, get rid of it. Even if that person was your spouse, don't stoke the fire of that connection in any way.

Putting an abusive or demeaning relationship behind you

Even harder than rejection is the recognition that you were in an abusive or demeaning relationship. It shakes you up to realize you were a case study of allowing someone to treat you badly.

You may worry that you could find yourself trapped in a relationship in which you feel helpless again. Rest assured that you can avoid repeating that experience. You probably know the warning signs from your own life, but just in case you're mystified about how to recognize people who may abuse you, here are some cues that are always worrisome:

- They're super charming, they come on strong, and then they run hot and cold. That's to make you try harder and lose your sense of personal pride.

- They're jealous and possessive and they accuse you of flirting with other people so that you'll believe that you're flawed.

- They cut you off from your friends and family. They may be subtle at first, but they don't like anyone you're close to and make it hard for you to see others, so you don't have other voices to tell you that you're in trouble.

- They're high maintenance. Taking care of them is a full-time job.

- They hit you or threaten you and then apologize, saying it will never happen again. They'll move your heart with their remorse and then, of course, do it again.

- They destroy your ego. They say you're dumb, fat, or a number of other hurtful things and that you're lucky to have them, because no one else would have you. They want you to be emotionally destroyed.

- They ask you to perform sexual acts that you think are demeaning. They have no respect for your feelings.

Any of these awful behaviors should set off alarms in your head. If you meet a person who reminds you of your past abusive lover or who exhibits any of these behaviors, you need to get away quick. There are a lot of good, loving people to date; you don't need to face abusive or demeaning behavior ever again. If you need help getting out, consult a professional.

If you're attracted to someone you're dating who displays some of these characteristics, call a friend who can remind you of how awful your past partner really was. Your friends and family can help give you the strength to resist any unhealthy relationship.

Rejecting the idea that no one is worthy of you

Insecurity comes in many forms. The idea that no one is worthy of you is one type of insecurity that can keep you from dating. If you assume that no one is perfect enough for you, the chances of you finding someone are low. You may actually feel that you're so extraordinary that few people are worthy of you, but even if that's true, where does that attitude get you? The point is that perhaps your big opinion of yourself is not working for you. This isn't to say that you aren't great or that you should "settle" (a dreaded word to most daters) but rather that you might consider that your position is keeping you lonely and you may want to change it, at least somewhat. Some things to consider:

✔ **Some amazing people are single — not all the "good ones" are taken.** This is especially true for people over 50 because divorce and tragedy strike quite a few folks over the life cycle and throw them unexpectedly back into the dating world.

✔ **If you always find some flaw in an otherwise promising person, you may be creating standards that would also disqualify you in someone else's eyes.** Can any human being really meet your standards?

✔ **Think of people who you were involved with when you were younger.** Were they really perfect? If not, ask why your standards have gotten "higher" than they used to be. Maybe you've forgotten how endearing "imperfect" people can be.

Perhaps your high standards are a defensive maneuver. Maybe your insistence on so many good qualities and appearance requirements is actually a fear response. Perhaps your real issue is fear of committing to one person, feeling trapped, or being in another disappointing relationship. If these fears hit home, then you need to deal with it before you start dating.

I'm a big fan of talking to a therapist when you feel blocked or stuck in the same loop and can't seem to talk yourself into a new mode of thinking. A good therapist can help you react to your fears with more positive thoughts and actions, allowing you to appreciate good people when you meet them.

Feeling Good about the Way You Look

The entire world conspires to make people feel bad about the way they look. Thousands of diets, gyms, and health gurus tell people that they're too fat, skinny, or flabby. Liposuction ads feature photos of women and men who look great except that they have a little tummy. Even people who have great bodies by most people's standards can feel bad if they don't have muscle definition or six-pack abs.

You'd think the pressure would let up when you hit 50 — and perhaps it does a bit. But it doesn't go away completely. So you need to take on some of the myths that may stop you from entering the dating world simply because you feel so bad about how you look. What you may think of as disadvantages aren't disadvantages to many people you'll meet.

Make sure you have flattering light in your bathroom or wherever you look in the mirror as you get ready to go out. Part of how you act comes from how you feel you look. Harsh fluorescent light makes you appear unnecessarily blotchy and overexposed. That cuts into your self-confidence, and you can't afford to start out the evening feeling unworthy and unattractive.

Changing the words you use to describe yourself

Not everyone wants someone slim or thin. Some men say they like a date with some "meat on their bones" — and they mean it. Some people like their guys to be big "bears," meaning they like hairy men and men with a tummy. Others prefer bald men. Some men want women with an hour-glass figure — busty and curvy are their kind of wonderful. There's no such thing as only one acceptable shape, so let that misconception go.

You can begin a redefinition of yourself if you revise the language you use to describe yourself. Seriously. Try these new terms — and don't lapse into the old ones!

- ✔ **If you're a heavier woman or have bigger hips or a large chest:** Use words such as *luscious*, *voluptuous*, and *sensual*.
- ✔ **If you're a heavier man:** Use words such as *solid* and *substantial*.
- ✔ **If you're skinny:** Use *wiry*.
- ✔ **If you're short:** Use *compact* or *petite*.
- ✔ **If you're a tall woman:** Use *statuesque*.
- ✔ **If you have a flatter chest:** Describe your build as *athletic* or *trim*.

You're a person, not an evaluation. You can look attractive in so many ways. Don't let general cultural preferences keep you from loving yourself and feeling good about how you look.

Accepting the flaws that everyone shares

Older people are more likely to accept flaws because they have them too. It's humbling to lose all your hair or have it so thin that it's almost transparent. But everyone has something going on — even if not all of it is visible. Almost all people in their 50s, 60s, and 70s have had something to contend with: bad backs, hair loss, scary diseases, lost flexibility, and aching joints, to name a few. Women have menopause to contend with; men experience changes in their erectile ability. People try to handle these issues and flaws with some grace and fight back with good diets, exercise, and various kinds of coping mechanisms. Most people are tolerant of the issues of others because they have something of their own that they want others to overlook. So forget about being self-conscious about wrinkles and saggy body parts. You've earned these changes over the years, and that doesn't mean you're undesirable or unattractive.

Getting fit

You don't have to be fit and healthy to date, but it sure does help if you are. If you're neither of these things, you don't have to give up and think it's too late to get there. Many people start fitness regimes as late as age 70, and they find that if they work hard enough, they can have a hard body almost comparable to people 30 years their junior. No one is saying that muscle definition is a necessary goal, but strength helps you live longer and reduces your risk of accidents. Core strength (stressed in yoga and Pilates) improves balance and supports your back, making it less likely you'll tear something or experience pain. The payoff for exercise is so great in every category. It's a wonderful way to prepare for dating because it makes you look and feel good, makes you healthier when you do find a partner, and gives you motivation to last to extreme old age.

If you're having trouble convincing yourself to take the time for regular exercise, consider subscribing to any of the great health newsletters for tips on exercise and healthy aging. Check out the Nutrition Action Health Letter (www.cspinet.org/nah), the Harvard Health Letter (www.health.harvard.edu/newsletters/Harvard_Health_Letter), the Johns Hopkins Medicine e-newsletter (www.hopkinsmedicine.org/news/e-newsletters), or Consumer Reports Health (www.consumerreports.org/cro/health/index.htm).

Doing 20-minute workouts at home

Getting fit doesn't take much time. One of the most encouraging findings of the last few years is that just 20 or 30 minutes of exercise a day contributes to a significant degree of fitness. You can spend those 20 or 30 minutes aerobic walking, weight training, jogging, or engaging in an active sport.

Just 20 minutes of exercise a day not only changes your shape but also changes your attitude. You'll feel stronger, fitter, and more confident, even if you don't lose any weight. Just think of how much better you feel about yourself if you can climb a flight of stairs without huffing and puffing. If you can run or jog a half marathon, you'll feel even better!

Joining a gym and hiring a trainer

If you'd like to get more exercise and shape up some but you just haven't been able to discipline yourself to get into exercise, then consider buying some discipline. You can join a gym cheaply these days, and many classes are likely included in the price. Apartment and condo buildings, offices, and community and senior centers often offer free or affordable gyms and classes. Or, if you have the money, consider getting a trainer to meet at the gym or come to your home. (You can get a group rate if you join up with a few friends and split the cost.) Consider it an investment in your health, because it truly is.

A trainer keeps you honest about how much effort you're putting out and also corrects mistakes of posture or muscle use that could undermine your body-shaping effectiveness and may even hurt you. Even if you hire a trainer just a few times to get your routine started and your mistakes pointed out, the investment would pay off. Don't be scared — not all trainers are as tough as the ones on *The Biggest Loser!* When a trainer compliments you, you'll feel great, and your added confidence will help you when you begin to date. There's something about being stronger and fitter than you were that does wonders for your self-image and emotional readiness.

Considering a nutritionist or a diet plan

Though someone will love you even if you're heavy or skinny, it's true that some people won't consider dating you if you're overweight or too thin. If you want to broaden your opportunities (and live longer), consider investing in yourself by consulting a nutritionist. Most hospital plans have a nutritionist on board, and now you can find help on the Internet. You can reeducate yourself about how much protein, carbs, and sugars you should eat.

Diets have changed in recent years. For example, the new Weight Watchers program is totally different from the old one, and it's effective for many different kinds of people. Other programs exist that are excellent, some supervised by doctors for people who have diabetes and other serious medical issues to deal with. If you've wanted to lose weight or gain muscle for a long time, use dating as the motivation that actually gets you into an online or off-line program that will foster health and a healthy weight. You can also check out *AARP New American Diet* by Dr. John Whyte (Wiley), at www.aarp.org/NewAmericanDiet.

Examining and Updating Your Wardrobe

Sometimes the way you feel about your attractiveness can be fixed by something as superficial as dressing differently. In fact, sometimes one's real attractiveness just needs a clothing update to shine through! For example, if you've been in a comfortable, long-term relationship, the sexiest thing you may have to wear is your college T-shirt or a pair of jeans that still fit well. But depending on who you are and where you're dating, the old clothes may not be flattering or alluring anymore. Granted, if you're a cowgirl or cowboy, well-fitting jeans and a dress shirt may be enough to rope someone in, but other people may have more extensive wardrobe requirements. Designer clothes aren't necessary (unless you run in a fast New York or Los Angeles crowd that can recognize a Jimmy Choo shoe), but new dates will look at how you present yourself and draw conclusions from it. This section outlines a few basic rules to follow as you examine your current wardrobe and make some updates to boost your self-confidence and increase your chances for successful dating.

Picking clothes that strengthen your personal brand

How do you want to come across? Metrosexual, athletic, nonchalant, very stylish, or just a guy or girl in jeans? Whatever it is, how you appear should back up how you want to be perceived as a person — your personal brand. Stylishness turns on some people and turns off others. The way you dress should be in sync with how the person you're looking for would want you to look. So if you want to be in the country-club set, you'll have a different look than if you were in the New York fashionista brigade.

If you're not sure how to put yourself together and haven't cut your hair a new way or bought a new outfit in a long time, you may want to go to a good department store and work with a fashion consultant. That sounds pricey, but really, in most cases it's only as pricey as you make it. If you give the consultant a budget and your goal (to look good and not to look dated or give the wrong impression), she can do wonders for you — and be the objective audience you need. Remember, people aren't always their own best judge of how they look, and sometimes their friends are too kind to tell them how they really look in some outfit they love and wear a lot. Men are at a particular disadvantage because unless they wear something dramatically awful, their male friends won't notice. Female friends may need to be prompted to tell you that your hair makes you look ten years older than you are, but a consultant won't mince words. Consider giving yourself the luxury of a makeover: a new hairdresser, a couple of new outfits recommended by a consultant, a manicure (you may need toning down as well as making sure your hands look nice), and a new cologne or perfume!

If you wear cologne or perfume, make sure you apply it with a light touch. Don't be one of those men or women who make people gag in an elevator. People shouldn't be able to smell your scent unless they're in intimate proximity to you.

Five common fashion mistakes for men

Most men aren't fashion-conscious. It's not a real problem because most women don't expect them to be. But that doesn't mean you can wear anything to a date and expect it to help support your quest. The old saying "Clothes make the man" actually has something to it. Think about society's romantic figures — cowboys (ooh, those chaps and spurs), military men (dress whites and beautifully fitting uniforms), and CEOs (power suits and Armani budgets). Granted, most men don't fit in these categories, but still, a nice sport coat and pants that fit and hang correctly, or perhaps a stylish leather jacket, make a man more handsome to most women. You can advance your "handsome rating" a lot if you dress well, but even if you wouldn't go that far even for love, you can avoid these pitfalls:

- ✔ **You wear the same thing over and over.** Showing up for your second date wearing the same thing you wore on the first date isn't advisable. You may not even remember what you wore, but your date is likely to remember and think that you don't care about making a good impression. She may also incorrectly imagine that you don't ever change your clothes — a distinct turnoff.

- ✔ **You never dress up.** There's nothing wrong with wearing jeans, tennis shoes, boots, or other casual attire most of the time. But if you're going out to the theater or a really nice dinner, looking like you took the time to pull yourself together is a must. Your date will probably look extra nice and dressy, and you don't want to look like you don't belong with her. I'm not suggesting that you wear a tux (although men really look gorgeous in them), but it's important for her to see you looking like you clean up well. If you don't, well, okay, there's no use in false advertising. But if you do like to look nice from time to time, this is the time to do it.

- ✔ **Your clothes are wrinkled or dirty.** Even women who think the word *metrosexual* is a dirty word don't like dirt. If you look like you just slept in your clothes, a significant number of women will immediately write you off. (Gay men will probably be even harder on you.) Messy, dirty, or badly wrinkled clothes show a lack of consideration and respect for your date. After all, she probably went to some length to look good for you — and she wants the favor returned.

✔ **You never get a style that flatters you.** Women have gotten pretty good at hiding figure flaws, but most men have not, and it's a pity. Pants that are too loose and baggy or cinched up tightly to accentuate your stomach are unnecessary fashion mistakes. You can wear something that doesn't accentuate body issues. If you have a lean body, wear a slim turtleneck, jeans that don't hang on you, and even a form-fitting sport coat instead of a boxy one. Celebrate your youthful appearance, because if you think only men ogle women's bodies and not vice versa, you're wrong!

✔ **You don't listen to what your date compliments you on.** Many dates telegraph what they'd like you to wear. They say, "I really like you in that jacket" or "You looked great in that windbreaker and jeans." What they're really telling you is which style they'd like you to repeat. Listen closely for these compliments; the women who make them are telling you how they'd like to see you in the future. If you ignore the comments, you rob yourself of an advantage, and your date will wonder why you don't dress in a way to please her when she has already told you how to do it!

Five common fashion mistakes for women

Many women don't know much about how to dress and what kinds of clothes make them look their best. This lack of passion for fashion may be no big deal in a long-term marriage, but it can affect your chances of attracting someone new when you're meeting people who may evaluate your romantic potential during a 20-minute coffee date. Here are some clothing issues you should consider seriously:

✔ **You haven't changed your style in 20 years.** Men are lucky in that their fashions change slowly or, in some respects, not at all. But women's hairstyles, hemlines, shoes, and dresses change every year — sometimes radically. Some looks are classic and never go out of style, but others (think bell-bottom trousers, empire waistlines, and beehive hairdos) go out of fashion and pretty much stay there. Whether you're 50 or 80, if you haven't changed your look in forever, this is a good time to do so.

✔ **You wear clothes that hide your shape and aren't flattering.** You may have gotten stuck in styles that suited you a long time ago but that no longer show you to your best advantage. For example, just because you've gained weight doesn't mean you should hide your body. Oversize garments may make you feel hidden and secure, but they make you look worse, not better. Even if you're a perfect size 6, you may be dressing too conservatively or in somber colors that drain you of any life and color.

Go clothes shopping and ask the salespeople to help you find something that makes you feel attractive and look pretty. Remember, however, that salespeople may not know your "look," so you're only obligated to consider their suggestions, not to follow them.

✔ **You dress ultra-sexy and show lots of cleavage.** If you go fishing with a certain kind of bait, you're going to catch a certain kind of fish. Do you really want the guy who is mostly attracted to you because of your generous cleavage or slit-to-there skirt? Yes, a sexy picture on the Internet will get you lots of interest, and those interested parties will be expecting more of the same, but some subtlety may get you a better class of guy.

There's no reason to believe that posting a seriously sexy picture on the web that shows a lot of skin puts you at more physical risk or attracts a rapist. However, given that you don't know the people you'll be meeting very well, it's probably safer to have a less explicitly sexy picture and to dress more conservatively than you may otherwise when you go to a first meeting. Turn to Chapter 7 for more advice on optimizing your first meeting and first date.

✔ **You dress like you're going to a business meeting.** If you're very conservative and you're looking for a man who is similarly inclined, then perhaps modest dress and unobtrusive color suits you best. But for most people, a little verve helps crank up the energy at the table and makes you memorable. If you dress whimsically, and that suits your personality, by all means do it. You want to seem like you could be romantic in another situation, so while you don't want to dress like a vamp, you don't want to hide your feminine, potentially sexy side either.

✔ **You wear your old wedding ring or other flashy jewelry.** Rings from your ex or deceased husband have no place on your hand when you're dating. People want to know whether the person they're thinking about dating is truly over an ex-partner, and keeping a ring on pretty much answers that question.

In addition to not wearing a wedding ring, you should watch how much jewelry you wear in general. You may not care about how much money a man has, but you'll intimidate him if you flash jewelry he can't afford. You can introduce good jewelry later if you usually wear it, but it's wise to leave it at home for your first meetings and first dates. It could signal expectations that you don't really have.

Polishing Your Social Skills

Are you anxious about prepping yourself for dating? Most people are. It's been a long time since you spiffed up for a date, worried about your clothes, or thought about how you would look to someone who doesn't already know and care about you. You may find yourself wondering how you're going to introduce yourself, how animated you should be, what to do if you're an introvert or meet one and have to carry the conversation, and more. These are all reasonable worries, but remember, you're on a learning curve, and though your first dates may be a bit harrowing, they'll get easier, and you'll discover who you are now along the way. However, you can do a few things before you strike up your first conversation with a stranger, go online, meet someone at a dinner party, or get fixed up. You can brush up on your social skills by practicing on family, friends, or just about anyone.

Tell your friends that you'd like to role-play a bit to see whether you can hold your part in a conversation and help move a topic along and make it interesting. (You don't want your friends to wonder why you've suddenly become a storyteller, are more animated than usual, or are laughing more at their jokes.)

Friends generally want to help you, and you can tell them you've had enough help at any time. But don't refuse well-intentioned friends who have some skills in this arena. They can give you badly needed feedback about your approach and conversational style. If possible, pick a friend in your age group who was dating not so long ago and who has found someone to love. Such friends can be both helpful and inspirational.

Social skills are like any other skills. Leave them dormant for a while and they get a bit rusty. Take them out and start exercising them and they get better. You need to practice to learn how to bring someone else out and also to make sure you present your personality, interests, and values well.

Part II
Where and How to Go Looking for Love

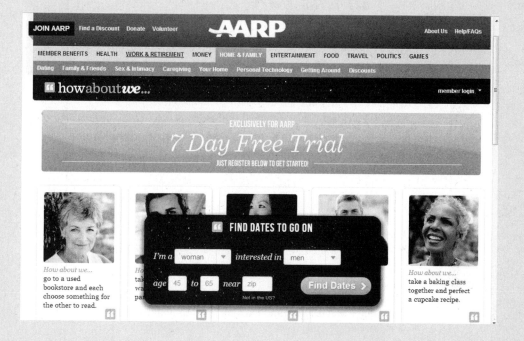

The world of dating is always evolving, and what you knew and did many years ago may not be as relevant as you get back into the dating game after age 50. Head to www.dummies.com/extras/datingafter50 for some tips and special skills that will help you prepare for a successful dating future.

In this part...

- Reduce your feelings of insecurity and increase your confidence about dating. Sometimes all you need to know are the steps to follow, and the whole mystery of dating just fades away, leaving you feeling competent and motivated.

- Role-play with a friend so that when you start dating you're more comfortable doing what you rehearsed.

- Identify the best places to find people in your age group. Bars don't cut it at this age, but plenty of other places do. Explore organized activities, singles groups, hobby clubs for singles, travel, and connections from casual acquaintances.

- Navigate the world of online dating, where you'll find the most singles. Consider the do's and don'ts that make a huge difference in who you meet, how safe you are, and how successful you are at attracting and dating the people you're interested in.

- Get advice for mastering the first date, including the right places to go, the right things to say (avoid hot-button or worrisome topics and issues), and the way to let someone know the best parts about you.

- Find out how to play it safe in every dating situation. You owe yourself a safe dating environment.

Chapter 5

Putting Yourself Out There

· ·

In This Chapter

▶ Formulating a plan for your first steps into dating

▶ Getting ideas about where to look for dates and which dates to look for

▶ Approaching dating prospects successfully

· ·

*I*t's time to stop thinking about dating and actually start doing it! The first step may feel like the hardest, but you can make it easier on yourself if you're mentally prepared and informed about your best options. This chapter may be the most important one you read because it starts you out with the core information you need — from formulating a dating plan to finding dates and approaching people — to stay on course while dating.

Getting Over Your Insecurity by Knowing How to Begin

You may feel less than confident about venturing into the dating world again after age 50. The first thing to do is think about what kinds of environments you feel most comfortable being in. For example, you may be interested in people who work at your company, or that may be the last place you'd want to look for a date. If you're interested in someone at work, you can do a little detective work to find out more about the person. It may be awkward and take a little courage, but you can ask coworkers about the person's marital status and other details. However, if you end up asking the person out and she declines, or if you do go out and it's awkward, you may have to face the person in the workplace occasionally. Whether bumping into a failed date is a big deal is a point of personal preference.

Settling these kinds of details can make you feel more secure about the whole dating process. Figuring out where to go to find someone and why you'd go to that specific place anchors enough details so that you start to feel more control over your future.

But then there's the issue of what to say to potential dates. How do you begin a conversation? How do you know whether you're monopolizing the conversation? What kind of signs should you look for to get feedback? If you find that you're nervous about every aspect of dating, you may want to take a class or work with a coach to hone your skills.

Getting help from classes on how to date

Dating classes can help give you courage and teach you skills if you feel that you're so insecure that you can't even begin to begin. Of course, classes vary by the teacher's psychological and educational skills, but many of them really shore you up with both information and technique. Classes give you exercises to do, like role-playing with a classmate that you're on a real date. You may even have homework. One homework assignment that was given in a class told students that they had to accept a date with absolutely anyone who asked, no matter what! The purpose of the assignment was not to let any preconceived ideas get in the way of finding out who the other person really was.

The downside of dating classes is that they can be expensive and time-consuming. Also, your teacher may have different values than you do. But you may also find an excellent instructor who can address your specific needs and jump-start the dating process for you.

A true story of dating class homework that worked out

Linda was 40 and hadn't dated seriously since she was in her 20s and married her husband. The marriage ended, and it was tough on her. She had dated a bit over the years, but nothing had resulted in a profound relationship. So she took a dating class, and one of the rules was that you had to accept a date with anyone who asked.

Linda owned an art gallery, but one of her other passions was athletics. She was a serious jock. So she wasn't too interested when an attractive, younger man in a wheelchair rolled into her gallery one day and, after chatting a bit, proposed that they go out together. She would have said no — it just wasn't a likely match — but because she had promised to say yes to anyone, she went on the date. The date was wildly successful, they got serious right away, and they ended up in a very happy marriage.

Role-playing with a friend

If taking a class turns you off or costs money you don't have, another way to learn techniques and get some direction is by role-playing with a friend. If you haven't flirted or related to someone in a romantic way in 40 years, you probably do need to relearn the art of making yourself interesting and also figure out how to get a good sense of who your date is.

Role-playing is reproducing the actual situation but not with the actual people. So you play yourself, and a friend plays the person you're trying to ask out or talk to. That way you can find out how to start, where you get stuck, and what you should and shouldn't say. A typical role-playing situation could go like this:

1. **You set the scene: a cocktail party. You practice the approach. What's your opening line?**

   "I saw you at the meeting last week. What's your name? I'm _____."

2. **What's your follow-up line?**

   "It's really nice to meet you. Aren't you a good friend of Sue's?"

3. **If your follow-up line leads nowhere, what's your potential backtrack line?**

   "Oh, you're not a friend of Sue's? So what's the connection that got you to this party?"

4. **The after chitchat opening: Now you're trying to get into the personal in a complimentary but not presumptuous way.**

   "So, you're wearing this fantastic piece of jewelry. Are you involved in the arts or music or am I totally and completely wrong?"

5. **You respond to the person's question or find an opening to say something interesting about yourself.**

   "I have absolutely no artistic talent, but I love design and have some friends who helped me renovate this old barn in the country that is my pet project."

Do your role-playing twice, under two different conditions: one where the person is easy to talk to and the other where the person is distracted or not too interested. In the latter case, see whether you can figure out a way to make the person more attentive and pleased with your company and what you're saying.

Try role-playing with more than one friend; each person will react differently, and you'll get broader experience that way. Make it entertaining, try different scenarios, and lighten up. You want the real thing to be fun too, and if you get used to keeping things interesting and even humorous when you role-play, you'll find it much the same when you're doing the real thing.

Real profiles of people over 50 looking for someone

If you consider yourself picky (and most people do), then you need to be reassured about finding people who really are exciting potential partners. Here are some real people whose profiles I adapted from online dating sites — all of whom I have met and think are amazing people.

✔ 61-year-old man, handsome, healthy, love and collect wine. Live on a small horse farm within commuting distance of the manufacturing plant I started and function as CEO for this and other endeavors. Love travel and dogs, have two adult children, and am looking for a life partner in a similar age bracket and place in life.

✔ 83-year-old woman, ex head of a large charitable organization. Zest for life undiminished by years — still travel, serve on boards, and crusade for public education. Happily married for 43 years and hope to have the same kind of fun, communication, and affection with someone now. Financially independent. Have loving adult children, and it would be nice if you did too.

✔ Successful independent woman, consultant, 55 years old. Serious athlete — if it floats or can be climbed or skied, I'm doing it. Run half-marathons now; used to do the whole thing. Would love it if you also placed fitness at the center of your life. Winding down my career but not finished with it; it would be nice if you weren't ready to retire either.

✔ Divorced, 58-year-old man. Successful entrepreneur, told I am good looking. I work with my adult child and have a teenage son at home from my second marriage. Family is very important to me. Prefer to meet a woman within ten years of my age; a good sense of humor is a must. Not religious, middle of the road politics. Pretty good cook!

✔ Attractive 73-year-old woman, ready to relocate for love if required. Surprised at how much fun the 70s are — hope you think so too. Been a wife and mother most of my life, but now I find myself running a small garden design business. If you like gardening a lot, we would have a lot in common!

These are just a few people who have been vetted and found to be admirable, attractive, and nice. Most of them have found someone to love and be loved by. They don't have excessive baggage, and they're smart, lively, interesting men and women of varying ages. Some of them are quite well-off; others do well enough not to be worried. Two have had life-threatening illnesses but are fine now. They have a mix of life experience. There's a good chance you'll meet someone as wonderful as they are.

Knowing Where to Find the Best Prospective Dates

If you accept the proposition that tempting and exceptional people are reentering the dating world just like you are, then the next thing to sort out is where to find them. Happily, you have a number of different routes to travel, any or all of which may be successful.

Making connections through friends

Friends may seem like the least likely people to help you find a great date. After all, you may assume that you know all their friends or that if they knew someone to set you up with, they would have already suggested it. But that's not the case. Friends often think you'd be insulted if they offered to fix you up, or they worry that if it's not a match, you'd blame them, and the friendship would be endangered.

If you release your friends from responsibility, you may find out that they know some possible dating candidates. Here are a few things to tell them to make them more likely to refer you to someone:

- **It doesn't have to be a perfect match.** You're looking for dates right now, not a spouse. Just providing company would be a service. In fact, any live body that isn't dangerous is a good idea because you're just starting out, and you can learn from any experience.

- **You won't blame them if it doesn't work out.** Reassure friends that you'll be pleased with any introduction and that no matter what happens, you'll hold them blameless and protect the friendship.

- **They don't have to know the person well.** If this is a friend of a friend, that's fine with you. Tell friends to keep you in mind as an eligible person because they may meet someone interesting for just a fleeting moment, and if they're thinking about you, they could slip the person your phone number.

Friends can be squeamish about playing cupid, but if you're direct and even a bit forward about asking them to help find you someone, they may feel that they really have to put out extra effort — and that may net you someone special.

Sometimes you can help friends remember people they know but aren't thinking of off the top of their head. For example, instead of asking a friend, "Do you know anyone?" try asking, "Do you know anyone who really loves bridge like I do?" Asking more specific questions may jog a friend's memory. Or if you say, "Do you know anyone who may have single friends that love hiking like I do?" they may think of who they know in a new way. If you let people know that you're serious about finding someone, they may spend a little extra time thinking more creatively about who they know.

Being open to help from acquaintances

Find strength in weak ties. The man who cleans your clothes may have the secret name you need. Or you could find a promising date through a student of yours, a client, or the woman who cuts your hair. Much of what people accomplish in life happens through the suggestions of people who aren't in their inner circle. You may see your hairdresser only occasionally, but she knows your life, at least on a superficial level. And if you tell her that you're looking for dates, she may come up with some great suggestions about a friend or another customer.

Here's an additional list of people you may mention your new mission to:

- ✔ Your child's teacher
- ✔ The people you bike or run with
- ✔ Colleagues
- ✔ People you're working with on a committee
- ✔ People at a cocktail party
- ✔ Distant relatives
- ✔ Friends you know and keep up with through social media
- ✔ The people who work at the stores you frequent
- ✔ Anyone with whom you get into more than a five-minute conversation!

Keeping an eye out in public spaces

One of the places you find people outside your usual network is in public spaces. If you commute by train or fly a lot, check out people in the waiting room or airport and see whether they look good to you. Go sit by them and engage them in conversation by bringing up your day or talking about commuting or travel issues. People who don't want to be social will answer in brief sentences and turn away to their work or something else. If they do want to talk, you can express how difficult it is when schedules get fouled up because there's no one at home to feed your dog, or something like that — something to give a hint that you're single. Ask the person if he's planning the upcoming holidays with his family or some other question that may tell you whether he's married or in a relationship. This isn't always the case, but more often than not, people will tip you off as to their marital status on purpose or just because of the questions you ask.

These "stranger interviews" can quickly become flirtatious and build positive energy. Sometimes the person isn't available, but the conversation is still fun, and you're building your dating skill set! Other times, the connection is fast and powerful, and you start dating. What you have to do, though, is be observant and pick out someone you may like to talk to, and then actually do it. Neither step is easy, but after you get the hang of it, you may like the challenge.

Looking for love in all the right public spaces

You never know when a brief interaction with a stranger might turn into something more. Case in point: Judy worked in a spa and beauty business, and she almost never ran into men at work. So whenever she was in a public space, she kept an eye out for men who seemed interesting, and she would try to start up a conversation. She never missed an opportunity, and this was never truer than when she went to the dog park with her fox terrier. Her dog was just as social as she was, and he would greet other dogs and try to tempt them to play. This offered Judy some good opportunities to chat about dogs with other owners, and she met several men she dated that way. One day she met Adrien, who was walking his sister's dog, and a polite exchange of superficial remarks about the weather turned into a larger discussion about dog habits, which then turned into a conversation about family relationships, a subsequent coffee date, and later a trip to visit him in his hometown. This simple encounter at the dog park turned into a commuting relationship, and ultimately, Adrien moved from Minneapolis to Los Angeles to live with Judy.

One way to know if a person is interested in meeting you is to make eye contact and see whether he holds your gaze for a few seconds. If he does, there's a good chance he's interested and is giving you a bit of encouragement to engage with him.

Here are some other public spaces and events at which you may find dating candidates:

- Playgrounds you visit with grandchildren
- Waiting rooms for medical appointments
- Sports events
- Fundraising events
- Concerts, especially at the intermission
- Dog walking
- In line at a restaurant, grocery store, or just about any place

Most cities have announcements of special events, festivals, and performances that are happening that week. Read about them and try some out.

Mining your hobbies and regular activities

A good place for you to start is where you already are. If you're a runner, pay attention to who is running where you run and what kind of running clubs exist that you haven't joined. Keep running but pick a new part of town, where you can meet new people.

Think the same way about your gym. You may love your gym, but can you meet anyone new there? If you can't, then it's time to try a new location. You need to maximize ways to meet new people while still doing what you love to do.

If you're active in local or national politics, look for races to get involved with. A lot of older people take the time to put their energy where their values are promoted, and working on a campaign can build group camaraderie and individual relationships. The group camaraderie is important because it opens up new networks on the "strength of weak ties" theme. The closeness of working together may lead to an attraction that you wouldn't have felt otherwise.

It's important to keep doing the things you love and are good at, but it's also important to use that precious time in places that may introduce you to someone special. It's a pain to find a different dog trainer or wine club or pool to swim in, but these are the changes that may find you your perfect match.

Figuring Out How to Approach Someone

If you haven't dated in a long time, approaching someone may feel awkward, and being approached may feel embarrassing or even a bit scary. If you're freaked out, let me reassure you that while customs have changed, the basics will come back to you. I hate to say it's a little like remembering how to ride a bicycle — but actually, it is. If you haven't been on a bike for a long time, you're a bit wobbly in the beginning. But then it all comes back to you, and you're on your way!

There's an art to approaching someone. If you're awkward, even someone who was intrigued by you may move away. She may feel annoyed or even threatened. If you do it right, even someone who wasn't interested at first could come around and want to know you better. She may feel flattered or intrigued.

The most critical act, however, is to gather up your courage and do something! As the old saying goes, "He who hesitates is lost." True, if you never start, you can't be rebuffed — but then you stay alone.

As you start, the first thing to remember is your most important tool. No, it's not your opening lines. Even before the first word is mentioned, a successful beginning starts with your eyes . . . and the other person's eyes.

Making eye contact

When you first see someone, the instinct is to look down, to look away, to look anywhere but at the person. So my first instruction is, "Don't look away." The eyes have it. They're the first way you both signal interest in each other.

Don't look away if you're interested. The person may feel rebuffed. If you do look away, force yourself to look up again quickly. Beginnings can be over in the blink of an eye — literally.

Here's the gazing protocol:

1. **You glance at someone.**

2. **He glances at you.**

3. **You both return the glance and hold it until one of you breaks into a smile.**

4. **The smile is returned.**

5. **One of you walks over to start a conversation.**

Of course, if the other person doesn't glance your way, or you don't get a return on your glance, or your smile isn't returned, you'd be right in thinking that this is not a promising situation. You can walk over without this sequence, but your approach is likely to be unsuccessful. If you're bold, however, it's still worth a try.

The first step in approaching someone is to focus on him and allow him a moment to focus on you. If you come up to someone and start a conversation looking down at the ground or across the room or only intermittently meeting his eyes, you'll come across as shifty, not really interested, or even crass. You have to meet someone's eyes and then hold his attention and keep him focused on you. This is the beginning of connection, and if you don't create it at once, you may not get it at all.

After you approach someone, it's true that it may take you a few sentences to get the other person to really "see you" and take you in. If he's busy or distracted, he may not want to meet your eyes initially. That's when you have to combine eye contact with something really interesting to say or demonstrate. If your target person is in a grumpy or self-absorbed mood, getting him to focus on you is hard but not impossible. Men and women, however, have to use slightly different strategies, which we detail in the upcoming sections.

Don't try any of this with sunglasses on. Sunglasses may look sexy, but they hide expression and can make people nervous.

Approaching a potential date: Etiquette for women

In general, there's still an expectation that after eye contact is initiated, the man will walk over to the woman rather than vice versa. This is particularly true when a guy is older; the last time he dated, these were the rules — and he's sticking to them!

On the other hand, if you're an assertive woman who wants to take control of this little dance of eye contact and approach, you need to pull a man over to you without giving him the idea that you're interested in sex. A good deal of research indicates that men often misinterpret women's friendliness as a sexual come-on, and women often mistake a man's sexual flirtation as just friendliness. You can see the problem!

So if you're going to approach a guy, you want enough of a direct gaze to get him interested but not so much that he feels he's in for an immediate evening of hot times. One way to temper your forwardness and direct gaze is to make the conversation lighthearted, fun, and not too intense. Think of some topics you have in common (say a delayed airplane or a destination) and chat up your potential date on some of these topics.

If you feel you're not making headway, tell him directly that you're just entering the dating world again and that you wanted to meet him because he's so attractive or interesting looking or on the same commuter jet that you take — whatever applies. Granted, this can be embarrassing if he whips out pictures of his six kids, but be ready to laugh at yourself and the situation and say something nice: "Well, your wife is a lucky woman" or "I could tell you were a family man type. I was just hoping it was in the future, not presently!"

You risk a bit of embarrassment if you directly approach someone and say you're interested in him, but men do it all the time and live through the always present possibility of being shot down. There's nothing wrong with failing; there's only something wrong with not trying!

Women are used to being able to touch a man to indicate interest and as a sly promise of possibilities to come if things go right. But when you're just approaching a man, he may feel either that the touch is a solid promise and prelude to something totally sexual or that it's really too pushy. Younger men may not care, but older guys have learned that getting involved with women they don't know well can be trouble if they're not careful. Don't touch early on and give the wrong impression or scare the man away.

Approaching a potential date: Etiquette for men

Women generally appreciate an admiring glance, but make sure you know the difference between an admiring glance and a leer. Don't even think of any other gesture when you look at someone. No hand gestures, no mouth gestures, no finger clicking — nothing but the frank stare of appreciation and a slight or even big smile.

You need to convince a woman that you think she's attractive without coming across as a threat. Men often don't realize the level of fear many women have about meeting a stranger, so show interest while at the same time showing that you're a good, friendly guy and that she doesn't have to be afraid of you.

How do you do that? By approaching slowly and carefully and saying something kind and friendly. After she acknowledges your several-second stare from afar, you have to dial down the intensity by walking over, smiling, and keeping your eyes focused above her collarbone. You don't want her to feel like a piece of meat; you want her to feel admired in a nice way.

When you walk over, approach in a gentlemanly fashion. Don't interrupt her if she's in the middle of a conversation. Wait for a break in the conversation and then introduce yourself, and be sure you have a follow-up line to avoid an awkward silence after you've said hello.

Your opening line should say something about why you noticed her, such as her laugh, her smile, her overall attractiveness, her clothes, her style, or the way she talks with her friends. In other words, something nice that has nothing to do with her chest, her butt, or even her lips (even if that's what you did notice). For example, you could say, "I'm drinking pale ale too. Can I buy you one?" or "You seem to be having a lot of fun here. I wondered what you were all laughing so much about."

If you can avoid it, don't have a drink in your hand. You want her to believe that your interest in her is genuine rather than the result of moderate to extreme intoxication.

If you can find something in common as soon as possible, that will reduce her fear ratio. Perhaps you both work in the same building or both know the wedding party at a wedding. Or you can just straight out say, "Tell me a bit about yourself" and search for common networks or neighborhood- or work-related things that may be mutually interesting.

Men are often expected to make the first move, so you have that going for you. At the same time, there is such a thing as being too forward or aggressive, so you have to moderate your approach so it feels comfortable to both of you.

Getting help if you're shy

The very thought of glancing at a stranger and smiling may fill you with dread if you're shy and you don't like to approach people. You may even have trouble being approached. Perhaps you get tongue-tied and awkward on first meetings. So you need support approaching someone or accepting someone else's approach.

It's helpful to have a friend with you when you're out and about trying to meet people. Pick a friend who can take on some of the beginning approach or response for you. You can focus on someone together, walk over, and let your friend start the conversation and bring you in on it. Or you can be there together and when someone approaches, your friend can rave about you and ask you questions to get you started until you feel comfortable talking on your own.

Don't feel bad about yourself if you need this kind of help. Many people do; ever notice how few people go to a bar alone? Conversing with strangers is a daunting challenge to many people, and most people do better with a friend who helps grease the conversation and brings them out of their shell.

If you're painfully shy, you may be tempted to drink a lot more in social situations in order to get braver. This is understandable, but in almost all situations, drinking for courage is a self-defeating coping mechanism.

Avoiding the lame pickup line

Give a bad opening line and all is lost. Give a good one — even a passable one — and the door is at least halfway open. A good pickup line is complimentary without being extravagant. It compliments the person, not the body. It doesn't involve bragging. It locates you (the neighborhood, the hangout, your work) and gives you a topic to proceed with. And it sets the stage for the next sentence. Otherwise, there really isn't much to talk about, or at least much to talk about that would be interesting. And most important, a good opening line doesn't scare someone and perhaps put the person on the defensive. Here are some examples that start out the conversation in a nice direction:

- ✔ "I just came here from work across the street. Do you work around here?"
- ✔ "You have the nicest smile. You seem like a really nice person."
- ✔ "I'm not a bar (party) kind of animal. It's nice to see someone who looks friendly."
- ✔ "Do you come here often? This is my neighborhood hangout."
- ✔ "I like your laugh. I saw you with your friends, and you seem like a really happy person."

As a general rule, don't open with a joke. You don't know this person very well, and sometimes, jokes come off as snarky, impolite, puzzling, or just plain stupid.

People generally say something corny or insulting when they're nervous or drunk. You can avoid approaching a person when you're drunk, but being nervous may be a bit harder to fix. That's why you have to practice not just your first line but a few follow-up lines to make sure you don't say something you'll groan about later. After something comes out of your mouth, it's hard to take it back, even if you apologize.

Here are some good things to avoid:

- **Anything about extreme emotions:** "I fell in love just seeing you walk across the room."
- **Anything with excess flattery:** "You remind me of (name of movie star)" or "You had me at hello."
- **Anything overtly sexual:** "You are so sexy" or "What a sexy dress."
- **Anything that's obviously false or sounds like bragging:** "I have a summer home near here; weren't you around my beach yesterday?"
- **Any quotes by Shakespeare or any other writer:** It just sounds too slick and practiced.

You'll be walking a tight line between just being warm, friendly, and sincere and clearly asking the person out for a date. You don't want to come off as an overeager puppy, nor do you want to look insecure and too shy. The important thing is to make sure you clearly ask the person out. Otherwise, the person may be confused about your intentions. Your biggest fear may be coming on too strong; actually, the more common mistake is not to come on strong enough! As long as you're not draping yourself all over the person or acting cheesy or arrogant, a clear expression of interest is the right way to go.

Worst of the worst: Lame pickup lines

A bad pickup line is met with derision and contempt. Here are some of the worst lines for men to say to women:

- "I'm here because you're the most beautiful woman in the room."
- "You and I were meant for each other. Fate has brought us together."
- "Baby, where have you been all my life?"
- "Don't I know you from somewhere?" (This one is a cliché, so you should avoid saying it even if it's true.)
- "You seem to be all alone...need company?"

Women are less likely to initiate contact. That's too bad, because some men are shy and need someone else to take the first step. But if you do initiate contact, avoid being too seductive and steer clear of the following openers:

- "I saw you looking at me."
- "Want to buy me a drink?"
- "Hi handsome."
- "That's an expensive suit you're wearing. Is it Armani? Or Hugo Boss?" (said while stroking the material)
- "I was just trying to figure out your sign. Are you a Gemini?"

Taking care not to scare

If you approach a total stranger in a public place, she may regard you with caution. Most people are what they say they are, but that's not true for everyone. A woman doesn't know whether a man is dangerous, and a man doesn't know whether a woman is setting him up for something. You need to send out signals that you're safe. How do you do that?

- Don't come on too strong, no matter how attracted you are.
- If you're there with friends, introduce them.
- Talk about your work, your day, or upcoming plans. Show that you have a normal way of talking about things.
- Suggest getting together sometime soon in a public place for lunch — not a drink (causing the person to question what you expect) or dinner (setting up images of drinking and late-night activities).
- Hand over a card with your number on it, showing that you are who you say you are.

If you meet someone and it feels wrong, listen to that instinct. If someone gives you a creepy feeling, you should heed that feeling and cross that person off the list. Who knows what it is? It could be an inappropriate laugh, an inability to keep eye contact, or perhaps some contradictory stories. It doesn't really matter what's bothering you or even whether you're wrong or right about your feelings; if you have them, you need to honor them.

Because you're strangers to each other, there is, and should be, a certain amount of caution during the early stages of meeting. Because you may be nervous or unpracticed in how to begin talking to someone you're attracted to, something you say or do could scare the other person, and she may quickly end the conversation.

You may think that this is only a problem for men, but it's not; both men and women can appear scary. Women may fear the man who is hiding a tendency to be violent or sexually aggressive. Women don't generally frighten men physically, but they can frighten them with their emotions, such as if their neediness is so apparent that the man fears that the woman may harass and hound him if she doesn't feel accepted or well treated. Men are more cautious than you think, and they've heard true tales of women who became stalkers or engage in other bizarre behavior when they were alone with someone.

So you really have to come across as an integrated personality: solid, with no big swings of emotion, no hyper energy, no anger, no bitterness, and no excessive neediness. If you have a big personality or tend to be a little too touchy-feely with people early on, do some role-playing with a friend to calibrate your actions so that you don't bowl someone over. A little insight into how you come across can save you a lot of disappointment.

Don't drink at all when you're just meeting someone. Alcohol tends to make people an expansive version of themselves, and sometimes they get carried away, and their personality is way more exaggerated than it normally is. Take alcohol off the menu for quite a while and you'll be much more likely to act the way you intended to act, modify your approach to the right pitch, and meet a person who's attracted to your authentic self.

Considering Online Dating

The elephant in this room is the possibility of online dating. Online dating has been growing exponentially over the last decade and has become a dating resource for millions of people. It isn't for everyone, but it's a godsend to people who like it. It opens up many more new networks than you would discover by yourself, and you get much more information about the person you're looking at online than you would with most of the methods to meet someone described in this chapter. Of course, the major drawback is that you may be attracted to someone's picture, her voice on the phone, or her writing on the Internet, but in person she somehow doesn't hold up the way you hoped she would. Still, there's a reason why almost all the dating sites report that their biggest percentage increase in membership has been with the 50 and older crowd.

Chapter 6 takes an in-depth look at online dating and how to do it successfully.

Ask some of your friends who've met someone recently how they met their new partner. It's very likely that they'll surprise you by saying they met online!

Chapter 6

The Online Dating Scene: Choosing, Learning, Winning

• •

In This Chapter

▶ Considering the promise of going online

▶ Finding out about different sites and which may be best for you

▶ Picking up on warning signs online

▶ Writing an appealing profile

▶ Dating safely online

• •

*W*hen online dating first emerged, older people were particularly cautious about it. People over 50 were rarely first adopters of technology, and it took a lot of time just to send e-mail, much less use Facebook, tweet, and start online businesses. But that's all changed, and online technology has become part of almost everyone's life.

With more knowledge and more facility negotiating the Net, online dating becomes more ordinary and acceptable. In the beginning, there was a feeling of uncertainty; after all, what kind of person would go online to find a mate? Now people know what kind of person would — themselves! People have heard so many stories of people meeting each other online that the stigma is gone, and some of the fear as well. But you may still need convincing. Not to worry — there are plenty of reasons that make going online to find a mate a very wise move. And once you're ready, I offer tips and advice to make your experience easy and enjoyable.

Why Go Online?

Online dating for people over 50 has become normal. Most people have thought about it, and a lot of people have done it. You may have tried it yourself but found it daunting or had a bad experience and gave up. Though I'm not saying online dating is for everyone, I'll go out on a limb and say it's for almost everyone, and one try doesn't fully explore its possibilities. Online dating is, in most ways, the most efficient, best way to date a lot of people, and it's particularly functional for older people.

Discovering new networks

People generally start thinking about online dating because they aren't meeting anyone new. Most people would prefer to meet someone in person, so they do all the usual things to find dates, like going to art openings, open houses, and cocktail parties and taking on new sports — in general, opening up their life to the possibility of chance encounters of the romantic kind.

It's the right theory, but sometimes it just doesn't work. People in smaller towns and cities exhaust their possibilities pretty quickly, and even people in big cities find themselves meeting the same people over and over again or not meeting someone who feels like a good match. So, reluctantly perhaps, they turn to the idea of online dating.

And they should! Online dating's greatest contribution is that it opens you up to new people. You can meet literally thousands of people in your age group, some of whom you may have passed on the street or at the airport but whom you never would have met in person because you were in different circles that never intersected. You were not in the same network of folks, but after you go online and enter a new group, you realize there are terrific people out there but they're living in parallel worlds. Here's what some people have said about this phenomenon:

> Woman, 68: "We were both teaching at the university, but I was in romance languages and he was in fisheries. It's a big campus, and the places we eat are in a completely separate complex of buildings. If we hadn't met online, we would never have met, even as co-faculty members!"

> Man, 59: "I'm in the import and export business, and I go to China all the time, but I had never been to the Chinese suburb she lives in. I have a certain snobbishness about suburbs, and it's not a place I would have looked. She travels a lot for her work too, mostly to Europe, and maybe we would have bumped into each other in the airport, but probably not. Meeting her online was the only way it would have happened, so I'm very grateful to the web!"

Getting more information upfront

It's kind of ironic that most people would prefer meeting face to face because while doing so gives you the most information about being attracted to each other, it gives you the least information about everything else. The best part of dating online (besides getting into new networks and having lots of choices) is how much information you get about people beforehand. You can find out their hobbies, feelings about children, political persuasion, religious beliefs, and a lot more. You can also find their "deal breakers" — things they dislike so much that they list them so that they aren't matched up with anyone who has one of these habits or beliefs. Common deal breakers that appear in online dating profiles are:

- ✔ Smoking (nonsmokers are sticklers for this one!)
- ✔ Wants to have kids with their new partner (or doesn't want to be around their partner's kids)
- ✔ Political beliefs (conservatives who want other conservatives; liberals who want other liberals)
- ✔ Cats or dogs (against, usually because of allergies; or for, because they have them)
- ✔ Distance (some people won't consider someone far away)
- ✔ Religion and religiosity (or lack thereof) — some people want someone who practices the same religion they do; others just want someone who is very religious or not religious at all
- ✔ Weight (very fit people often make it clear they'll consider no one who is heavy or unfit)

Some of these deal breakers may sound obnoxious or narrow, but at least you know where someone stands — and you can make your own preferences very clear. In thinking about what you want and don't want, you also get to know yourself better, and that's no small advantage.

You only want to list your absolute "will not consider" items under deal breakers. If you list a lot of them, like almost everything in the previous list, and also add desirable physical attributes like "must have blue eyes and be over five foot ten," you start to narrow your possible dates quite a bit!

Finding people you have things in common with

Sometimes a characteristic or set of characteristics that you prize in yourself and others is so important that you only want to choose people that fit that description. For example, if you live on a ranch or you show horses and horses are your life, you may only want to look at other horse people for partners. You can find them on general sites, but you can find a lot of them on www.equestriansingles.com. Likewise, if you're a trainer or yoga instructor and would like to meet another enthusiast, you may want to go to www.fitsingles.com.

Social networking sites and your long-lost love

If you're interested in online dating, you might consider using the general networking sites that bring people together who used to know one another but have lost contact over the years. Remember that great guy from 8th grade or your girlfriend in high school? Reaching out to them through Facebook or Classmates.com may prove to be an interesting and rewarding experience. Sure, they may not be available (you can usually find out quickly from their bio whether they're single), but even if they seem single and turn out not to be, you'll still have the fun of checking in and finding out about their life. Better yet, they may be unattached.

An ongoing study started in 1993 by Dr. Nancy Kalish found that 51 percent of the people in her study who had reconnected with a lost love were 40 or older — 37 percent were in their 40s and 50s, 10 percent were in their 60s, and 4 percent were over age 70. Kalish found that older people who reconnected to childhood or previous sweethearts usually fell in love faster than other kinds of daters and got married more quickly. Many of these people felt immediately comfortable with the person from the past because they shared a history, even if it was long ago. This may not work out for everyone; people almost certainly change a lot over the years. Still, even if your memory of a special person doesn't match the person today, it's certainly worth the effort to track the person down and find out whether an old flame can still heat up.

Some boutique dating sites come and go quickly, but options include sites for Greek singles and African-American singles. You can also find sites that prioritize religious compatibility, like those targeted at Christian or Jewish singles. You can even use sites for alumni of Ivy League and elite schools.

Other sites cater exclusively to people over age 50, so you're more likely to meet someone you can connect with. Here are some good examples:

✔ http://dating.aarp.org (see Figure 6-1)

✔ www.seniormatch.com

The advantage of these sites is that they bring you a group of people that fit your criteria and help you narrow your search and potentially save you some time. If you want to meet another Jewish person, going to a Jewish singles site helps you do that. The only drawback to these sites is that they generally have a lot fewer people than the big diverse sites, so you could miss out on a potential match who only uses the larger sites.

Meeting a lot of available people

You've probably met everyone at your church group who you're going to meet through that venue. Maybe a few new people will pop up, but not too many, and not many of them single.

Figure 6-1:
The home page of AARP's senior dating site.

But the web is different. New people are always showing up. Relationships break up, spouses die, or perhaps a connection that started on the Net isn't quite strong enough to go the distance, and so a person reappears to try again. The Net is constantly refreshing itself, which makes it always interesting.

Furthermore, the web has so many sites, and few people go to all of them. So if you switch a site you may find a new set of people. This is particularly true if, for example, you've been on one of the big sites and then you go to a boutique site. You're almost guaranteed to find some new people who didn't want to try the larger, less-tailored sites.

Narrowing your dating search can pay off

If you have a specific passion that orients your life, it can help if you go to a site that is specifically for people who share that passion. The chances of finding a person who can share your lifestyle with you increase exponentially! For example, the avid athlete like the man in the following anecdote may do best if he looks for someone on a site that's all about being fit and into sports.

"I live and breathe athletic competition. I've tried being with women who aren't just as crazy about athletic competition as I am, and it just doesn't work. I spend so much time training, and it's also the way I relax and blow off steam. So I just looked at dating sites that focus on fitness, and that worked really well for me. Mari is a swimmer and was once a champion. She enters other athletic competitions as well; right now she's training for the senior Olympics. We understand each other; it's such a pleasure."

Some people who are very motivated to find a partner are on and off a dating site as soon as they can possibly manage it. So if you see a new face and you're interested, contact that person immediately. The person may be gone very soon, and you want to have a chance to meet.

So many people are on the Net that sometimes people get addicted to staying online, intrigued by the next wonderful possibility. Don't let that happen to you. There will always be intriguing people, but if you're really looking for a partner, you don't want to get seduced by the idea that the grass is always greener someplace new.

Some people online are just serial daters who don't want to commit to anyone, but the vast majority of people are looking for a serious partner. Yes, you may also run into the occasional person who pretends to be free and is not, but fortunately, there aren't too many of them. If you do meet someone who is engaged, married, or otherwise committed, don't get so discouraged that you drop out. You've just been unlucky; most people are what they say they are, and if they say they're looking for their one and only, that's likely to be the case.

When you get interested in someone and are thinking about dating the person, do some due diligence and conduct a web search on the person. With not too many clicks you ought to be able to find out whether the person is single or married.

The exception: The married guy

Occasionally, someone pretends to be available when he's really not. Married people posing as single daters aren't common, but they do exist — and you should be aware of the warning signals that someone may be lying to you. You may think it's not nice to check up on someone to make sure he's telling you the truth, but unfortunately, sometimes it's necessary.

Consider this real-life example: Patti had had great experiences dating online but still hadn't found anyone. Then she met Ira — handsome, an entrepreneur, new in town. She was smitten, and they started seeing each other every other week. He said he couldn't see her more often because he still had some obligations to his old job and was still living part time in his former city. She was in love, but he was never available on weekends, and this aroused her suspicions. She looked up a previous company he said he had started, and indeed he had. Unfortunately, with not much more digging she found out that he had a wife at that time. When she searched the wife's name online, her worst fears were confirmed: Ira and his wife were still married. She was extremely upset and depressed, but she broke it off and a year later was in love again and engaged to a trustworthy guy.

Meeting quality people

Some people still believe that people who date online are substandard. But that couldn't be further from the truth. Celebrities (Martha Stewart, Joan Rivers), CEOs, lawyers, doctors, military officers, and other accomplished and attractive people eventually go on the web to meet someone. Perhaps when online dating was new it was reasonable to assume that only the daring and the desperate would be early adopters, but it really wasn't true then, and it certainly isn't true now. You can be sure that there are people online whom you'd be thrilled to date — no matter how you meet them.

Setting Your Online Expectations

As I explain in Chapter 2, working on your attitude and expectations is a critical part of getting ready for dating and being able to have a new relationship. That applies whether you're dating online or taking the more traditional route. To increase the chances of online dating success and to maximize your enjoyment of the experience, you need to be aware of some common errors in judgment, including unrealistic expectations, lack of preparation, and issues of trust and honesty.

Sidestepping common mistakes

You want to avoid setting your sights so high that you have a hard time finding someone. Here are three things you may expect that, unmodified, will undermine your success:

- **You think you'll find someone fast.** Some people have great luck and find someone on a first date, but some people also win the lottery. It's about that common. You really have to stick around and go on a lot of dates before you find "the one." You may find people to hang with sooner than that — in fact, you most assuredly will. But finding the person for you takes time, a bit of luck, and perhaps a mastery of the dating system.

- **You go after someone whom everyone goes for, and thus, your chances are low.** Some people on the web are spectacularly good looking, or spectacularly accomplished, or write a particularly moving profile. These people get hundreds of approaches. If this is the only kind of person you aim for, your chances of finding someone are correspondingly lower.

✔ **You don't try to sell yourself.** You may expect that others will see the inner you without a lot of salesmanship. This isn't true. People read a lot into these profiles, and some online daters craft detailed profiles and figure out a way to make themselves shine. You need to put the same kind of thought, effort, and probably a friend's editing into your search. Otherwise, you may not look as interesting as the people who put together a really good presentation.

Watching out for white lies and whoppers

Though some people lie in their profiles, most only shade the truth. The areas that people fudge the most are their age, weight, and height. Few people (with the exception of the whoppers I talk about shortly) lie about anything major (like being married as opposed to single). Still, the question of whether it's a white lie or a whopper often lies in just how close to the truth it is. For example, common categories to describe weight are "slender," "fit," "average," and "a few extra pounds." Most people are afraid to pick "a few extra pounds," and readers usually presume that everyone is gilding the lily, so that the people of "average" weight are actually heavy, and the "few extra pounds" people are really heavy.

Maybe if you're not slim or fit, you think people won't consider you. But the truth is, you have to go with what you have. A little lie like not fessing up to a few extra pounds isn't little anymore when the actual difference is 40 pounds. These white lies may not cause a problem if someone was already flirting with you in person and obviously didn't think your weight was a big issue, but they matter a lot when the first time a person sees you, you're 40 pounds heavier than you look in your profile picture.

People can get angry and rude when they think they've been misled. If you're much heavier than you said you were, someone meeting you for the first time may just turn right around and decide not to stay. Save yourself from mortification. Don't lie substantially about what you look like.

Whopper lies are the dark side of online dating. Many predatory people are on the Net. The most common deception is a married man or a man who lives with someone and says he's single. Another variation on this theme is a man who strings along three or four women and tells each that she's the only one. Some women do the same thing, but I've found that to be less common. You may also encounter people who misrepresent their financial status.

On some sites, professional sex workers contact men who are there looking for dates, not sex. These professionals figure that some of these men will be flattered by attention from a very attractive woman (or a man on gay sites), so that even if they didn't go to the site looking for sex, they may be very happy to get some. Of course, not all of them lie and present themselves as just sexy potential partners. Some of them are straightforward about being "affectionate" if they "are treated right" or just ooze sexual promise — and then, when contacted off-line, say that the "affection" comes at a price.

Male scam artists generally have an impossibly handsome picture — but that's not the tip-off, because of course there are other handsome men on the Net. Two things should alert you to the truth about these guys. Some of them only want to communicate by e-mail and have all kinds of excuses why they can't talk on the phone. This is because the Nigerian men who do this would be calling from another country, and they have accents that usually don't match their picture. And second, they'll tell you they love you madly within a very short time. They may wait six months after that, but eventually, they'll ask you for money so they can come visit you while their money is tied up because the bank made a big mistake and it has to be cleared up, or something like that.

One bite of a bad apple and the whole online dating space can seem threatening and dishonest, but don't think this is a common occurrence. The majority of people online aren't scam artists, and you can avoid these scammers if you follow my advice about safety on the Net in this chapter. (Flip to Chapter 8 for general safety rules when dating.)

Don't get turned off because there are a few dishonest people on the web. People lie in every kind of dating or casual meeting situation. This problem isn't confined to Internet dating, but you have to be somewhat more cautious online because it can be harder to check out the facts.

Crafting Your Profile: How to Be Honest and Appealing

To date online, you need to be able to write reasonably well. And that's not the only skill you need that's more specific to dating online than any other kind of dating. You need to know, for instance, how to write a profile, how to make and respond to inquiries, and how to judge other people from their profiles. If you don't have those skills now, don't worry. I'll walk you through it.

Putting some thought into your picture

The first thing in your profile that people glance at is your picture . . . and I do mean glance. Many people spend only a few seconds checking out your picture before moving on to the next picture, and the next, looking for a face or smile that appeals to them. It's not fair, and it's not even in the web browser's best interest, but it's pretty much the way it happens.

The picture is more important than it should be. In real life, people take in a lot of cues at once about a person: her voice, her facial expressions, her dress, and of course how she says what she says. But online dating's first introduction is a picture, and so appearance in online dating is more important than in real life.

Still, you can create a mood and convey more information in that picture if you pay attention to these points and take them seriously:

- ✔ **Don't use a blurry picture.** Most people just bypass a blurry picture, assuming that you used that picture because you don't want to be seen — and perhaps that's your reason! In any case, it's a bad idea.

- ✔ **Don't use an old picture.** Pictures of you in high school will cause people to think that was your best moment and that you're hiding your true self. Any picture older than a year or so isn't a good idea.

 Consider getting a special picture taken just for this occasion. Women have an advantage in that they can wear makeup and get their hair styled to look their best. It's not cheating to go to a salon and get professionally made up and then get your picture taken. You'll look your very best for your profile picture, and you also may get some pointers that will help you look your best every day. It's truly amazing what a skilled makeup artist and hair stylist can do to bring out your best characteristics.

- ✔ **Don't use half a picture.** People often take a picture and then cut their ex-husband or wife or kid out of it, and it looks funny. It looks like you don't care enough to put a good picture of just you on the site.

- ✔ **Don't use a raucous party picture.** Unless you think each one of the people in this picture reflects well on you, you'll be judged by how your friends look as well as yourself.

- ✔ **Do post a picture that looks friendly, open, and warm.**

- ✔ **Do post more than one picture if the site allows it, but remember that each picture is as important as the next.** Each picture should portray you at your best. It does help if you show some pictures of you doing different things: boating, traveling, hiking, painting, and so on.

- ✔ **If you post only one picture, don't use one with your children in it.** Doing so makes the viewer uncertain about your priorities or what role potential dates would be expected to play with your family.

 Be careful if you post a picture with your adult children — sometimes they look like they could be a partner. Likewise, be careful of a picture that shows you with a grandchild; that could look like you have a young child at home. For some people, that would be a deal breaker.

> ✔ **Don't pick a picture that doesn't look like you when you sit down for coffee.** People get angry if a picture misrepresents you. It can be a good version of you — but not so good that it doesn't look like you in real life.

Writing your profile

Your profile is a combination of answers to specific questions for a specific site and the free-form text that describes who you are and who you want, in your own words. This written part of your profile is extremely important. I can't emphasize your essay enough. The first thing people do is look at your picture, but the second thing they do is look at the written section. This is the place where potential dates get a sense of what kind of personality you have. So it isn't just what you write but how you write it that makes a difference. Here are three things to make sure you do:

> ✔ **Use spell check.** If your profile has typos or misspelled words, many people will look no farther than the first mistake and delete you from consideration. They'll figure that you're uneducated or at the very least uninterested in anything serious. They'll assume that if you took so little care about spelling, you're probably not very invested in the whole process.

> ✔ **Show your heart.** People are looking for authenticity. If you put down a lot of superficial thoughts and nothing about what you want out of life or what's truly important to you, you'll be more interesting to people who are looking for fun and less interesting to people who are looking for someone who could love them.

> ✔ **Take the time to tell your story; don't be too brief.** Remember, this is the only place a person can get a sense of your personality. A few sentences don't give enough information. And you need more than information — you need to let your writing style speak for you (so that you get a chance to speak in person). If you're funny, be funny (but remember that humor can translate in different ways than you intend). If you're earnest, be earnest. But give yourself at least a couple of paragraphs so that your personality emerges.

Write a convincing description of yourself, but don't go much longer than a couple of paragraphs or it may not get read. People go through pictures and profiles very quickly, and you don't want to look like it's work to read your thoughts.

Making sure your profile meets basic requirements

A good profile has two required parts: a description of the kind of person you are, including a section on your hobbies, passions, and outlook on life; and an appealing description of who you're looking for.

In the first part, give some background information: married, divorced, with kids, and the like. You can talk about what kind of work you do, or did, and how you spend most of your free time. You can talk about your lifestyle and what kinds of things you'd like to share with someone. After that discussion, you can talk about who that someone might be.

Here you want to be careful. You want to be clear about who you're looking for, but you don't want to sound like you want the perfect human being and nothing less will do. This isn't the time to give long lists of characteristics and physical attributes. You want to prioritize your preferences and list the most important ones. If you write a laundry list of requirements, most people will be offended and think you're arrogant (even though they may secretly have a pretty long list, too). You want to say what's most important to you and what's preferable but not necessary. Help people know whether you're looking for them, and save both of you wasted time and effort if they obviously don't fit your most important priorities.

Comparing your profile to other great ones

A great profile makes you want to meet that person. It also resonates with you; you feel like you and this person would get along and share values and an approach to life. You're reassured if you think this person would share some of the same passions and ambitions you have and that the person would add to your life. Following are some written parts of profiles that would attract the right person — and discourage the wrong one.

Profile: Animal Lover Looking for Another

I'm a 55-year-old, active, and cheerful woman who loves gardening, old movies, an occasional game of poker, and great food with great wine. I am, without a doubt, a dedicated and imaginative cook! (I used to have a catering business but sold it last year.) Most of my hobbies would, I hope, be easy to live with, but one passion of mine will need a special guy. I love dogs and have three of them, and I often foster pets for the Humane Society until they find a good home. Not liking dogs is a deal breaker!

I'm looking for someone who is optimistic, knows how to have a good time, and also likes some solitude and space. I don't ask anyone to love my hobbies, but I need time for them and want someone who also wants time for himself from time to time. I do love to cook, so it would help if you liked fine food and were particular about your wine or at least would like to learn about food and wine with me. I also love to read and discuss books and classic movies, and if you were a movie buff I would be thrilled, but all I really need is someone who likes to read and talk about what he has read.

I'm tall, but I have no height requirements for someone to fill. I'm more interested in your character, your enthusiasm, and your positive attitude about life and the future. I don't smoke and can't deal with it, so if you smoke, I'm not your girl. But I'm open to many different kinds of people — as long as you don't dislike dogs!

Profile: I Have Wanderlust; Hope You Do Too

I've traveled the world, and I'm not done yet! Sixty, as they say, is the new 50, but right now I'm feeling like it's the new 40. I've gone through a rough patch — I lost my dear wife of 34 years, and it's taken me about 2 years to get back to enjoying life. But I'm ready now and looking for someone who is also ready to love.

I've worked as a travel agent for many years and also consulted with hospitality clients on technical programs for booking trips. I'm a bit of a nerd, but not so much that I don't enjoy swing dancing and dinner parties. My main passion is travel, but I'm open to how we do it; I must say, though, that my camping days are pretty far behind me.

I have three adult sons, a warm, full-of-life Italian family, and I want someone who feels the same way about family that I do — the more the better. I promise you I'd feel the same way about your kids and whoever else is in your life.

I think life is to be lived now. I believe in family, friends, God, and country — all the old-fashioned virtues. If this sounds like you too, I hope you'll contact me — and, of course, I'll be looking for you.

Profile: You're Never Too Old for Rock and Roll

I've never completely grown up I guess. I'm an almost 70-year-old woman who still likes rock and roll, late night movies, and experimental theater. Like many of you, I don't feel like 70 sounds, and you can decide whether I look it (whatever 70 is supposed to look like!). I'm healthy enough to go to concerts that start at midnight and end at 3 a.m. (although to be honest, that is a pretty rare occurrence for me these days). But I do love music, and I try to keep current — and when I fail, my adult children fix up my iTunes so that I know what's happening in the music world.

I've been a designer most of my life. I no longer have as intense a career as I had before, but I still have a longtime client list, and I work part time for a major sports design firm. I'm pretty athletic myself and have run quite a few 5K runs, and I'm trying for a half marathon. I'm passable at tennis and golf, and I know how to crew a sailboat. I love the city but can do well in the country; when I was married, we split our time between the two.

You should be fit, fun, and intelligent; love music; and it would be wonderful if we shared a sport in common. That isn't necessary, though; if you're an attractive person inside and out, I can make plenty of compromises. One compromise I won't make, however, is dating someone more than an hour away from me. I've tried that and it just doesn't work for me.

Profile: Worked Hard, Now It's Time to Play!

I'm a retired principal of a large inner-city high school. I've enjoyed this work enormously, but sometimes it's time to move on to another phase of your life. I still do a lot of charitable work for my college (Howard University) and my undergraduate fraternity. I live on the East Coast but I'm movable. I have great affection for the Los Angeles area, where most of my family lives.

I also have a great affinity for other people who've worked with young African-American men and women and who are committed to enabling the fulfillment of their potential. Most of my close friends are teachers, counselors, and activists who, like myself, have dedicated themselves to social justice and liberation by education. In addition, I come from a family of social workers, another profession I respect.

I'm particularly interested in meeting an active or retired professional woman somewhere between the ages of 45 and 65. I'm 62 myself, a divorced father of two adult children. I'd prefer meeting someone who also has adult children. I'm far beyond wanting to have additional children and also prefer not to go into active day-to-day parenting again. I have had an intense career, and I'm ready to enjoy life. I have a fishing cabin that I love to go to in upstate New York, and it would be a plus if you liked to fish. I'm an active guy — I work out several times a week — and I admire women who take care of themselves and would like an active lifestyle. I'm also open to learning about the things that you enjoy and trying them. Above all, I want a woman who is able to love, who is kind, and who is not held back by past experiences.

Before you write your own profile, read a lot of them on the dating sites you join. You can learn a lot about what you want to say (and what you should avoid saying).

Showing what's truly important to you

One of the important things about these profiles is that they clearly show your personality and preferences and make a few statements that begin to tell the reader your priorities and values. You want to write about what's important to you in the hopes that it will attract like-minded individuals and also that it will send people on to someone else's profile if your profile doesn't appeal to them. Turning people away who wouldn't be interested in you saves time — yours and theirs. The clearer you are about what's important to you, the more likely you'll attract the attention of someone you'd be very interested in and not someone who is totally on a different page in life.

Being specific about details of your experiences

Don't be generic in the way you describe things. For example, instead of saying, "I like hiking," say, "I love hiking in countries with historic sites. Last year I hiked to Stonehenge, and this year I intend to visit similar sites in Ireland." Or, "My ambition is to hike some part of all the national parks because I'm never happier than when I'm camping in and walking through magnificent mountains."

Be specific about experiences, even if you're just describing your day-to-day life. For example, "My favorite kind of weekend day is to get up early, take a two-mile walk on one of my prescribed routes, go back and have an ultra-hot shower, and then meet a friend for coffee. After that, it depends on the day, but it can be anything from fixing things around the house to going to one of the many blues or bluegrass clubs that are within walking distance of my place."

Giving off an air of confidence and positive energy

The more confident, friendly, and happy your tone, the more people will be drawn to you. Most people on dating sites are complete strangers to one another, and they're looking for reassurance. They won't think a lot of you if you sound depressed or angry; they want someone who is self-confident. This can be a little tricky though; you want to sound self-confident but not arrogant. For example, "I started from nothing but slowly built up a business that now employs more than 100 people, many of whom, like me, came to the United States without speaking passable English." That's self-confident. This, however, is arrogant: "I'm a very successful CEO, the first in my area of business to ever get the Sam Smith Award, and there have been a cascade of honors since then." Hopefully, you can see the difference!

Part of how you sound depends on the words you use. Use bright, active words to describe your approach to life. Use evocative scenes to let someone see your soul.

"I'm always excited when I start a new continuing education class."

"I'm such an avid sports fan that I have to be careful not to scare the people who sit near me when I scream with delight when we get a touchdown."

"I'm a managing partner of an old, traditional law firm, so no one would know that I cry at sad movies, but I do, regularly."

What to Look for in a Date's Profile

As you get into online dating and start to read profiles of potential dates, you may feel overwhelmed by all the information posted, and you may be unsure of how to separate the wheat from the chaff, so to speak. This section helps you become better at evaluating profiles, because when you know what to look for and how to interpret what you see, your chances of picking the right person (or at least some solid contenders) are much improved.

Here are the basic things to look for in *any* profile:

- ✔ Decent writing and spelling
- ✔ More detail than "love long walks on the beach"
- ✔ A reasonable number of descriptive leads that cue you about who the person is looking for
- ✔ Absence of insulting or angry remarks
- ✔ Absence of touting the person's own special superiority
- ✔ Absence of overtly sexual language or demands

Specific insights about what men say in their profiles

The following list contains lines that men often use in their profiles, what those lines mean, and how you might react to them:

- ✔ **"I'm fit, and you should be too."** This means you should have zero body fat. No kidding. Even if you have zero body fat, you may not like a man who has that entry-level requirement. But if it's important to you too, recognize that this is seriously important to him.
- ✔ **"Don't answer this ad if you have any baggage."** Men who say this have had some bad experiences dating or at least what they perceive as bad experiences.

They may be bitter about those bad experiences and bring those feelings even to the first coffee. They may be suspicious and grill you — which isn't a pleasant or bonding experience.

✔ **"Don't answer this ad if you're looking for a sugar daddy."** This one isn't too hard to decipher: These men have experienced women who only wanted them for their financial support, and that's exactly what they don't want to be. Some of them are happy to share the financial costs of dating and being together, and some may be generous after a good relationship is established, but in general, this is someone who doesn't want a traditional relationship that assigns a man the total financial responsibility. In addition, never disregard the tone of a comment. The tone here is angry and defensive, much like in the preceding bullet, so you have to decide whether you want to meet someone who's in that state of mind.

✔ **"You should be very attractive."** He means beautiful. He thinks he deserves it or is worth it, but you better be way more attractive than average. Unless you're beautiful and like being admired for it and wanted for it, this wouldn't be a good ad to answer.

✔ **"I believe in chemistry."** "Chemistry" can be a code word for beautiful, but not always. What it does mean is that this person is looking for an instant connection that's part personality and part sexuality (heavy on the second part). This is one of the reasons you can have a perfectly wonderful coffee with someone but it doesn't go any further. At least for one person, "chemistry" didn't happen.

Specific insights about what women say in their profiles

Like men, women also telegraph messages that may or may not be what you want, and so it behooves you to understand what key words and expectations are embedded in their profiles.

✔ **"I'm looking for the love of my life."** She really is. If you're just looking to date or even to take it slow, this woman is probably not for you. She doesn't want to date just for the sake of dating, and she may abruptly discontinue seeing you if she decides that, although you're a perfectly great guy, you're not "the one."

✔ **"I'm a traditional woman."** You'll be expected to pick up the bill, and you won't have sex early on in the relationship.

✔ **"I can be very good to the right man."** Depending on the site you're on, this woman could be a sex worker. If she's very explicit about sexuality, she often has another agenda.

✔ **"My children are the joy and center of my life."** You better love kids, and you better be ready to wrap your life together around them. Younger or older, she interacts a lot with them and won't be totally devoted to you.

✔ **"I'm a widow who was married to the most wonderful man."** Good chance she's still in love with him. On the other hand, there's a chance that, because her previous marriage was excellent, she faces dating in one of two ways: There can never be another man like him, so all these relationships are secondary; or, because he was wonderful, she's open-hearted and ready to love again. You'll find out which mode she's in soon enough.

Evaluating a man's profile

Try to spot the warning signs in this man's profile:

I'm 55 years old and handsome — at least that's what I'm told by my friends and the women I know. I look and act much younger and would like a very fit woman between 30 and 50. I'm looking for someone like me — good looking, smart, and well-off. Is that too much to ask? Please don't reply if you're overweight, loaded with baggage, or still have children in your household. You should look great in a simple black dress, pearls, and high heels, but also on a golf course. (It would be highly desirable that you play golf well.) You should like to travel. I'll treat you very well, but you have to be ready to go at a moment's notice. I need someone who is free from everyday entanglements. Don't worry — you'll get plenty in return. We would have access to my house on a golf course in Arizona and also my condo in Hawaii. I'm retired from a corporate job, but I still have many of the perks, and I'd like you to enjoy them with me. I'm very generous to the right woman.

Here's what you should have noted in this profile:

✔ He brags about his looks. Not terrible, but a warning. He goes on to tell you how wonderful his life is and basically how you should hand yourself over because he has so much to offer. Read closer: This means everything is about him, and your life either folds in completely or he won't find you acceptable.

✔ He's looking for a woman 25 years younger than himself (he does go up to 5 years younger), so if he's seeking a much younger woman, there's a good chance he won't appreciate you if you're close to his age.

✔ He has quite a few requirements: His date has to be good looking, smart, and well off. He even tells you how to dress and what you should weigh! You should not only play golf; you better be good at it. Can you spell "controlling"?

✔ He doesn't want anyone "loaded with baggage." That's usually a signal that he doesn't want anyone who has anything that will impede his particular desires — in particular, he finds having children around annoying. He says he doesn't want them in the household, but even if you have kids living outside the home, he may not want them in your life!

✔ He indicates he can be "generous to the right woman." This is pretty close to saying that if you can meet his requirements, you'll get money and perks in return. At least you know the exchange rate, but maybe you want someone who doesn't think he can buy you!

Evaluating a woman's profile

Consider this woman's profile:

> I'm a 64-year-old widow with four wonderful children and nine fantastic grandchildren. We're a warm family, and they're at the center of my life. Life has been hard without their father, who died suddenly three years ago and left us without some of the comforts we were used to. But I soldiered on and am proud of the life I've put together since his passing.
>
> My children have been encouraging me to start living my life more fully, and I'm prepared to do that now. I love to cook and bake for the man I love, and I'm a supportive and fine friend. I'm looking for a man of good character who lives by Christian principles and doesn't smoke, drink, or gamble. He should also be neat and gentlemanly, and it would be very comfortable for me if he were also a Lutheran.
>
> I haven't seen much of the world, but I think it would be nice to do some traveling. I have an RV that my husband and I intended to use after retirement, but we never got a chance to use it. One hobby we enjoyed was ice fishing (popular here in White Bear Lake, Minnesota), and I still bundle up and go ice fishing with my children. I've also joined a walking club, and I'm looking for someone in good health who can do some of these activities with me.

Here's how to interpret this woman's message:

✔ A woman who mentions her children (and how wonderful they are) in the first sentence is telling you about her priorities and, perhaps, her central self-concept as a mom (versus as a partner). If you're going to be involved with this woman, you're going to be involved with her kids, and it's probable that her kids come first.

✔ If she mentions how hard her life has been without her children's father, she isn't into establishing her independence as part of her identity. You may or may not like this. However, because she also mentions economics, the loss of creature comforts, and traveling opportunities, there's a good chance she's looking for someone to help correct the situation.

✔ She's telling you she likes to take care of you in traditional, womanly ways. If she's traditional about some things, she's likely to be traditional about others.

✔ She wants a man who's free of "vices." And she has a long list of other requirements that she really wants met. She's quite judgmental, so if you don't fit her rather strict idea of the perfect man, you may want to pass on this opportunity.

✔ Many older women are worried about finding a partner who wants to be "nursed." Wanting a partner in "good health" is often a code word for "don't expect me to take care of you if you have anything seriously wrong with you." It can also be a code word for not wanting to date anyone older than they are (or sometimes even the same age).

Online Matching Systems: Do They Really Work?

Online matching systems don't necessarily send you your true love, but if you think of them as narrowing down the pool of eligible people so that you know more about them and they about you, you'll be pleased with the results. These tests aim to get you to someone you may love by helping you discard people who just don't have the personalities or characteristics that you find pleasing. A good matching system not only helps you avoid people whom you've expressly said you don't want but also helps you know yourself better and feel more comfortable about whom you should look for. In this sense, quite a few of the matching systems are very helpful. In fact, one good reason for trying several of them is because they give you different kinds of insights into who you want and what your own personality type is, and these insights can help you be more effective in relationships.

I'll give you an example I know well. I created a matching system for www.perfectmatch.com called Duet, based on the theory used by the Myers-Briggs test, a highly successful matching system developed for organizational teams to understand one another and to see how different ways of approaching a problem can actually be helpful, even if the parties experience frustration because of their differing approaches. If, for example, one person is a *closer* and likes to come to conclusions rapidly, and the other is an *extender* and likes to think about all aspects of a problem before rushing to judgment and execution, the two may get aggravated with each other, not realizing that they actually make a pretty good team, even if it isn't an easy fit.

In Duet, the system matches people based on characteristics — both similar and somewhat different — where the combination of characteristics produced some degree of predictability about how compatible the two people might be. Four characteristics are listed in the personality category, where similarity generally works best:

- Risk-taking versus being risk-averse

- Active types versus more laid-back people

- Optimistic versus cautious approach to life

- People who like predictability and replication of places and people versus people who like variety and change

The characteristics and preferences that may work with similarity or difference are:

- Flexible people who accept many solutions to an issue versus people who want things to be done a certain right way (structured)

✔ Calm people versus people who are excitable and usually passionate about their feelings

✔ People who like to lead versus people who like to follow or compromise

✔ Extroverts versus introverts (defined here as people who get energy from being with people versus people who feel depleted by a lot of interaction with people)

These tests, done on www.perfectmatch.com (and in my book *Finding Your Perfect Match,* published by Perigee Trade), aren't a panacea for matching, but they do give personal insight, and they're based on solid social science data. Many of the other sites, such as www.okcupid.com or www.chemistry.com, also have interesting and useful matching systems that may be worth looking into.

What I think is not particularly valuable are sites that give you long lists of questions and then fix you up with potential dates without telling you what your answers said about you or why you should be matched with this particular person. They may be good matching systems, but they don't give you any additional insight into yourself or the other person.

Getting Help from a Wingman or Wingwoman

You need someone who keeps you on track, motivated, and supported when you start to date again. You also need someone to review your profile, to help you look at other people's profiles, and generally to keep you dating when you go through a rough patch and want to throw the whole enterprise out the window! A friend will be there to help you get over a discouraging period and can also help you see what you may be doing wrong.

Giving advice on your picture and profile

It's hard to see with another person's eyes, which is why you need the other person. Maybe you think you look cute in that dress or think the picture with your buddies fishing is a really good shot of you. But your wingwoman may say that the dress makes you look like you're still living in the 1960s, and your wingman may say you look like a macho guy in your waders and you're a bit scary looking. You need to have your friend's comment because the people looking at your pictures and profile don't know the real you. You need a friend to help guide you so that strangers don't get the wrong idea about you.

You can bring your wingman or wingwoman in at any time, but a really good time would be right at the beginning, when you're polishing your profile. You may not notice sentences or words that may bother someone or give the wrong impression, but your friend will, and that will help you out a lot. Likewise, if you've been on a dating site for a while but haven't attracted the notice of the kind of person you're looking for, you can bring in your friend for a little surgical help. Your friends can excise an offending paragraph or put in a better description of you, and your whole experience could change for the better!

Helping you pick potential dates

If you've been a dating dynamo and always picked the right person, if you're doing great online and never hit a dud, well, you're the exception, and you probably don't need a dating sidekick. But if you're like most people when they start online dating, you're guessing wrong a lot, and you're getting frustrated. This is where your wingman or wingwoman comes in. They go over the candidates with you and help you see those little details you didn't quite notice (6'5" and looking for a basketball player). They may also deliver a psychology lesson every now and then about how to pick someone different from the people who have let you down or been a bad fit in the past (because they know). Wise advisors are worth their weight in gold, so if you know someone you think can act on your behalf that way, don't hesitate to ask for help.

Protecting Yourself Both Online and Offline

Online dating is safe — most of the time. But like anything, there's an opportunity for taking advantage of people. There are a few malicious people who are out for themselves and can be dangerous to you. You need to have some rules that you follow all the time to be safe. (You can find more on protecting yourself and ensuring your safety while dating in Chapter 8.)

Keeping your address private

When you first meet someone, it should always be in a public place. In fact, until you know *a lot* about this person, the person should never know your home address. Someone can seem like a regular guy or a well-balanced woman and turn into something else. Until you're absolutely positive that's not going to happen, the person should never know your address. In fact, if the person acts hurt or angry because you don't want to share that information, take that as a bad sign.

Doing your due diligence

The great thing about dating in the digital age is that you have so many ways to track someone and find out whether the person has been truthful with you. If he says he graduated magna cum laude, you can look that up through school records (and, incidentally, find out whether he actually went to a specific school). If he says he worked in a bank, that's pretty easy to trace too. If you're suspicious or a tiny bit paranoid, why worry? Use your favorite search engine to find basic information. Online search firms can find out whether your date has ever had a misdemeanor or felony.

You can do some direct due diligence, too. Ask to meet friends and do a little networking. For example, you can find people who went to the same high school that your date went to or people who know someone who went to that high school. Sooner or later you can find people who were in your date's class and maybe get a look at the yearbook.

In most cases, you'll be able to find some mutual friends or at least acquaintances, even if you start out quite unknown to each other. A little bit of detective work isn't unethical; most people expect it nowadays!

Sticking to paid sites

There are paid and unpaid online dating sites. For your own safety, I recommend that you fork over the cash for the paid ones. The reason is that it's hard to track people on unpaid sites. Because the paid sites have credit card information, they can check up on people who have complaints lodged against them and find out whether there's any truth to the complaint. If there is, they'll toss the people off the site and make it safer for everyone.

Setting up meetings during the day in a public place

First meetings should be at a coffee shop in daylight and should last about 20 minutes. If the meeting goes swimmingly, you can always stretch it out. But agreeing on 20 minutes allows for polite interaction if there's no chemistry or interest.

You shouldn't meet at night for a while, nor should you meet somewhere isolated. Furthermore, if you're a woman, never let the guy walk you to your car, even in the daylight. Ninety-nine percent of the time that would be just fine, but I'm worried about the 1 percent.

You're going on the web for online dating to meet people you wouldn't have met otherwise. You not only don't know these people but also may not know anyone else who knows them. This kind of anonymity presents its own risk, so you really have to be careful not to put yourself in an awkward situation where no one would notice if you were threatened.

Handling Communications and First Meetings with Online Dates

First meetings from online dating are their own special kind of first meeting. You're going to be meeting someone with whom you've only corresponded via e-mail and maybe talked to a bit on the phone. You'll have ideas in your head about how she really looks, but even if her picture is a fair representation of who she is, people almost always look different in some way from their picture. So make sure that if you're disappointed or surprised (in a good way), you don't show a startled expression. You need to enter with an open mind: Everyone jumps to conclusions on first sight, but you don't have to keep that conclusion.

Of course, the other person is also making snap judgments about you. Here are some pointers to help you negotiate what is a slightly (and sometimes extremely) awkward moment.

Starting with e-mails and phone calls

After you've picked someone out by sending her an e-mail expressing interest and she responds with interest, there can still be an exchange of e-mails to determine whether you'll proceed to a phone call. The following sections outline things that dates may want to know at the e-mail stage.

Why you e-mailed the person (and what you may have in common)

You'll probably have just a short exchange telling the person exactly why you e-mailed her (you found her attractive, you felt you both shared similar lifestyles, you were impressed with something she accomplished, you liked the way she wrote, and so on). Short, however, doesn't mean unimportant. You have to convince her that she should take the time to talk to you further and actually speak orally rather than via e-mail. If you're the person who is contacted, these are likely the same kinds of concerns you'll have before you proceed further. In addition, both of you will be looking for the first signs of chemistry — an ease of talking with each other and a genuine interest in what each other is saying.

If you do find something interesting about each other, you may suggest the next stage, which is to talk on the phone. Women, who are more likely to be careful about safety and security, may insist on getting the man's number so that they can call without giving their own number. Of course, many modern phones have caller ID unless the owner of the number has blocked the number from being shown.

If you really don't want someone to have your home or cellphone number, call from an office or a friend's place, or get your phone number blocked.

Whether you sound grounded, nice, courteous, respectful, witty, or smart

The phone call is the first time the other person will hear your voice, laugh, inflection, speech patterns, and overall speaking style. You have to be careful to sound pleasant and interesting but not dominate the conversation too much. Some people are good on phones; other people, not so much. If you find yourself inhibited on the phone, tell the person that you feel constrained on phone calls and say you'd like to meet in a café sooner rather than later. Be prepared, however, for the other person to insist on more than one conversation before meeting you. Some daters are super careful and want several conversations before they feel assured about what kind of person they're meeting.

If you're the one who wants several phone calls before you'll meet in person, remember that you're at a disadvantage on the phone because you can't see the person's expressions. You may be talking too much, laughing too much, or sharing too much information, but you may not know that if all you get is silence on the other end. Don't have too many conversations before you meet or the other person may get tired of waiting and simply decide to go elsewhere.

Whether you sound like the same person as on the site

People worry that what others write on their profile doesn't really reflect who they are. So the phone calls are partly to help establish that the profile is correct and authentic. If you said that you're a college coach, talk about your life in a way that incorporates that identity and gives reassuring details. If you sound younger or older than you actually are, mention in passing that sometimes people mistake you on the phone for someone of a different age. Your job here is to authenticate yourself.

Prelude to a date: Meeting face to face over coffee

Don't mistake the coffee meeting for a first date! Think of it as more of a job interview. You have a very limited time to make an impression, so you need to get on the right track and know how to change the conversation if it starts to veer into dark or trivial subjects. Here are some do's and don'ts for this first exchange:

- ✔ Do smile, laugh, and be pleasant.
- ✔ Do talk about why you liked the person's profile.
- ✔ Do talk about some similarity between the two of you that you discovered from the profile.
- ✔ Do mention something really interesting about you. For example, floating the Grand Canyon last summer, tutoring inner-city kids, and so on.
- ✔ Do listen a lot and make sure you ask questions about what the person says and what's listed in the person's profile.
- ✔ Don't talk about your ex.
- ✔ Don't talk about something bad that's just happened to you, even if it happened on the way to the coffee!
- ✔ Don't agree with everything the other person says, unless you really do. People are looking for an authentic person, and though they want to have things in common, they don't want to feel manipulated.
- ✔ Don't let this meeting go on too long, even if it's going well. Make sure the other person doesn't feel pressured to stay longer.

This isn't only you in a job interview; you're interviewing the other person too. Make sure you get enough information about the person to come to some conclusions about whether you'd like to see him again.

Keep the meeting to 20 minutes, or half an hour tops. Set the time limit in advance and make sure you tell the person that you have something to do afterward. You can always have another meeting if it's a real match, but you need a pleasant way out if the meeting is nice but you're not interested in the person — or not so nice and you can't wait to get out of there!

Online Dating Downers: What to Expect and How to Be Resilient

It would be great if every date were a home run and the first date lasted the rest of your life because you fell immediately and madly in love. This has actually happened — but it's pretty rare. You have to expect that some coffee dates and even some extended dates that come out of online dating won't go the way you want them to, especially because this is someone you've never seen before. Here's the rub about online dating: You can't establish visual chemistry just from your e-mails and phone calls. When you first see each other, it's almost always a little bit different from what you expect. Sometimes it's a welcome surprise, but other times, it's disappointing.

There are two classes of these kinds of disappointments: the ones where you wish you weren't there, and the ones where you're extremely attracted to and interested in someone and she doesn't return the feeling. The following sections look at some of the common ones in both categories.

Your date is rude and obviously not interested

You sit down to coffee, and it's clear that you're not what your date expected. Maybe your pictures gave a much different impression, and she thought you were a better dresser or were taller or thinner, or perhaps she's just in a bad mood that day. Whatever the reason, because online daters can go through so many people quickly, they often become causal about their manners and even downright rude. When someone is like this, you can tell from the beginning that she isn't interested in the slightest. She may be sarcastic or ask you rude questions ("Why did you go into social work? It's such a dead-end profession!"), or she may just act rude, not making eye contact or looking around the room at other people while you're talking to her.

If that's the case, just chalk it up to bad luck and count the minutes until your getaway. Of course, there's an online tradition that protects you: You only owe her the full 20 minutes if she's reasonably decent to you, but you're not interested in making a scene. Just suffer through it and chalk it up to one of those moments that tests your character and fortitude.

You have a great first date and the person disappears

This one is really hard because you were excited during the coffee. The two of you hit it off, you both laughed a lot, and the conversation was fluid and fascinating. It was a wonderful moment, and at the end of it you said, "I thought this was great!" and the other person said, "It was. I really think you're an amazing person." Maybe one or both of you mentioned something about looking forward to the next meeting. But then the person never calls you or you call and he never answers. You e-mail and get no response, and you feel disheartened. What happened?

You may never know the reason. Online people disappear for no reason much more than people in other kinds of dating. It may be because he doesn't know you from any other part of his life so he feels less guilty (or embarrassed) for dropping you without the slightest explanation or attempt to make you feel better. Sometimes people go online and then make up with their ex-partner and drop everyone else like a hot potato. Sometimes they like you, but not as much as they thought they were going to like you. Whatever the reason, they have that enormous pool of online options, and so it seems that online daters are more likely to just vanish than other kinds of daters. Sometimes, however, the reason is just the opposite. The person is on a frantic hunt for his "one and only," and though he liked you a lot, it wasn't perfect, and the great number of possible dates online allows him to move quickly to another person rather than concentrate on seeing what may work out between the two of you. These situations are hard on the ego, but you have to learn not to take them personally. They happen for a number of reasons, and they may have nothing to do with you.

Your date doesn't want to see you again

Your date may tell you that you aren't right for her. This can happen in any kind of dating scenario, but people who go online because they're highly motivated to find someone may be seeing other people besides you and can simultaneously be evaluating who's the best person to proceed with. If you had no idea that you were not the only person your date was seeing, you may be surprised to see the relationship end without much discussion.

But the bad news and the good news here may be the same. The fact is that most people dating online who are over 50 are genuinely dedicated to finding a serious relationship, so even if they like you a lot, they may know that you're not "the one." This may mean that pleasant dating situations end rather soon. You, of course, may not have come to the same conclusion, and so the news that the person doesn't want to see you anymore hurts. But she's doing you a favor, even though it may not look like it. You don't want to be with someone who already knows you're not the one, and you can take some solace in all the millions of people still online, one of whom will be the right person for you.

Chapter 7

Mastering the First Date

*I*f I were asked, "What's the hardest part of starting to date again?" I'd say that it's becoming comfortable initiating contact or showing interest in someone else. The very beginning of contact is full of suspense. Will she accept an offer for coffee? Will he respond to an invitation to a play? How do I show I'm interested without looking pathetically interested?!

That said, planning a mutually comfortable and fun first date and figuring out a way to make yourself memorable (in a good way!) doesn't happen automatically. Many people (including many experienced daters) flounder when it comes to conversation and modern date etiquette. In this chapter, I make sure that you feel secure about having a successful first date by discussing places to go, conversation topics, flirting, and who should pay the bill.

Setting the Stage: Where to Go and What to Do

The first date sets the stage for whether the two of you will have any more dates. It's an audition, and as such, it needs the right setting. The place you pick, the time you meet, and the careful planning of details all make a big difference. You want to have fun, and you want to get to know each other better. In this section, I outline the strengths and weaknesses of different kinds of first dates to help you decide what the best options are for you and your date.

Doing the dinner date

Meeting over food is great. Good food and good wine (especially good wine) create an amiable environment. You inherit the mood of the room: quiet and contemplative or lively and animated. The food and ambience give you something to talk about, and if you're foodies or wine people, you can delve into your hobby and use it to further conversation. Going to a fancy restaurant allows you to dress up and look elegant; if it's a more casual restaurant, it can be relaxing and show off your sportier self.

If your date asks you where you'd like to eat, pick something less expensive but not noisy — less expensive because you want to reassure your date that she's the point of the date (not the dinner) and less noisy because it's really important to be able to talk. Having to ask, "What did you say?" after every sentence can really ruin a date! Not hearing each other well can lead to embarrassment and somewhat odd or inappropriate answers. Don't make the ability to hear each other a challenge.

Other things that can ruin a dinner date include

- ✔ Wolfing down your food
- ✔ Slurping your drink
- ✔ Picking the most expensive thing on the menu (unless you're paying)
- ✔ Checking out the other diners instead of your date
- ✔ Touching your partner (this is the first date!)
- ✔ Deciding what your partner should eat
- ✔ Talking about weight or diets

A dinner date works best when you know the two of you have a lot in common and a lot to talk about. If you hardly know each other at all, a dinner date isn't the best option because it requires a lot of conversation before you've gotten to know each other. You could be stuck with those awkward silences you definitely want to avoid!

Going to the movies

There are two great reasons to bring a first date to the movies. First, you don't have to talk as much as you do when you're on a dinner date (see the preceding section), and that can be good when you don't have a wealth of experiences together. And second, after you see the movie you have plenty to talk about — if, that is, you pick the right movie. Some films are perfect date movies, and others are perfectly awful date movies, so you need to take into account some general guidelines.

Don't depend on a film one friend recommends. You can find dozens of movie review sites to consult online, such as www.imdb.com and www.rottentomatoes.com. Look at what both men and women have said; this movie has to appeal to both.

Things to consider:

> Do: Pick something funny and perhaps romantic.

> Don't: Pick either a "chick flick" or a "guys night out flick."

Why? Because you don't know each other's sensitivities, and movies that come from only one gender's point of view are often insulting to the other gender.

> Do: Pick a movie that has won some awards; there's a better chance you'll both like it.

> Don't: Pick a movie that's a marathon.

Why? You want to have some energy left after the movie to go to dinner or have coffee and discuss it together. Do your due diligence and choose a movie that has been well reviewed so you both aren't feeling that you wasted your time. You want something to talk about but not something that uses up all your time and emotion.

This is about the date, not the movie. Just because you've been meaning to see a certain flick doesn't mean that this is the time to see it.

Speaking of movies . . .

Some people are quite sensitive about movies they love and quite vocal about those they don't. If a movie date is on your agenda, here are some things to avoid when talking about movies:

- Don't trash your date's evaluation of the movie, even if you want to. At most, politely disagree.

- Don't lecture, even if you know everything this director ever made.

- Don't go all dewy-eyed over a romantic lead. Doing so may bother some people, as if they're being compared — and found lacking.

- Do try to find something in the movie you can both agree on.

Choosing something athletic or outdoorsy

If both of you are athletic and have talked about how much you like physical activity or outdoor adventures, why not start with a mutual interest and strengthen that bond between you? A really great day outdoors can be romantic and exhilarating. Remember to choose a popular place where you'll be surrounded by other people; you don't want to be isolated on a first date.

Be careful, though, that you gauge both your abilities and your date's; otherwise, one of you could end up spending the afternoon at the emergency clinic.

Here are some great athletic activities for summer:

✓ **Take a short hike to something beautiful.** Be sure to keep the hike to no more than a few miles each way, and make your destination a waterfall or a place with an amazing view.

✓ **Rent a couple of kayaks and paddle down a river.** If you're experienced, you can get a double one.

✓ **Bike to a fun destination, such as a winery, a summer concert, or a picnic.** Many cities have a large network of bike paths, and many of them get you out of the city safely to great events or beautiful parks.

Here are some great athletic activities for winter:

✓ **A walk in the snow:** It's quiet and beautiful, and there's time to talk.

✓ **Day skiing:** If you're both really good at it, it gets your adrenaline going — and there are those great after-ski fireplaces and hot chocolates. But keep it to a day. This is your first date, after all.

✓ **Snowshoeing:** Pick a scenic spot and rent some snowshoes, if you don't own them. There's less chance of getting hurt than with skiing.

✓ **An indoor aerobic or yoga class:** You get a great workout and you get to see each other look sexy.

Change your plans if the weather turns nasty. You don't want your first date to be a grim weather scene. It could be dangerous or just seriously uncomfortable. Be flexible rather than determined when you're dealing with weather conditions.

This is about having fun together, not testing either of you at your utmost ability. Pick an activity that's easy and offers time to talk; afterward, savor the experience together. This is the first of what you hope to be many experiences together, so keep it simple. Being rescued off a mountain isn't romantic.

Finding the right level of activity

When planning a first date, it's important to correctly gauge what level of expertise or athleticism is comfortable for both you and your date. You don't want to be so exhausted that your primary feeling is frustration or even anger. That's not the feeling you want to develop here! Just to make sure that dates don't try to please you so much that they take on something above their ability to enjoy, I list a few questions that may help you know what kind of activities are appropriate. You can add a few more for a specific sport that you know well if you think it's safer to probe a bit deeper. For example, if you're thinking about kayaking in open water, ask whether your partner has taken some kayaking lessons.

That will tell you a lot about how experienced your date is. Here are some questions to ask to gauge the ability of your date so that you pick the right level of activity (and be honest about your own ability!):

✔ How long have you been doing this?

✔ Tell me about some great experiences you've had doing this.

✔ I've taken on a few things I shouldn't have. Have you?

✔ How long do you think an optimal time out would be?

Opting for a cultural event or performance

If you love plays and concerts and you find out that your date loves them too, then get the best tickets you can to an event you both agree upon. Don't assume she'd like a Broadway musical just because you do or that everyone loves Lady Gaga. But if you both follow a certain performer or type of theater, this is a great date idea. You can have dinner before, exchange impressions at intermission, and go out for dessert afterward. It's almost foolproof as long as you check out the reviews and make sure that there's a general enthusiasm for the tour or performance.

In general, pick something else if the only seats available are in the nosebleed section or have limited views. This may be okay for later on, when you both make a decision on whether it's worth it, but right now you're aiming for as close to perfection as you can get.

Some helpful hints about cultural events:

✔ Think about the noise factor. If possible, pick something that doesn't make your ears hurt.

✔ Think about the mood factor. Is this the world's most depressing play? Go for something that doesn't leave you both thinking the world is hopeless.

✔ If you choose to go to a lecture, see whether you both have the same perspective on the issue. Hot-button topics like war and euthanasia may not be exactly what you want for a first date.

Always keep in mind that this is a first date. Even though strong emotions may arise after seeing a beautiful vista or a touching romantic movie, you need to take physical affection slowly. Don't assume you can hold hands in the movie or snuggle around the fireplace after skiing.

Keeping the Conversation Flowing on the First Date

Ultimately, the date's success depends on how well you connect with each other, and that really depends on how well you communicate. Communication is a combination of what you say, what you don't say, how you listen, and what your habits and body language transmit. Communication helps build chemistry. All these things to remember may seem complex or even overwhelming, but the basic rules of communication are actually pretty straightforward.

Before your date, think about what to talk about and what to say or not say. If you don't, you may bring up topics that create tension, disinterest, or even anger. You want topics that interest both of you, that are respectful, and that help you get to know — and hopefully like — each other better.

Chatting about what you do and how you like it

Much of who people are is defined by how they spend their days. Here are the principles to keep in mind when talking about work:

✔ How you feel about your work and how you describe it says a lot about you. Think about what this listener would like to know about you: Are you disciplined? Hardworking? Imaginative? Say something that gives your date an idea of your work and shows good sides of your character.

✔ Dates feel comfortable if you start out with what you like about your job. You can always add some criticisms later. If you get into a rant, you may come off as a malcontent. Complain with a close friend, not with a first date.

✔ Figure out how to make what you do interesting to someone not in your field. Don't use technical terms (boring). If you don't work outside the home, talk about something you do that's interesting and important to you. Are you on a board, do you run something for your church, or do you handle a complex web of duties related to your children's school? Say things that give your date a sense of what you do on a regular basis.

Expressing your passions and other fun things your life includes

Even if you live a relatively quiet life, you surely have some fun and fascinating stories to tell, and people love stories. Perhaps you can tell your date about how your work with global health has changed you. Or, on a less serious note, describe your first encounter with painting a nude person in an art class. How about giving your impressions of your last high school reunion? Pick a story that's funny or puts you in a good light, and let your date know how you handle life.

Use only stories that make you look pretty good, but don't brag. Bragging or being arrogant is one of the main things that turns most people off.

A lot of love is about lifestyle and passions that you're committed to. Let your date know yours and find out what makes his heart sing. It's heartwarming when two people discover that they both share some well-loved interest or activity. It's also intriguing when someone has a passion you don't share but you admire, find interesting, or would like to get into. Don't go on too long, though — especially if your date doesn't share your passion.

There's a difference between a passionate hobby and an obsessive one. You don't want to look like you're in the latter category. If you love dogs, for example, make sure your partner doesn't think you love dogs more than you could ever love him! If you love golf, make it clear that it's a hobby, not a lifestyle — unless it is and you don't want to be with someone who will treat it as anything less.

Staying away from some conversation topics

Some topics are never okay for a first date. Never! That's not to say that they aren't tempting, but I urge you to avoid these subjects. They rarely reflect well on you, and there's time for tough topics later — but if you bring them up now, there may not be a later. Here they are, in descending order of danger:

- **Why your ex was so terrible:** I don't care if your ex was the worst person on the planet — don't go there. Even if you have true stories that would curl the hair of anyone listening, the ultimate impact is one of distaste. This thought will occur to your listener: "Maybe this person brings out the worst in someone!" or, "I wonder what the ex's side of the story is. . . ."

- **The money you lost in your latest divorce:** There are two offenses here. One, complaining about money, even if you were economically pillaged, isn't a good idea. Your listener may feel that you're cheap, overly materialistic, or just not being fair. Even if your date commiserates, the impact is sordid. This gets further compounded if you've been married multiple times. Divorce happens, so people understand once they know you. But in the beginning, your date may feel that she can't be special in your life, and you eventually end up blaming your partners instead of being thoughtful about your own role in making a relationship work.

- **Portraying your dead or divorced ex-spouse as a saint:** Don't create an icon of your deceased spouse. If you feel that you must talk about your beloved ex-spouse, then you're probably not ready to date again. That's okay. There's no shame in realizing that you aren't emotionally ready to let another person back into your heart. But it's not fair to be with a new person, especially on a first date, and have your heart and mind elsewhere.

  You may, however, just be talking about your ex because so much of your life was intertwined with her. It's understandable, but avoid it because it will make your date feel that you're not emotionally free yet. It's even worse if you only speak of how amazing, fabulous, kind, and loving your partner was. Who's brave enough to try and compete with someone who has achieved sainthood in her ex-spouse's mind?!

When talking about your past, use the word "I" as opposed to "we" — even if you're describing something that you and your ex did together. If you use the word "we" all the time, you'll make your date feel like you still think of yourself as part of a couple.

- **Health:** If you feel your date is a compassionate person, you may be tempted to share some of your physical challenges with her. This isn't a good idea because you're telling her that you are or have been physically vulnerable, and this could scare her away. After she gets to know you, she may be willing to take on everything about you — including a serious illness — but if you set up a frightening picture of your health on hello, she may think it's safer to avoid you. You don't owe her all this information now. Later, probably, but not now.

If you're a jock and you seek someone who is very active, ask her whether she likes to hike. If she does, you can talk about specific hikes she or you have taken, and that should tell you enough about her level of ability to enjoy the same activities that you do.

✓ **Sex:** Keep it zipped when it comes to sex. I don't care if she's dressed like a sexy babe or he has bedroom eyes, a first date should avoid the topic of sex at all costs. I know of plenty derailed first dates on which a man — and less often, a woman — brings up how important sex is and what he expects out of a partner. In general, he grosses out or scares his prospective partner. Unless you're just looking for a hookup and know that's what your date wants too, this topic is almost guaranteed to turn off the other person. So even someone who loves sex is likely to cross you off the list.

✓ **Kids:** It's okay to talk about your children — but just a little. You don't want your date to think that you're just looking for someone to parent or grandparent with! So:

  • Don't show more than one picture of your kids or grandkids.

  • Don't rhapsodize about their lives, trips you've taken together, and so on.

  • Don't mention that they would have to approve of any serious relationship.

  • Just say you love your kids and other kids (if you do), and you have a good relationship with them and their families (if you do).

Remember to avoid the tough stuff. If your child has challenging health, has been in trouble with the police, is neurotic — whatever — leave it be. Again, you want this date to be about the joy of discovery and having fun together. If you're suited for each other, you'll talk about these and other issues as the relationship deepens.

✓ **Money:** You can talk about your job, your trips, and your hobbies, and these topics will reveal whether you have discretionary income and also tell you something about your partner's lifestyle. But any direct questions such as "How much do you earn?" or "Has it been economically hard on you being a single mother?" are a very bad idea. People don't want to feel that they're being assessed as a potential business partner, an economic life jacket, or a lifestyle bonanza.

Stay in the present. Talk about each other and what you're doing. Don't bring up the past too many times except as a charming or illustrative anecdote that helps your date understand who you are now. Don't weigh this first date down with sad details or the glowing memory of a deceased spouse. Create fun, laughter, insight, and warmth.

Sharing while keeping some of the mystery

Sooner or later you'll want to exchange more intimate information with your date because you'll both need to know each other's reactions to issues and lifestyle choices that matter to you. But err on the side of waiting rather than leaping in with deeply personal and emotional topics. Likewise, avoid asking extensive questions that look like you're conducting a job interview.

There's something about being a little mysterious that seems to intrigue people more. It's like the tease on the news or the headlines that grab you. Some pointers:

- ✔ **Don't overwhelm your date.** You want to have a lot to say, but you also want to make sure that you're not so eager to be memorable that you overwhelm your date with your life story.

- ✔ **Let interesting stories develop from the topics at hand.** One way to avoid getting in too deep is to let interesting topics develop out of who you are, who your date is, and interests that overlap. For example, say that you're both crossword puzzle fans. You can do the *New York Times* puzzle together and find out what each of you knows through the game. Or a news story that refers to something you've worked on or studied could spark an interesting conversation.

- ✔ **If it's starting to feel like you're telling your whole life story, screech to a halt and hand over the conversation.** Try to avoid recitations of your life story and instead discover each other through stories, affinities, and in-depth conversations about things you care about.

- ✔ **If you're telling sad stories, back away and think of entertaining, amusing, or intriguing ones.** Laughing together is one of the best things you can do on a date; it builds intimacy and pleasure.

Try not to be too earnest. Remember to have fun. Vary serious conversations with topics and activities that make you laugh and lighten up.

Marketing yourself in a safe and winning way

You want to be real and authentic. It serves no one if you pretend to be someone you're not. But be yourself on a good day rather than a bad one. Don't oversell who you are — and don't undersell! Be patient and let information flow as appropriate over time.

Overselling	*Underselling*
I bought and sold two companies last year.	I went bankrupt during the recession; I just couldn't save the company.
I'm a take-charge kind of person. Give me a problem and I can solve it.	I'm just an average kind of person.
My children adore me.	I don't know how parents do it. The teen years were an awful time.
I've never had a sick day in my life.	I just can't hear or move like I used to.

Reveal some accomplishments, but don't overdo it. Don't list all the great things you've done, and certainly not all the great things you own. You don't want to come off as an egomaniac. Playing Donald Trump doesn't look good on anyone, including Donald Trump.

Making sure you're a good listener

Here are the top five elements of effective listening:

- ✔ Steady, focused eye contact
- ✔ Smiles and facial expressions that show you've understood and that you're attentive
- ✔ Questions asking for more information
- ✔ Allowing breaks in conversation so that you don't jump in just because there's a pause in your date's comments
- ✔ A compliment about what has been said to show your appreciation of something that struck you as interesting, clever, or moving

These aren't optional. To be a good listener, you must follow each of these points. Otherwise, your date will feel unheard and unappreciated. Furthermore, these instructions help you avoid the worst thing you can do: bore your date to distraction. The most boring conversation is a conversation where only one person talks.

If you're nervous, you may be prone to fill up any white space with conversation because you don't want any awkward silences. Your motives are good, but the outcome is bad. How prone are you to talking too much? Here's a set of indicators; if you answer affirmatively to anything on this list, you may need to work hard not to dominate all the air space.

✔ When I'm nervous I tend to talk more.

✔ I feel responsible for keeping the conversation lively. If there's too long a pause, it makes me uncomfortable.

✔ When the conversation lags, I'm likely to jump in, often with some anecdote about myself.

✔ I think I'm pretty entertaining. I often keep the conversation going in my group of friends.

✔ I often end up telling a lot about myself, but I don't hear as much about the other person.

To become a better listener, think of questions you want to ask ahead of time. If your date is in marketing and you're not sure what that is, ask her what kind of training and education she had that gave her the skills she needed. Or, if your date works for a community organization, ask what kinds of projects or campaigns she's worked on. Here are some other listening and general conversation guidelines:

✔ Restrain yourself from jumping in on a topic of your own as soon as your date stops talking. You don't want to sound like the only reason you asked a question was to get your turn to speak!

✔ Restrain yourself from giving long-winded answers or lectures. Answer briefly and see whether your date asks you a follow-up question on the same topic. If she asks you a follow-up question but on a different topic, chances are she'd like to change the subject.

✔ When your date tells you something interesting, go deeper. Ask a follow-up question that shows you understand and want to know more. For example, if your date mentions that her classrooms are overcrowded, making her teaching job difficult, ask her what she does to compensate for those conditions or whether there's any effective movement going on to change the situation. Here's a sample exchange when a person asks his date why she became a police officer:

- "Because I wanted to help communities be safe and because everyone in my family was in that field."

- "But weren't you worried about the dangers?"

- "Things happen, but no, I was never afraid."

- "Is that because no one in your family or squad was ever hurt or because you've never been roughed up or shot at — or have you just always been brave?"

Here's what happened in this short exchange: The person closely tracks what his date says, digging deeper to know more. She can see that he's really interested and wants to know her better. Then, he gives her a compliment (intimating that she must be brave) that's appropriate to the conversation.

Don't dominate the conversation, but don't be passive, either. If your date is dominating the conversation, help him out by turning the conversation toward something you think he may be interested in. It's too much effort to be the only one who's talking. If he feels like he's the only person putting out any energy, he's going to be bored or annoyed.

Encouraging Chemistry: How to Flirt

Dating isn't all in your head — some of it's in your heart and hormones. Though it may be true that your hormones aren't quite as intense as they were when you were 25, they're still very much active, and you'll find that you still have a different reaction to someone when there's chemistry than when there's not. No doubt about it, chemistry is important.

But chemistry isn't preordained. You don't have chemistry with every smart person you meet or every blonde or redhead. Chemistry is partly about how people look and greatly about how people act. Connections can be made over a smile, a sense of humor, or what you see in someone's eyes.

When these signals are intentional, it's called flirting. And flirting is definitely a form of communication. It tells the other person that you're interested in her as more than a friend, that you're a sensual person, and that you can be playful. All that information can be communicated with just a few bold looks. One flirtatious move can definitely telegraph your interest instantaneously, and the reception to that move will tell you a lot about whether someone is interested in getting closer to you.

If you haven't dated in a long time, you may have forgotten how to flirt. The good news is that it's not too hard to learn how to do it again. You can jog your memory with these core elements of flirting — and then, of course, you must practice! It's worth doing because this is the way you start the other person's heart to thump a bit faster and, in fact, increase your own heart rate as well. Here are the key moves:

- ✔ **Eye contact:** Holding eye contact without blinking or looking away is so sexy that you'll find you have to look away a little just so the whole sequence doesn't become combustible. Let your eyes "soften" and smile just a little while you lock your eyes together. If your date refuses to hold your gaze, the moment won't work. But if she does, you've got something going!

- ✔ **A certain smile:** The smile that works is a little mysterious, with the ends of the mouth slightly turned up — not a big, broad smile. This is a smile that promises more, if everything goes right. It's a smile that indicates the beginning of desire and availability.

✔ **Words:** Words matter. If you're drawn to someone, let her know it, but don't go overboard. Watch her reactions carefully.

For example, if you say, "Your hair is beautiful; I find myself wanting to touch it," the response should be something like, "I'd like that very much" or at least, "Thank you" with a smile. If she ignores it or says, "Oh, not really . . ." back off. The first reaction shows that the person is willing to flirt with you. The second reaction shows that you've made her uncomfortable.

But flirting does require playful, intimate sentiments or a bit of sexual innuendo. Such verbal flirting shows that you're attracted to the person and tests the waters to see whether the person is also attracted.

Does this sound like dangerous territory? It is. A gifted flirt is a bit scary because she can charm the socks off of anyone. But flirting isn't necessarily manipulative if the sentiments are sincere and performed to encourage a relationship rather than just a ploy to get admired or a deliberate prelude to having sex with someone.

Flirtation is, at its most helpful, a way to help move things along. It differentiates the attention you get from someone who's just being friendly from the attention you get when someone desires you in a romantic or sexual way.

It can be hard to differentiate a flirt or "player" from someone who's interested in only you. Only time will tell whether you're just getting lines or a true expression of deeply felt chemistry. Go ahead and flirt and enjoy flirtation, but take it all as just a first step toward knowing more about each other.

Flirtatious phrases

Here are some flirtatious phrases that you should use only if you really mean it:

✔ "You have great eyes."

✔ "You have perfect skin."

✔ "You're incredibly handsome."

✔ "You look a lot like _____ [movie star your date really looks like]."

✔ "I think you're so attractive — much more attractive than your picture."

✔ "I can't stop staring at your lips."

✔ "I love your hair."

✔ "You're incredibly sexy."

✔ "Those are really sexy shoes."

✔ "I love the way you dress."

Picking Up the Check: Who Pays?

These days, who pays on a date has to be negotiated. This can be quite a delicate process. Sure, it used to be easy: It was the guy. It wasn't even a question. It was the guy under any and all circumstances.

And that still seems to be true for the first date (although if it's two guys, it gets a bit trickier). For heterosexual couples, particularly for older daters, it's still pretty clear that the man is supposed to pay for the first coffee and most likely the first date. But after that the view gets a bit cloudy. (For more discussion of money and sorting out who pays for what, turn to Chapter 13.)

Sticking to tradition: He pays

In general, the man pays for the first coffee date and the first date date. The more traditional the man or woman, the more likely he'll want to pay and she'll want to be paid for. There are exceptions, of course, but if she wants him to open the car door for her, and he wants her to wait for him to open that door, it's likely he's traditional about paying for the bill as well.

Men with traditional values still feel they should pay. They're surprised and sometimes a bit put off if the woman offers to chip in on the first date. They wouldn't dream of it.

But that's not true for a lot of men these days. Dating can be expensive, and some men have rightly wondered: If all the other rules about who does what in relationships have changed for men and women, why shouldn't the system for paying for things also be on the table? So some men ask the woman to split the cost of the first date, and this can be awkward for people who grew up at a time when men always paid for everything to do with dating.

Nonetheless, asking a date to pay half on a first date is a risky move. Even the most ardent feminists figure in a certain amount of gentlemanliness for the first encounter. True, a man may be tired of paying for the umpteenth coffee, but insisting on the new rules on that first encounter will probably be a buzz kill. Wait until further dates before you talk about how to deal with money.

Each date is different, and there are no hard-and-fast rules about how to split bills. You have to negotiate with each person you're with.

Trying the new normal: Sharing costs

Presume that unless you're a very traditional male or female — both of whom would like the guy to pay for everything — the "new normal" is that anything goes. That means you have to negotiate because there's no template to rely on here. You need to talk about it. Here are some opening lines that may be useful:

- ✔ "I'd love to go to the play, but the tickets are really expensive. How about if you pay for the tickets and I get dinner?"

- ✔ "You paid for our first meeting, and I'd like to contribute to the dinner tonight. It only seems fair, and I'd like to do it."

- ✔ "I'd like to split the costs if you don't mind. Why don't I pay for the wine and we split the dinner?"

- ✔ "How about I get the dinner tonight and then you get the next one?"

  This one is particularly nice because it indicates that there will be a next dinner and perhaps a continuing relationship.

Yes, this is hard for some of you. Men can feel awkward asking and women can feel offended at the very idea that they would pay. But times have changed, and as women have asked for their place at the table and men's help in the home, it only stands to reason that other older customs should also be revised. So welcome to the new world of sharing.

If sharing costs seems incredibly awkward, tell your date your dilemma. Just say that you really don't know how to handle this but that you need to bring it up. Your date may feel the same way. This way you can discuss your feelings and mutually decide the next step.

If you want to avoid the sharing costs question on the first date or so, suggest a picnic with simple sandwiches or think of another truly inexpensive way to get together. Go to a high school football game or an art fair. Get a better feel for each other before you have to face the money question.

Chapter 8

Staying Safe While Playing the Field

Many people are afraid to date people they don't already know because doing so seems inherently unsafe. After all, the person you're meeting could have malicious intent. Apprehension and caution are understandable. Scammers, players, and some people with low impulse control are lurking — and yes, there are a few genuine crazies, too. But the overwhelming majority are folks like you who are lonely, honest, and looking for someone special. Yes, some of them may fib a little about their height, weight, or age, but only a tiny percentage of the millions of online daters are people you have to watch out for.

You can prepare for the worst, but you're unlikely to be with anyone who even causes you to worry, much less threatens you. The old saying about a little prevention being worth a pound of cure is spot on. This chapter helps keep you safe and gives you the confidence you need to meet all these new people in your life. (For information on safe sex in particular, turn to Chapters 11 and 12.)

Following General Safety Rules

The safety rules for men and women are different, but they're not as different as you may assume. Both sexes have exposure to risk. Both men and women can meet someone whom they no longer want to interact with but who may have trouble taking no for an answer.

Don't make the mistake of thinking that safety advice is only relevant for online dating. In fact, because online dating has an unjustly bad reputation, people forget that any kind of date with someone you haven't known for a long time has an element of risk. Even dating someone you know well but have never dated may reveal some unpleasant surprises.

In this section, I cover general safety recommendations for dating — regardless of whether you're a man or a woman and regardless of the type of dating you're doing (online or all face to face). Consider this advice and then supplement it with the gender-specific recommendations later in the chapter.

Doing your due diligence

Some problems are avoidable if you do some research on anyone you're interested in before you flirt with him, and certainly before you go out with him. Thanks to the Internet, you have many easy ways to look up someone's background, and sometimes reading between the lines can teach you a lot. If you find a person's résumé, for example, a string of jobs that lasted only for a short time could indicate instability. Public court records can tell you whether the person was ever convicted of a crime or a DWI. Doing a little junior private-eye work saves you some grief or, better yet, shows that the person is everything he says he is and is worth investing emotion and trust in.

The downsides to dating a coworker

Meeting someone at work can be a sticky situation when the person who seemed fine in the office turns out to have some significant downsides, as the following story shows:

Marlie was sitting across from Stewart in the company lunchroom when he started talking to her about an article he was working on that he thought she might be interested in. She was interested in the article but even more interested in him. An attractive man, well dressed with glamorous streaks of white at his temples, he had been a senior editor at her magazine before he was promoted to another magazine owned by the same corporation. Talking to him was easy and stimulating, so she asked him if he wanted to come by her place for a drink after work. He couldn't do it but said that he'd like to come after an early business dinner that night that wouldn't be too late. But by 10 p.m. he still hadn't appeared or called, so she decided he wasn't coming and turned off the lights. About 11, she woke up to insistent buzzing from the condo intercom system. When she asked who it was, a very drunken, slurred voice came across the intercom, and it took her a minute to realize it was him. She was put off by the hour and the drunkenness, and she told him she was sorry but it was too late for her to see him. He unleashed a stream of profane insults, and she hung up on him. They avoided each other in the cafeteria after that.

Don't let your guard down completely at dinner parties

Be cautious with people you meet at dinner parties. Just because you're interacting with this person at a mutual friend's house doesn't mean the person is being honest — despite flirting with you like crazy. Case in point:

Dave met Rosie at a dinner party. She was with another guy, but she seemed very interested in him. She ignored her partner and turned to Dave all night. At the end of the dinner, she slipped him her phone number and said to call. He did, and they went out for coffee a few times and then dinner. They kissed after the dinner, and he was looking forward to getting more serious about her when he mentioned the growing relationship to the host of the dinner party. As he was talking, he noticed that his friend's expression was somewhere between skeptical and incredulous. When Dave asked what his friend was thinking, his friend said, "What are *you* thinking? Don't you know that Rosie is engaged and getting married next month?" Dave was dumbfounded. When he called Rosie, she said, "I thought you knew! What's the harm in a little flirting? Are you upset?" He was more than a little upset; he felt humiliated and very disappointed.

The moral of the story? Some people like to flirt even when they're unavailable. So do some checking and don't wind up like Dave!

If you're dating someone from outside of the country, it's much harder to do due diligence. Consider hiring a professional to find out more about your date's background. Nine times out of ten the information you receive will be accurate, but you have to watch out for that tenth time. I've heard some sad, sad stories of people falling victim to scams, and I don't want you to become one of them.

Knowing your comfort zone

Your gut feelings are important. If someone doesn't feel safe, listen to your instincts and honor them. Yes, you may be wrong, but it's far better not to trust an innocent person than to trust the wrong person and get in a terrible situation. You may not know why you're feeling threatened or cautious, but your instincts are picking up something subtle that your conscious thought pattern hasn't figured out yet.

Even if you aren't getting signals, here are a few wise precautions to take:

✔ Don't give your date your home address until you've done your due diligence and feel very reassured. (Jump back to the section "Doing your due diligence" earlier in this chapter for advice on researching your date.)

✔ Don't go away on a weekend trip together until you know your date quite well and have all the information you need to feel safe and secure.

✔ Don't get in a car with someone — either as a passenger or driver — until you know him or her very well and have a more established relationship.

Sometimes a date will try and talk you out of your decision. For example, he may say, "Hey, I'm just going to drive us to the movie. Don't you trust me even that much?" Your natural reaction may be to give in and get in the car because you don't want any hurt feelings. But don't do it. A good person will understand that you don't know him well yet and will respect your feelings.

Refusing to be isolated

The world has a few sociopaths, and you don't want to meet them. And if you do, you don't want to be alone with them. What does "alone" constitute?

✔ Taking a walk in a secluded park

✔ Visiting your place or his place

✔ Going on a car ride with just the two of you

✔ Walking to your car in an empty or busy parking lot

✔ Meeting out in the country

You get the idea — avoid any place that people can't hear you or wouldn't know you were in trouble. There's no need to be paranoid — most people want the best for you — but these guidelines cover the ones who don't as well.

Refraining from ever giving anyone money

Your date should never ask you for money. You may feel that such an attitude is hardhearted, but the fact is that 99.9 percent of money requests, heart-rending as they may be, are scams that were always the point of the relationship for that person.

There are thousands and thousands of scammers — so many, in fact, that the U.S. Office of American Citizens Services and Crisis Management has been going to meetings to warn Americans about various ways people prey on others. In one common scam, someone with an absolutely gorgeous picture contacts you and within weeks, maybe days, tells you she loves you. She's usually out of the country and tells you she can't get hard currency (or something like that), so she asks you to front her $500 for your share of the plane ticket. In the next call, she claims she's being held by a corrupt passport official and needs $800 to get her identification back. And it goes on and on. Thousands of similar scams happen to people who are smart enough to know better but kind enough to want to help someone they believe is truly in love with them. You need to be savvy because many of these scammers specifically target older men and women.

Protecting against the dangers of alcohol

People shouldn't consume alcohol when they're planning to drive, but traffic accidents aren't all you have to worry about when it comes to alcohol. Drinking lowers inhibitions and makes it hard to make wise choices. Even a little bit of drinking loosens your natural instinct for editing what you say. You lose oversight of the situation, and you add that lack of objectivity to nerves and the result can fatally undermine a chance of a second get-together.

Drinking too much makes at least two things more likely: more disclosure and more sex. Suppose you're really attracted to someone and you decide to slide from coffee at 5 p.m. to drinks at 6, and then dinner with a few more drinks. You didn't gulp down all those drinks in one sitting, but that doesn't change the amount of alcohol you've consumed in a relatively short period of time. By the time dessert comes around, you're either truly looped or at least buzzed. Neither is safe, and far too many promising beginnings have been compromised early on by getting in too deep too quickly. Even if you consider yourself a power drinker not bothered by a few drinks, and you show no exterior changes in mood, remember that your date is watching you throw those drinks back and most likely crossing you off the list because of that performance. Play it safe and pass on drinking at early stages of the relationship.

Depending on your weight, even one drink can cause some impairment in judgment. So any alcohol at all may change you enough to make a difference in how the date works out.

Watching out for mood swings

Sometimes, people with mood swings (or, in a more extreme example, bipolar disorder) are among the most attractive people on earth. In their manic or most happy and energetic states, they're fun, funny, full of life, and captivating. But this condition usually has another side — either extreme lows or depressive cycles that are a lot less fun to be around. Some people can control this with medication, but if they don't medicate or work on this problem in therapy, they can be a handful.

What's most worrisome in a dating situation is if someone's mood swings include an angry streak. Does your date get white-hot with anger if the waiter doesn't show up for a while? Does he talk about his ex with extreme fury in his voice? If he does, take this as a good reason to make this a one-date experience. You don't ever want that anger directed at you, which can happen quite easily if you stick around too long. In fact, if you encounter someone like this, be nice, but be gone. You just don't want to get him too interested in you.

Look for patterns in a person's more manic periods. Is his intense energy commensurate with what's happening around him? For example, if he's doing a happy dance at midnight for no good reason, chances are this kind of energy is manic rather than the result of anything happening between the two of you.

Worrying about jealousy and possessiveness

Jealousy and possessiveness are a serious red flag for both men and women. You've heard the stories, but perhaps you don't think such a bad situation could happen to you. After all, you're loyal and straightforward, and when you commit to someone, the person has nothing to worry about. Right? But that's rational thinking, and pathologically jealous people aren't rational. If they like you and you encourage them, their insecure ego will start bothering them almost immediately. They'll become suspicious every time you're unavailable or you go out with friends, or even when you spend time with your children or grandchildren!

The signs aren't clear at first. The jealous person is interested in you, and you're interested in her, and it seems delightful. But a telltale sign of possessiveness is lots of questions about your whereabouts, or even worse, unexpected visits because she was "in the neighborhood." If that starts escalating or she acts possessive and jealous very early in your relationship, extricate yourself as soon as possible. Be clear, firm, and nice. Tell her that you're too different or you're not ready for a deeper relationship. If she persists in calling or stopping by, you may need to threaten calling the police (and in some bad situations, you may have to do just that).

Real stalking or telephoning multiple times a day to check up on you is rare but not unheard of. You have to nip it in the bud or it can flower into a man-eating plant.

Men may not take a woman's jealousy seriously, which is a mistake. A woman who won't let go, is extremely jealous, and pursues you is no laughing matter. She could be dangerous or disrupt other dates and scare off someone you're interested in. A jealous person, male or female, is to be avoided.

Becoming more than neighbors — or not

Think long and hard about getting involved with someone in your neighborhood, especially if you know the relationship isn't going to become a serious one. People may talk a good game about just wanting to have a good time or just wanting a "friends with benefits" situation, but they often don't mean it or aren't being honest with themselves. When dating gets sexual but not emotionally committed, the person who wants more but gets less can feel gravely insulted — even if the person promised not to be. So be careful what you get into, because getting out of it may be harder than you thought it would be. For example:

Ross had lost his wife to cancer after a long, heartbreaking illness. He really didn't feel like dating, but he was slightly depressed and wanted to head that off, so he went out from time to time even though his heart wasn't in it. He had a single neighbor down the hall who was quite solicitous, and they became friendly. She would come over for a few hours, and they'd have a glass of wine, talk, and watch some TV. He wasn't that attracted to her, but he liked her. One night she propositioned him. He was hesitant for a number of good reasons. He didn't see a future with this woman, and he didn't want any complications. She said she understood and felt the same way, but they could give each other some "comfort." He was needy too, so, against his better judgment, he had sex with her one night. They both enjoyed the evening, but the next evening she was knocking on his door again. Ross restated his emotional situation and his need for no entanglements, and then she got verbally abusive, saying that he was heartless and that he led her on. She also wrote him a nasty note and pinned it on his door. In the end, he was forced to move.

Outlining Special Safety Rules for Men

Most dating safety issues affect both genders, but some are far more likely to affect men than women or vice versa (see "Spelling Out Safety Rules for Women" later in this chapter for recommendations for ladies). Men are definitely at less risk than women of being raped or beaten up, but there are plenty of other risks out there to be careful about. Even if you're smitten with someone you just met, you have several reasons to go slow before you arrange to be alone in a romantic and sexual situation.

Avoiding sexually awkward situations

Few men worry about unwanted sexual situations until it happens to them, and then it's really upsetting. Though the last thing most women would do is proposition someone who doesn't show extreme interest in them, occasionally a man will run into a woman who doesn't want to take no for an answer. Consider this true story, for example:

> Boris, age 65: I met this nice lady about ten years younger than me. I thought she was lovely, and we went to the ballpark a couple of times. The second time was when things got uncomfortable. At first I thought I was imagining it, but she was pressing her leg against me during the game, and then there was the hand on the thigh . . . I moved away but her hand moved with me. I didn't want to make a big deal out of it — you know, embarrass us both — but I didn't like it.
>
> So I didn't call her after that, but she called me, and I don't feel like I should turn down a lady, so we went out to a show and dinner (she had the tickets), and there goes that hand again. So this time I tell her that I like her but not that way, and she gets really insulted and says that maybe I'm gay. I say I'm not, and she says, "Prove it." It was hard finishing dinner. Then she gave me a big hug and a big red lipstick kiss on the lips at the cab door. I honestly didn't think this kind of thing could happen. It certainly didn't when I was young, before I met my wife.

Granted, this story reflects a situation that may be considered more annoying than scary, but be prepared for women who are far more aggressive than they would have been many years ago.

If you're uninterested, don't get into a situation where sex becomes expected, and you have to refuse someone's sexual approach. That puts you — and the other person — in a difficult situation that could have been avoided.

Protecting yourself against charges of sexual harassment

Being accused of sexual harassment isn't likely, but it isn't impossible either. These charges have multiplied over the years — sometimes because someone has tried to bully someone into sex, but other times because the complainant and the accused simply don't agree on what was happening, and each think the other is at fault. More rarely, but not unknown, is when someone just makes up a charge of sexual harassment because the person is manipulative, has a distorted reality, or is angry.

Make sure you're not alone with someone — even in a nonsexual situation — until you know what kind of person she is and you're confident that you won't be accused of something you didn't do.

Remember, sexual harassment is often defined as "unwelcome behavior," so be cautious, go slow, and communicate with your date. Here's an example of how things can go wrong:

> Gilbert, age 72: It was the second time we went out. We went back to her house and had a bottle of wine. We were both feeling amorous, and we started to kiss, and then it got going. She was this beautiful woman, smart, sophisticated, about 67. So she is half naked, and I start to unbutton her pants and she says, "What do you think you're doing?" Before I can say anything, she's standing up and yelling at me to get out. I'm so startled I can't move, so she starts pushing me and saying she can call the cops. So I hustle out of there. I call her the next morning to try and understand, and she won't pick up. So I e-mail and apologize for not understanding what she wanted, and she just sends one sentence back saying that if I ever contact her again, she'll call the cops. That stopped my dating for a long time.

Spelling Out Safety Rules for Women

No matter how fit they are, most women are no match for a man who is bigger and physically aggressive. Some women are capable of defending themselves against a sexually aggressive man, but most women would have to depend on their brains, rather than their brawn, to get out of a dicey situation. The best defense, of course, is never getting in that situation in the first place, but it's easy to misjudge a man's intentions if he's trying to mislead you.

Therefore, women have to be extra cautious about being alone with a man and not within earshot of help should they need it. Most older men are gentlemen, but if they misinterpret your intentions or if you get someone who is disturbed, it can be scary and dangerous. You should never be in a situation where you feel you can't make the choices you want to make.

Lucky you if you have great legs, a fine curvy body, or a chest that attracts notice and admiration. You should be able to look as sexy as you want to. In the name of self-protection, however, you may want to slow down the relationship and get to know each other, and if you dress very sexy, a lot of men take that as a signal that you're interested in sex early on.

Keeping yourself modest starts with your profile, if you're dating online. Don't use a picture of yourself in a low-cut top, a clingy dress, or a bathing suit. You can attract men in so many ways; you don't need to show everything on hello. Be modest for a while and ask for gentlemanly conduct for however long it suits you. If you advertise the wrong things early on, you may find yourself with the wrong shopper. For more advice on online dating, turn to Chapter 6.

How to Say You're Not Interested in the Nicest of Ways

Dating is the road to love, companionship, and often passion, but you need to exercise good sense and caution both online and off-line. Some people don't say what they mean or mean what they say, and others have not-so-hidden problems that make them unsuitable dates, much less partners. Still, if you run into one of these gems, remember that they're the exception, not the rule. And if someone is unpleasant, make sure you have a safe exit and a continuing buffer against any further interaction.

One of the toughest parts of dating is being rejected. It hurts. But it's also hard to be the person who calls things off. You want to be as nice as possible, and you don't want to get anyone angry with you. In this section, I cover some strategic, gentle ways to say goodbye.

You're searching for "the one"

Everyone wants to be wanted, but people don't expect everyone they meet to think that they're "the one." Obviously, you have multiple ways to get the message across, but the seriousness of your quest will soften the blow to your date's ego. So if you say to someone, "I like you, but this isn't going to end up as the love affair of my life, and that's all I want right now," most people will understand that and bow out gracefully. Or you could say something like, "You're great, but I'll know when I've met the person I was meant for, and I'm sure that this is not our future. I like you a lot, and we could have a lot of fun, but I'm on a hunt for the person I'm going to spend the rest of my life with, and I don't just want to date around. So this has to be it for us."

Your date may want to argue with you, saying, "I am too the person of your dreams; let me prove it to you." You have to be ready with an answer because you're sure that this person isn't the one. Here's one possibility: "I can't do that. Even if you're right, I need to stop here. Perhaps someday I'll feel differently, and I hope if that happens, you'll accept a call from me. But right now I think that ending this is right for me, and I hope you'll see it that way too someday."

Things are getting too serious

Say you find someone who has totally fallen in love with you, and it's too much too soon. Perhaps this person isn't the one, but you don't have to say that. You can say that you aren't interested in anything really serious right now, and you can see that this person is serious, and it's not where you want to be. You want to date around and get to know more about yourself as a partner at this age, and you aren't ready for any kind of deeper connection.

This may not be pleasing to someone who has fallen for you, but again, you can depersonalize it. You can say something like, "You're a fantastic person. In another time, in another mind-set, we may have been a great couple. But that's not where I am now, and we can't wind back the clock and pretend you don't want something more from me than I have to give right now. I'm uncomfortable with the difference between our feelings and intentions, so I need to end this." This isn't fun for the other person, of course, but it does put the explanation more on timing and intensity of feelings and less on personality or other flaws that you really don't want to mention!

Playing the friend card

You can say this and it can also be true: Your date is great friend material, but you aren't sexually attracted — and you aren't going to be. You may be having great times, but it feels like you're with your brother or sister. Telling someone you think he's wonderful and you want to be friends with him is a big compliment, but of course it's terribly disappointing to someone who wants to be more. In fact, some people may be insulted and say something like, "I have plenty of friends, and I don't need any more. If that's the way you feel about it, I'm gone."

That doesn't feel good to hear, but sometimes it's just ego, humiliation, and face-saving behavior, and it may reverse itself after the first shock of rejection mellows. Some people want to be friends later, just not right away. For others, their attachment to you isn't a big deal, and they're happy to become friends. In those cases, you may find yourself developing a really valuable friendship with someone, and you'll have a relationship that works well as long as it doesn't have to be romantic.

Don't use the friend card if you don't really want to be friends with this person! Also, don't use it if you're pretty sure that the person is only going to use friendship as a way to try and restart the relationship.

Chapter 9

Keeping Things Fresh and New: Dating Ideas

. . . .

In This Chapter

▶ Gaining knowledge about your partner through dating

▶ Doing familiar activities and trying out unfamiliar ones

▶ Taking classes together, playing sports, and volunteering

▶ Making your dates romantic

. . . .

Dates can become boring if you do the same thing over and over. But the good news is that it's easy to get out of a rut. Nothing's wrong with dinner and a movie — in fact, the reason it's the default date for singles and couples alike is that it's so satisfying. You get time to talk, a movie to discuss, and perhaps a heightened sense of emotion and connection, depending on the emotions the movie produces.

But if you go out for dinner and a movie date after date, month after month, it can start to lose its punch and pizazz. You want dates that help build your sense of togetherness and give you a sense of the kind of future fun the two of you can build as a couple.

Dates aren't just going out; they're opportunities to try out each other's lifestyles and personalities. What you do together matters, so think about what you can do ahead of time so you don't always end up in the default dinner and a movie. This chapter gives you some dating options to try out and provides some ideas on how to be more romantic.

Finding a Good Fit: What You Want to Know about Your Partner

Dates are part of the audition for both partners. So the question is: What parts of your personality do you want to express, and what would you like to see in your partner? Here are some questions to ponder:

- How competitive are you, and how competitive is your date?

- How collaborative are you?

- Does conversation lag or is there never enough time to discuss all you want to talk about?

- Do you feel funnier or smarter when you're with this person?

- Does your date come up with good ideas about what to do or where to go, or is it all or mostly up to you?

- Is your date solicitous? Does your date make sure you're having a good time?

- How do you each handle problems, such as one of you being late, getting stuck in traffic, or going to a restaurant that turns out to be closed?

- How does your date treat the people who you come in contact with?

- Do the differences between you and your date help you be a better person or are they merely irritating?

If you're smitten by your date's looks or wit, you may forget to take in this kind of information. Or if you hear a discordant note, you may be tempted to excuse it immediately or doubt your own perceptions. But you really need to keep these kinds of questions in mind. If your partner displays spoiled or egocentric behavior, it's better to notice it early on than suffer from it in a long-term relationship.

The most important part of the date is to expect that both of you will get something out of it, even if you don't end up together as life partners. You want to set up your dating experiences so that you have fun, try things you haven't done before, or go back to beloved places or activities that you haven't taken the time for in a very long while.

You want to make sure that your experiences start to stack up so that you're far happier than you were, even if some experiences aren't as consequential or emotionally fulfilling as you may have liked. You want to date in such a way as to build your optimism — if not about a specific person, about the fact that dating has given you so many new things to do and see, and so many new people to understand and converse with. When you genuinely enjoy dating, you'll feel more optimistic about eventually meeting a person to love and be loved by.

Discussing What You'd Like to Do Together

After the first couple of coffees and perhaps a few dinners or movies, you'll start to discuss things that each of you likes to do, and you'll eventually introduce each other to some new activities. First, of course, you'll try to find mutual ground — and hope that you have enough in common so that you'll have an immediate advantage of mutual interests. But probably sooner than later, you'll want to see what it's like to explore someone else's world. The trick of this is to try things with an open mind that you may have rejected in the past but not talk yourself into something where there's a 99 percent chance that you'll hate it, be afraid of it, or resent your date for getting you into this situation!

Trying out the things your date likes best

Suppose your date loves in-line skating (or some other sport) and you've never done it. In fact, it scares you a bit. On the other hand, you'd kind of like to try it. Should you? Sure, but here are some guidelines to observe:

- ✔ **Are you able to try this activity without getting hurt?** In your enthusiasm for your date, you may try something that you really aren't good at and hurt yourself. Breaking a wrist or ankle isn't romantic and can really derail a promising beginning to a relationship. If you're uncoordinated or really don't like athletics very much, don't make this your first foray into new territory.

- ✔ **Do you think there's really a good chance that you'll enjoy it or will you have to pretend you like it?** Don't start out your relationship on a false premise. You may like to please your date by doing something she likes, but then she may assume this is a shared common interest, and you'll eventually have to try and find a graceful exit from these kinds of activities, which makes you look less than authentic. Better to just say it isn't your thing in the beginning if there's little or no chance that you'll truly enjoy it.

- ✔ **Are you willing and able to be the student for an evening and follow your date's lead?** If you're going to do something your date likes, she'll probably take the lead and decide on the date's details. You have to give up some control and trust that your date will shape the day or evening in a way that's comfortable and appropriate for you. If you're unsure whether your date knows you or your abilities well enough to pull this together in an agreeable way, you may want to beg off on this type of date until you're sure it will turn out well. Don't forget, though, that taking a stab at things you don't do well has comic potential and can create a lot of laughs between you, which often creates a very endearing situation. For example, if your date suggests learning the samba, your inept attempts at shaking your booty may be just the icebreaker that bonds you.

Introducing things you usually do

Sharing something you love with someone you're interested in can be exciting, but you want to make sure that you don't take your date too far out of his comfort zone. You also don't want to make this into a de facto test of suitability. Here are a couple of pointers for introducing activities to your date:

- ✔ Do a very basic version of what you do.

- ✔ Engage in the activity for only a brief period of time; if your date wants to extend it, he can, but don't push it.

- ✔ Reassure your date that if he doesn't like it, it's no big deal.

- ✔ Try not to be too much the expert; your date may like some teaching, but do it with a light hand.

Trying out things neither of you have done

In some ways, trying out things that neither you nor your date has done before, which I discuss in the next section, is the safest choice. Discovery together is fun. Neither of you is on your own turf, so you learn together and can lean on each other without one person being the teacher and the other the pupil. If you don't like something, it's not a reflection on the other person — you just move on to another choice. Consider the example of Beryl and Paul: When they started dating steadily, they decided that they would always keep their relationship interesting by learning new things together. They started out trying skeet shooting, and that was so much fun that even after they got married, they kept up the ritual of learning one new thing a year.

Exploring New Dating Ideas

If you were married a long time or lived alone a long time and lived life exactly as it appealed to you, you may have accumulated some strong habits, and entertaining new ideas about how to spend time with someone else may be hard. Still, plowing some new ground together is a great idea. In this section I highlight some activities that are particularly likely to create some good feelings between the two of you.

Taking a class together

A great class taught by a gifted teacher is engrossing, entertaining, and enlivening. If you pick out a class that interests you both, you can become history buffs together or take an introduction to art history or geology. Learning something new together builds a sense of you two as a couple, and research has shown that doing something innovative together is likely to bring couples together more tightly than doing things they know well. But this is only a good idea if you don't have any of these issues:

✔ You're competitive, and if your date is better at something than you are, it will bother you.

✔ You're not willing to go the distance with the class if it stops appealing to you but your partner still likes it. (You can't abandon something when you're doing it as a couple activity! It's bad form and will hurt your blossoming relationship.)

✔ You have a short attention span, and you know you'll get tired of the class part of the way in (so it would be best if you didn't start).

A cooking class

Cooking is so tactile and aromatic that it can't help but be sexy. Making desserts is probably sexiest (using your finger to scrape that last bit of frosting out of the bowl is so sexy that it should only be done by very mature adults!).

A cooking class offers so many opportunities to feed each other (to taste whether the sauce is done, for example) and enjoy something sensual at the same time that it can't help but bring the two of you together. It's a playful way to interact, and it may also have some practical rewards. After you get proficient and learn to cook together, you may be encouraged to have more domestic dates where you cook and spend time together. An added advantage is enjoying extremely good food without spending a fortune at fancy restaurants.

If you're a perfectionist and you're going to complain or be upset if your souf-flé doesn't turn out right, you may want to skip this suggestion.

A language class

Language classes can be frustrating if you're lousy at learning a language. But if you're just untalented, as opposed to hopeless, it's kind of sexy to repeat sentences to each other in Italian, French, or Spanish (German, maybe not so much). You can also make dates to quiz each other and practice at home. And the prize at the end of the class? Why of course, a trip to Italy, France, or Spain! Or at least a European restaurant.

A film class

Experimental or independent films usually have provocative content and are fun to discuss in class. You can both contribute and learn each other's tastes. The point is exploring the content and not just being entertained. So if you're the kind of person who wants someone to discuss intriguing topics with and perhaps impress each other with insights, a film class may be a great date activity.

Film societies often offer interesting films all year long at very reasonable prices for the cost of a membership. Joining such a group may be an economical way to enjoy many interesting dates.

A music, dance, or art discussion series

Most of the arts are even more compelling when there's a discussion after the performance. A lot of heavyweight cultural institutions, such as the ballet, opera, and symphony, have previews that are sometimes free (or offered at a lower price) and often have a discussion component to them. You can learn more together and make it into your own special ritual.

If you enjoy these series, you may be moved to join one of the booster groups that help the arts raise money and put on events. Doing something like that together is another way to grow the feeling that you're becoming a couple.

Doing volunteer work

Showing your compassionate side is never a bad idea. Also, if you pick an emotionally fulfilling and touching charitable endeavor, the feeling of doing the right thing and being a good person will infuse the relationship.

You need to pick your joint commitment very carefully, however. You both need to feel that this volunteer work is a fulfilling and uplifting enterprise. It can't feel forced or inauthentic; that would have the opposite effect on the two of you. But if it's really and truly something that touches both your hearts, you'll admire that in each other, and your time spent volunteering will help each of you feel good about doing good in the world and feel proud of each other as a couple.

Getting sporty

If your life is organized around active sports, then you'll probably try and find someone who's at least somewhat enthusiastic about physical activity. You just want to set it up right.

One of the nice things about doing a sport together is that sports produce, or at least can potentially produce, adrenaline, which can affect the way you see someone and how that person sees you. All sports that produce a thrill induce the secretion of *endorphins,* the hormones that make you feel good and also feel good about someone else. You may consider using endorphins to help make your partner's heart grow fonder "cheating," but if your partner is athletic, she probably knows the effect of endorphins, even if she hasn't read this book.

Sports and physical activities are a great way to get the blood coursing through your veins. Some sports, like bungee jumping, are obvious thrills that get you excited (if you aren't so scared that you're angry). But other sports, like hiking or kayaking, are more blissful than hormone-producing (unless you're white-water kayaking or ocean kayaking, in which case you have gallons of hormones pumping through your system). Bicycling on a pretty day and skiing are wonderful ways of spending time together.

Learning a sport together

Learning a sport together is much like taking classes together, with some of the same advantages and pitfalls. If one of you is a natural athlete, that person will pick up any sport and be reasonably good at it. If both of you are, so much the better. Be cautious, though, if one of you is good at sports and the other person struggles. It's easy for people to feel humiliated if they totally fail at a sport, and that never helps build intimacy, much less love.

If you want to ensure you're on equal footing when it comes to a sport, choose something new and easy that won't stress out either of you. For example, go snorkeling rather than scuba diving, or bounce along the waves in an inner tube instead of trying to water ski.

Doing something new together that produces a little adrenaline is a good idea. Just make sure no one's pride gets banged up. If you want to do a sport together but worry that you won't be able to keep up, take some lessons separately as well as with your date. That way you can get the worst flubs out of the way before you try doing the sport together.

Fishing for trouble

When you invite your partner to join you in an activity, it's crucial to consider your partner's ability in said activity if you want to avoid stories like this:

Alice was intrigued when Chapin invited her to go fly fishing. She'd never done it, but it appealed to her. She had visions of a long cast during which the fishing line would hang in the air and then, after gently hovering over the water, gracefully land without so much as a ripple. After all, that's what she'd seen in the movie *A River Runs Through It,* and the quiet beauty of the scenes she remembered appealed to her. Unfortunately, her actual experience had no resemblance to that vision whatsoever. She and Chapin were up above

Lake Tahoe and had hiked to some of his favorite streams, but Chapin had neglected to realize that the banks of the stream were covered with trees and that a novice would have trouble casting without getting tangled in them. At the first cast, and every cast thereafter, Alice had her hook and line woefully twisted around branches and leaves. She never, not once in the afternoon, got her line in the water. Though Chapin helped her, it was hopeless. She put up a good front, but she was frustrated and finally ticked off. He apologized and she forgave him — but not before she thought seriously about never seeing him again. Ultimately, the two continued seeing each other, but Alice never went fly fishing again.

Creating a team

Sometimes, general camaraderie can be a support to your relationship. Maybe one-on-one sports put too much pressure on you, but trying a really low-rule, community kind of sport puts everyone in a happy frame of mind. For example, playing soccer with as many people who want to be on the field, playing no particular position, can be a lot of fun. You meet your date's friends or your date meets yours, and no one's performance is too central or obvious.

You may want to wait a while before you do "team dating." Sports create endorphins, which help bonding and attraction. You want to make sure the two of you are a pretty secure couple before you take the chance that one of you may take those endorphins and use them to be attracted to someone else on the team!

Opting for relaxing, low-key dates

Nothing's wrong with wanting slow, easy, and intimate times that don't require travel, physical exertion, or other people. If you're more of a cerebral type or you just want to share more discussion than vivid experiences, then you want to do things that give you time to just hang out. You can plan plenty of great dates with that premise in mind.

Exploring: The fun of the hunt

Collecting something together is really fun, and it implies a future. It really doesn't matter what you collect. It can be old teapots, quilts, or antique car posters, or perhaps you enjoy just looking around at garage sales or rural antique stores for something unexpected. This activity can make for an urban adventure or a country outing, and it brings with it the possibility for mutual fun and excitement and learning how to assess the other person's personality and companionship. You also may end up collecting something that adds joy to your life.

If shopping and collections aren't your thing, you can go look at wildflowers for the day or walk around the zoo for a couple of hours. If you want to get more ambitious and it's spring or summer, see some entertainment at a park or attend a weekend festival or parade. Check out nearby towns outside your city or explore new neighborhoods in your city. Take your date to your favorite local haunts or find new ones together.

Unwinding together

You also have the option of doing absolutely nothing besides enjoying each other's company in a nice setting. You can go to the mountains and have a cup of coffee in the restaurant at the top of the hill. You can go to the beach with a couple of good books or a board game. You can go to a marina and admire the sunset. Or you can simply watch your favorite TV series and veg out with finger food or a pizza.

You don't have to do much at all if you're interested in each other, but in the beginning of the relationship, it helps to have some point to the date so that you share something in those first weeks and months, when you don't really know each other very well.

Taking advantage of free and low-cost activities

Occasionally, people on a fixed or low income say they don't want to date because it costs too much money. That's not much of an excuse when almost every institution, from zoos to art museums to ballet companies, has free activities that invite the public. There are so many free and cheap community activities that you'd never have time to do even 25 percent of them! Here are a few ideas:

✔ Local high school football, baseball, and basketball games, or competitive trials for runners

✔ Symphony and ballet rehearsals

✔ University and high school recitals and practices for music and theater

✔ Book readings, poetry slams, and other events at local YMCAs, bookstores, and coffee shops

Consider just picking a book to read and discuss together. Done in a nice comfy place, reading aloud to each other can be positively romantic and intimate.

✔ Hiking and fishing and water sports along rivers in most states

✔ Most evening lectures at universities and colleges

✔ Trail-clearing for conservation groups

✔ Most federal and state buildings and exhibitions

For another low-key date that exposes you to new things, consider attending an AARP convention together. The cost is minimal (only about $25 for members and $35 for nonmembers), and you get access to three days of nonstop lectures and festival-like events with your peers.

Adding a Dash of Romance

When you find someone you're romantically interested in, it's important to have dates that advance the prospects of that dream. Some options for dates are intensely romantic, and that furthers the possibility of awakening deepening feelings.

Before you try one of these really romantic places, be sure your date is feeling exactly the same way about you. People aren't dumb (for the most part), and if you pick a restaurant with low lighting and soft music, they get the picture. You want to make sure a romantic date makes the person feel happy, not pressured.

What kinds of places and activities are best for romance? Here's a list, along with some details you can add if they're not already present:

✔ A small, intimate restaurant with fresh flowers, low lighting, and a feeling of conviviality without being loud. A really small place creates a feeling of intimacy, which is what you're after.

✔ Appreciation of the grandness of nature, which may include mountains, oceans, a sunrise or sunset, or a particularly amazing tree. All these majestic sights put awe and wonder in the air and invoke a sense of togetherness.

✔ A romantic dinner after a romantic movie. The movie sets the tone, so make sure that it isn't tragic or violent and that it has a happy ending. The dinner afterward allows you to dwell on it.

✔ An adventure that gets the blood pumping (asking hormones to be your helpmate again). Something exciting like going white-water rafting or even betting on a long shot at the races — and winning — gets you both excited, in a good mood, and rather ripe for each other.

✔ A special event like a concert or show. Get tickets to see a favorite band from the '70s or arrange something else special that has to do with you both having lived through the same period of time and events. These memories can produce a sense of closeness, understanding of each other's lives, and an appreciation of your mutual life histories.

✔ A hotel (a bed and breakfast can be romantic but often not private enough) that's luxurious and treats you both well.

What is anti-romantic on a date?

✔ The news. Don't watch it. It almost always has something depressing and/or violent.

✔ Almost anything you used to do with an ex or an old flame.

✔ Loud, bustling restaurants where you can't hear each other.

✔ Chain restaurants. You want each memory to feel special.

✔ Spectator sports. Fun, yes; romantic, not so much.

✔ Hikes on super-hot days or skiing on super-cold ones. Being uncomfortable isn't romantic.

✔ Hotels that are low end or look unkempt.

✔ A sleepover at friends' homes in their kid's bedroom or on the office couch.

Dating is an art, not a science. You have to keep checking in with your date to see what makes her thrilled or romantic. Maybe something worked once but it may not again. Honest communication is the key. For more ideas of dates designed to impress, check out Chapter 19.

Part III
Taking Things to the Next Level

Five Things to Avoid When Meeting Your Date's Adult Children

- **Don't act overly affectionate toward them.** You may have heard so much about them that you think you know them, but you don't. Inappropriate intimacy with family members before you know them and before a real friendship arises is at best an irritant and at worst presumptuous and offensive.

- **Don't say, "Your mother/father has told me all about you."** This could embarrass the children, but more than that, it presumes a lot of intimacy between you and your date, and that may be a shock to adult children. They want to think that no one is more intimate with their parent than they are.

- **Don't talk in the future tense; stay in the present.** You don't want them to get nervous at this point about their parent getting cornered into a serious relationship too quickly.

- **Don't talk using "we."** It sounds too proprietary and even competitive to adult children. Say "I," even if you're talking about something you and your date plan to do together.

- **Don't drape yourself over your date.** Even though adult children know their parent is an adult and may have a physical relationship with someone, they may be squeamish about seeing it and think it's in bad taste.

If your relationship is sexually intimate (or if you'd like it to be!), visit www.dummies.com/extras/datingafter50 for advice on being a great lover and creating a good experience for both you and your partner.

In this part...

- ✔ Prevent careless and awkward introductions that can sometimes spoil relationships. Find out how to ease into your date's family and friends and how to introduce him or her to your closest friends and family.

- ✔ Pay attention when meeting your date's family and friends. They'll tell you loads about your date by the way they interact. Pick up on what to do, and what not to do, if you're trying to impress them (and you should be trying, at least a little!).

- ✔ Listen to your friends' comments about your date — but know when to trust your own opinion. Find out what to listen to and what to be more cautious about.

- ✔ Take a survey of yourself to find out whether you're confident enough about your own sexual worthiness and whether you feel ready for an intimate relationship. Get yourself there if you're not there already, and understand how to negotiate safer sexual practices.

- ✔ Talk with your partner about sexual issues that you may have, such as erectile dysfunction, vaginal pain, or a bad back or knees, and learn how to work around these issues.

- ✔ Think about money and dating in a new way. Not all men are traditional anymore; many want to share expenses.

Chapter 10

Making Introductions to Loved Ones

● ●

In This Chapter

▶ Figuring out when to introduce your date to family and friends

▶ Having a plan and making observations when introducing your date

▶ Meeting the people your date is close to and gauging their reactions

● ●

*I*f you're excited about someone, you're naturally curious to meet the person's family. The family is always an important part of the puzzle.

When you're over 50, meeting family and close friends means meeting people who've known your date for a very long time and who also knew your date's previous partners. You come late to the party. You may also be meeting children, who may still be in school or may be adults with children of their own. They may be delighted to meet you or consider the very concept of their parent's date as a threatening and awful proposition. The scenarios are varied and complicated.

And you may not be exactly sure of the reaction of your children and your friends. You may want your date to meet them, and your date may be enthusiastic about the prospect, but don't assume your family is up for this until you think about when and how to introduce the possibility.

Timing Is Everything

Before considering the introduction of your friends and family and your date's friends and family at length, start with the most important directive: Do this at the right time or the consequences can be messy. The "right time" is different for every couple, but the following cues give you an idea of when you and your date may be ready for this next step:

✔ **When you feel that your relationship is secure enough that a bad reaction by someone wouldn't doom it:** You need to have had enough experience together so that if a parent or sibling doubts that you're the right partner, your date knows the grounds on which he would defend his choice. If it's too early in the relationship, he may not really know why the relationship is a good one or why you're a good person. You need enough time together so your date is sure of his choice and won't readily buckle under to another opinion. This goes for you as well when it comes to your family and friends.

✔ **When you've been dating long enough to plan these introductions together:** Meeting friends and family is consequential, and it shouldn't be a test that only one of you studies for. Unless you and your date want to plan these introductions together (for example, knowing what topics to avoid with which person), it's too early to meet the family.

✔ **When you have enough intimacy to discuss who would be a good introduction, who wouldn't be, and how to plan the order of who gets to meet who:** There are always people to avoid early on in the relationship. Maybe it's an uncouth relative who will offend your date or incessantly praise your departed spouse because she can't handle the idea of someone else in your life. Your relationship should be mature enough to explain why you should skip a specific introduction, and the two of you should have enough trust that your date supports your reasoning.

✔ **When you have a good idea what it means, and doesn't mean, to be meeting friends or family:** Understanding the meaning of any given act is critical. Some meetings show your parents or children that this is a serious relationship and that it may even be a committed one; other meetings are of a far less determined and perhaps more casual nature. It's so important to know which is which that you might ask your partner, "What does this get-together mean to you?" or "Are your children used to meeting your date?" or "Will this meeting be some kind of signal to your son or will he just be happy that you're dating?" You want to have as much of a framework as possible so that you gain some perspective on how to act or how to interpret the reactions of the people you meet. It's important, for example, to know whether his best friend will be scrutinizing you because he has never introduced anyone else.

Bringing Your Date into Your World

When you're ready to introduce your date to people who are important to you — your friends and family — it helps to give some thought to just how you'll take this next step in your dating relationship. Rather than throw everyone in a room together and cross your fingers, giving it a little thoughtful planning and observing everyone's reactions carefully helps smooth the transition and increase the chances that everyone gets along.

Making introductions in the right order

What should be the order of introducing someone to the people you care about? Here's the order that makes sense in terms of feedback, difficulty, meaning, and purpose.

1. **Your best friend(s).**

   Your closest friends want the best for you and want you to have whatever it is you want. They won't try and deep-six something just because it gives them less time with you or because you're not the person of *their* dreams. (If they're not this kind of person, perhaps you need to reevaluate the friendship!)

   So they're the likeliest people to root for you and hope that your date is worthy of you. They may have an inflated sense of your "worth" (God bless them), but with that in mind, they're still the best first introduction. They'll give you kind feedback (even if they think you're utterly deluded, they'll say so nicely), and if they really like your date, it will shore up your courage to move down the list to other people whom your date would like to meet and whom you want your date to meet.

2. **Your crowd or friendship circle.**

   Eventually, you'll want to see how your date fits in. She doesn't have to like everyone in the group (you probably don't even like everyone in your friendship circle!), but your group is a good testing ground to see whether your date sees people the way you see them and mixes easily with the people and events you like the most. People in your crowd may or may not give feedback, but because you have differing levels of closeness with them, many of their opinions don't matter that much.

   If you don't have an extended group of friends and acquaintances, take your date to an event where you know people to see how she adapts and works with you in a couples situation.

3. **Your siblings.**

   Your date is going to be very interested in your brothers and/or sisters if you have any — especially if you're close to them. They're a big clue to who you are (and are not), and your date will be very concerned about making a good impression if you tell her that you're close to your family.

   If your siblings are judgmental or treat your date indifferently, your date may wonder how many times you've introduced someone. If your siblings act like your date may become one of the family, it will raise expectations (or fears, depending on your date's state of mind), so basically, whatever way your siblings act will be meaningful.

   Introduce your date to your friendliest, least-judgmental sibling first. That person is likeliest to send around a good message about you to the rest of the family.

4. **Your children.**

Your children may be excited and happy for you. However, they may be happy simply because you're dating but not necessarily satisfied with the person you're seeing. And you may face a situation that really causes fireworks if your kids think that you're desecrating your deceased spouse's memory or if issues from a divorce rise again and your children and ex-spouse become enraged.

Consider putting off this introduction until you feel it's important enough to both of you to brave whatever happens. If you're positive that your children will be thrilled with your date, you can move the introduction up a bit. But be cautious: The reactions of children aren't always predictable.

Don't tell your children things that should never, ever be said, such as, "Don't worry, this isn't 'the one,'" or "I'm just dating, it's nothing serious." Relationships can change in nature, and you may fall in love with your date — and then hear your children throw those statements out to your beloved if they aren't happy with this person.

5. **Your parents.**

Your parents are probably quite interested in meeting your date, unlikely to curb their opinions, and perhaps worried about this new relationship. If your relationship is getting serious, your date will probably want to meet your parents. If you think this may be difficult but want to honor the request, set up a brief visit to start.

Seeing how your date relates to your good friends

The reaction of your friends tells you a lot about your date and a lot about your friends. You want to introduce your date to someone who has your back and will represent you well — someone who will be friendly and helpful to your date but who will also give you honest feedback. Your date is well aware that this is a mutual interview, and it's important to note whether your date puts in real effort to try and be friendly.

If you have snarky friends who are likely to regale your date with stories of your craziest behavior or of you and your ex-spouse, cut your date some slack and warn him ahead of time. Also, give strict instructions to your friends ahead of time to avoid this kind of behavior.

Give your date as much history and description of people as you can so he's prepared to have something to talk about. Do the same for your friends. Meeting someone new can be awkward, and it's doubly awkward when the relationship is even moderately on the line.

Funny first meetings

Sometimes, even when everyone is trying her best to impress others, things just go awry. A firsthand account:

"As I sat down to dinner to meet the people who would eventually become my in-laws, I was on my best behavior. Elsa, John's mother, was a lovely woman, brimming with goodwill and handsome, with snow-white hair and the bearing of an ex-schoolteacher (which she was). Louie was a kind man, retired from the university, easy to talk to, interested in what I was saying, and quite a storyteller.

"Charmed, and listening, I proceeded to eat the small piece of fish put in front of me and a small bowl of vegetables. When I looked up, I saw all three of them staring at me. Confused, I looked at John and said, 'Why are you staring at me?' Laughing, he said, 'Because you ate the bowl of vegetables that was meant for the whole table!'

"I was embarrassed, to say the least. Luckily, these were very kind, easygoing people."

Still, whether or not the introduction is a love fest, the important thing is that your date tries hard to please your friends. If he fits your group like a glove, all the better. But don't worry if they don't develop an immediate connection; you have plenty of time for people to get a deeper, better sense of each other if the relationship lasts.

Try and introduce your date slowly to friends, one by one. Meeting a room full of friends all at once is both daunting and confusing.

Getting your friend's honest take on your date

Your good friend's reaction to your date can be tricky. You need feedback from someone, and your close friend knows you well and has an opinion about who's good for you and who's not. So this person is important for a reality check. On the other hand, if the verdict isn't what you want to hear and you're going to date this person anyway, the feedback may be difficult to absorb and may put a crimp in your friendship or affect social situations that involve your close friend and your date. Consider describing to your friend what you do and don't want to hear from the beginning. For example:

- What do you think are her strong points?
- What do you think may cause some incompatibilities?
- Please don't comment on her looks or her clothes. I just want observations about how you think I seem when I'm with her.

✔ Please don't compare her to my ex. I know the situation is completely different, but even if you think it's similar, I just don't want to discuss that right now.

Never tell your date that someone in your inner circle doesn't like her, and never reveal any specific comments from a friend (or anyone else), unless it's a rave review. If your date knows about some negative remarks and you become serious, knowledge of this remark may seriously impede any friendship your date may have started with your friend, and she may even refuse to spend social time with your friend.

Observing and managing interactions between your date and your family

Your children or other family members may not be ready for you to date, now or maybe ever. What do you do if they're capable of acting badly? Your first move should be to head off that behavior by talking to people before the introduction takes place.

✔ Talk to your children and tell them what stage this relationship is in. If you're just starting to date, let them know that. If you think this person is really special, let them know that too.

✔ Tell them that you need them to be friendly and welcoming. If they can't promise that, don't introduce your date. Do tell your children that you want to include them in all parts of your life, but you're not going to embarrass your date, and you don't want your children to harm this relationship (or any relationship).

✔ Remind them that you've accepted the people that they've chosen to be with in their life, and you'd like that respect to be reciprocated.

✔ Reassure them that you understand their feelings (and don't talk about them until you do) and you respect their emotions, but they have to do the same for you.

The second move is to keep introductions short. Your date's curiosity and desire for inclusion will, at least in the beginning, be satisfied by an introduction. You don't have to spend a day at the beach together or even have a big dinner party in the early stages of dating someone. Let some time pass after the first introductions to let the reality of this new person being around become a fact of life for your family. Then gradually create visits of a longer length.

Your last move is a correctional one, if needed. Talk with any of your children, friends, or extended family who is acting badly. If such people can't

Introducing your date to your pets

Pets can be one of the most precious things in a person's life. Many (maybe most!) pet owners regard them as family, and how a date treats pets matters a great deal. If you live intimately with your pets (they sleep in your room or in your bed, they're at your side a lot, and so on), you may want to make sure your date understands that "love me, love my pets" is one of the most important cards in your deck. Furthermore, if your date is a dog or cat lover and has one or more of her own, she may have strong feelings on how her animals are treated. You want to be careful that nothing you do regarding her pet offends her. (For example, if she's permissive with her pet, and you're very strict with your own, you may want to check that out beforehand and not do anything that makes your date recoil, like ordering her dog around.) Remember, both of you may be assessing each other as a future partner, and the animals can represent all the issues (and fun) of a blended family.

That said, if you're very interested in your date, you may want to make sure that you stack that deck by making the first meeting with your pets a positive one. Here's a checklist to think about:

✔ Find out whether your date is allergic. If she is, vacuum your place carefully so that she can survive the visit. (She can also take an antihistamine before the visit, which may help.)

✔ Find out how much experience she has had with dogs, cats, or whatever pet you have. If she's at all afraid of big dogs or animals, find out what would make her feel at ease.

✔ Find out if she likes pets or loves them (this will be revealed upon meeting your pets, but it will help you know what to expect).

✔ When introducing pets, warn your date about their habits: Do they jump up, do they growl but not mean it, do they growl and mean it when meeting someone new, and so on.

✔ Protect your date from any bad consequences (a cat that scratches, a bird that lands on heads, a dog that nips).

✔ Introduce your date to your possessive pet gradually and underplay it. You don't want your possessive dog to make it clear that he's having none of this new person.

✔ Find out what your date's boundaries are — for example, she may love dogs or cats but not want them on the couch next to her, especially if she has nice clothes on.

Be very conscientious about this. People's pets, and owner's habits with them, can reveal a lot about the owner's temperament and lifestyle. You want your behavior with your pet to reinforce the positive impression your date has had about you up until now. The good news is that your interaction with your pet can show off many good qualities: your patience, affectionate nature, and attention to your pet's health and manners. What you don't want to do is lose your temper or act in such a way to make your date doubt your character.

modify their behavior, stay away from them with your date until they can support you. If it's children, you need to keep talking to them, trying to get them to see this from your point of view.

If you're close with your children, they may just be feeling territorial and not want to share you with someone else. Or they may feel it would be disloyal to their other parent to like anyone you're dating. But they may only be inhospitable to this person because they don't think the person is right for you. If so, listen to what they have to say, and at least consider it. They may be seeing things you need to see too.

Asking to Meet Your Date's Family

Of course you'll want to meet the important people in your date's life. When you get to the point that you're dating only each other and can easily presume that you'll be spending each weekend together, you'll want to dig deeper into his past and present. Hopefully, the family situation will be wonderful, but you may face a clash of cultures. Doing some due diligence before you meet the parents — like finding out as much as you can about their values and lifestyle so that you don't unintentionally insult them — is time well spent.

Your date may see his family differently from you, so don't expect everything he says to be your perception as well. Of course, he knows his own family better than you do, but sometimes, closeness colors vision, and what he has experienced over the years internal to the family may be quite different from what you see or are allowed to see.

Preparing to meet the family

When you talk about wanting to meet your date's family, you should be clear about which ones you want to meet and why you want to meet them. You have to think about how you'll present yourself. You must tread carefully, especially when you meet your date's adult children. Most adult children recognize that their parent may become attached to someone again if the parent is in her 50s. But as parents age, young adults may hold the prejudice that now is the time that their parent should devote to them and their grandchildren rather than falling in love again. Of course, you may disagree, and therein lies a rich environment for all kinds of misunderstandings and conflict.

This actually can get really dicey as the decades roll on and you're in your 70s or 80s. Love isn't impossible or unwelcome at any point, but children start to worry about intruders into their world late in a parent's life, and they may get increasingly touchy about a parent's dating. They may worry about everything from the parent's ability to make a good decision about romance to more materialistic fears (a new person will come in and snatch their inheritance). And of course, if there are several children, they may react quite differently: Some children will be thrilled their parent is in love again, or at least dating seriously, while others will vary from worried to furious.

So meeting the children can be a minefield rather than a festive occasion, which means you have to be very careful — and a good psychologist. You have to get good intelligence from your partner about who's who and who feels what, and you may want to avoid meeting the children who are truly hostile. Ultimately, if you become a committed couple, you'll have to meet even the hostile ones, but while you're dating, it may be wise to stall on dealing with the tougher issues.

If you ask your date to meet her family and she isn't comfortable doing so, check out the later section "Reacting if your date isn't ready for you to meet" for advice on where to go from there. If, however, the coast is clear, and the family wants to meet you with, if not open arms, at least an open heart, here are some guidelines:

- ✔ **Don't act overly affectionate toward them.** You may have heard so much about them that you think you know them, but you don't. Inappropriate intimacy with the family before you know them and before a real friendship arises will be at best an irritant to the children and at worst seen as really presumptuous and offensive.

- ✔ **Don't say, "Your mother has told me all about you."** This could embarrass the children, but more than that, it presumes a lot of intimacy between you and your date, and that may be a shock to adult children. They want to think that no one is more intimate with their parent than they are.

- ✔ **Don't talk in the future tense; stay in the present.** You don't want them to get nervous at this point about their parent getting cornered into a serious relationship too quickly.

- ✔ **Don't talk using "we."** It sounds too proprietary and even competitive to adult children. Say "I," even if you're talking about something you and your date plan to do together.

- ✔ **Don't drape yourself over your date.** Even though adult children know their parent is an adult and will have a physical relationship with someone, they may be squeamish about seeing it and think it's in bad taste.

- ✔ **Do be very friendly and hospitable, and listen more than you talk.**

- ✔ **Do meet on neutral turf, like a restaurant, rather than in your date's house.** If possible, treat them to dinner or do something else that's generous.

> ✔ **Do show that you have an interesting life of your own, that you're worth knowing, and that you're not some pitiful creature looking for a free ride or happy to have just anyone in your life.**

Be nice but don't try too hard. Let the children come to you a bit. Don't buy them all gifts, but if you're going over to dinner, do bring a small gift like a bottle of wine or flowers. You want to be generous and thoughtful, but you don't want to beg for acceptance or act like you're already in the family.

Dealing with an unfriendly reception

As already mentioned, there's a considerable chance that adult children and other family members may not be entirely welcoming. In fact, they could be downright hostile and even rude. That's unfortunate, but you need to remember that if they're like that when they meet you, it's unlikely that it's about you — it's about the idea of you.

Of course, there could be specific things about you that they don't like in general. If you're much younger or much older than your date, they may find it unsettling (especially if you're the same age as they are).

Likewise, if you're a great deal less affluent than their family, they'll worry about your motives. They may even worry if you're a lot better off and are going to be changing your date's lifestyle (and, along this line of thinking, becoming "too good for them"). People often jump to judgment and nurse some premature assumptions until they feel real to them. That kind of thinking may cause you to get a hostile reception before you've shaken the first hand.

So what to do? Basically, it's up to your partner to stand up for you and protect you. He needs to talk to his family first to make sure they act hospitably. If they don't act well, there are probably some family issues going on, and they're acting out.

What should be most important to you is not how the children or other family or friends act but how your partner reacts to it. If he doesn't call them on it or hustle both of you out of there, you should doubt your date's feelings about you — or his strength of character. His loyalty in this situation has to be with you, even if his more profound long-term bond is to the family. Your date has brought you into this situation, and he has to bring you out.

Later, you can discuss the situation, what could make it better, and what, if any, part either of you played in making it worse. Hopefully, another meeting with family or friends can iron out the issues.

But let's think positively here. The majority of relatives and friends are going to be delighted that the person they love has found someone to love. They'll reach out to you and make you feel welcome. Most of you will meet friends and family who offer friendship and goodwill.

Don't write off family members if you have an awkward or unfriendly first meeting. Who knows what else was going on in their lives at that time? Try to get over your bad first impression and try again. The same person may be totally different the next time.

Reacting if your date isn't ready for you to meet

What if your date is dead set against you meeting her family and friends? What does that mean?

Well, it could mean whatever she tells you, which may be:

- ✔ "We aren't at that stage yet."
- ✔ "If I introduce you, they'll think we're going to announce that we're getting married, and that will set up assumptions and questions we're not ready for."
- ✔ "My children are just visiting for the week, and they'll be resentful if I put another person in the picture right now."
- ✔ "It would confuse my grandchildren right now."
- ✔ "I'm not comfortable with letting them know about my personal life right now."
- ✔ "I'm having a difficult time with my child right now, so it's not a good time."
- ✔ "They're still not over the divorce, and this would stir things up."
- ✔ "They can't imagine me with anyone else but my ex-spouse."

There are a lot of reasons for family feuds that wouldn't be a parent's fault. But if the reason you can't get introduced to anyone is that your date has burned her bridges to her family or that a child or children have rejected her, see if you can find out more. There may be reasons that should make you cautious about this person as a serious partner.

Of course, the subtext on some of these answers may be one you're not crazy about, and that is, "We're not serious enough for me to interject this into my family life." The question for you is, do you think you're at a stage that would require an introduction, and if you think so, and your dating partner doesn't, what are you going to do about it?

You have a few choices. The first and smartest one is not to push it. You have to recognize that she's not ready to introduce you, and no matter what the reason, forcing the issue isn't in your best interest. When you meet the significant people in your partner's life, you need her to be totally behind you personally about the concept of the two of you as a couple. Meeting family and friends before the two of you have an identity as a couple and before your date feels comfortable creating these opportunities to meet is a recipe for disaster. If your date feels pushed into something she's queasy about and if it's awkward, it may actually change her feelings about the relationship. She may feel that there's a lack of fit or that you want much more than she does at this stage, and this may cause a different turning point than the happy inclusion you imagined. Creating this experience too early may in fact cause a dating partner to back away from the relationship rather than moving closer.

Of course, your other choice is to meet the real issue head on. If you feel you've been dating long enough to warrant inclusion in the rest of her life — and your date doesn't — you have to think about whether you *need* to be more involved in her other important relationships. Consider the possibility that your desire to meet her friends and family is actually more about your ego (being treated respectfully as someone who exists and should be recognized as a partner) than about knowing these children or her old friends. There's a chance that you may not even be too fond of these people, and if you do get introduced, you may have to be in more social interactions with them than you really want!

This is a good opportunity to think again about what the relationship is or is not and what you want out of it. If you want marriage and full acceptance or at least acknowledgment from the family, then you need to take her reluctance to introduce you to family and friends as a significant piece of information and think about whether the relationship is going to stay at the level it is now. It may change over time; relationships do grow. That means that how long you've been dating becomes a factor in what facts you bring to bear on deciding whether this relationship is going to be a lifetime commitment. If you've been dating only six months and you're anxious to be included, you may be putting more pressure on the relationship than it should have to bear at this stage. If you've been dating two years, it's a totally different situation.

You're at a stage of your life that gives you freedom about how to conduct a relationship. When you were 25, knowing the family would be critically important, but at 70, maybe it's not such a big deal. Or maybe it is.

The apple doesn't fall far from the tree

Your date's relationship to her family can be very revealing. For example, when Brian first met Sophie, he was amazed at how such a beautiful and charming woman could have such an explosive family situation. No one in her extended family was talking to anyone, and when she explained all the flaws of her parents and siblings, he wondered how she had managed to escape from such a damaged family background intact. However, as he continued to date her, he realized that perhaps she wasn't as different from her family as he had imagined. During their first disagreement, she threw a shoe at him with painful accuracy. After a tearful apology, they made up until she got into a fight with his kids and said nasty things to them that he thought were way out of line. They broke up, but she showed up at his door one night with a delicious dinner she had made for him, and he relented. Then about three weeks later, she called him up and accused him of all kinds of infidelity, which was a charge without any kind of basis. At that point, he broke up with her for good — and vowed never to ignore a date's relationship to her family again!

Chapter 11

Let's Talk about Sex

In This Chapter

▶ Getting acquainted with your personal love map

▶ Determining sexual philosophies

▶ Raising the issue of monogamy

Sex is an undeniably important part of a successful relationship. The better you understand how sex works in any relationship, especially at this point in your life, the more you can make sure it's a satisfying part of dating after 50. (No matter how you view sex and your dating life, you must take health precautions like the ones I cover in Chapter 12.)

Navigating Your Love Map to Chemistry Town

No one can deny the importance of sexual chemistry. When chemistry is present, eye contact is more constant, smiles are more frequent, and you have an instinct to touch the other person. This is someone you want to know more about. There's a spark that signals the beginning of sexual attraction.

Perhaps you've long thought of sexual chemistry as a magical, potent force that takes over and pulls you toward someone in a way you can neither understand nor resist. As it turns out, you *can* understand what creates sexual chemistry between you and another person.

All people have stimuli that turn them on — and off. Psychologist John Money defines the circuitry of the elements that create a person's individual criteria for sexual chemistry as the *love map*. The following sections help you determine what your personal love map consists of and what its influences are.

Identifying the components of your love map

Chances are that the gateway criteria that determine whether you feel sexual chemistry with someone are already deeply embedded in your psyche. Following are some of the characteristics you may be deeply drawn to . . . or not:

- ✔ **Age:** Some people like age mates, others want someone older, and still others (mostly, but not completely, men), prefer someone much younger. Youth, or looking youthful, is commonly sought after. This becomes an interesting issue after 50 because you can nominally maintain youthfulness, but you can't compete with people who are actually young. The aging of the face and body can be an issue for people whose love map can only sexualize people of a certain age (and who don't do so well with their own aging process, either). Some people can readjust their attractions based on their own and others' ages after 50, but some can't. Both men and women often deal with their aging appearance by dying their hair, having plastic surgery, or using anti-aging products, such as Botox.

- ✔ **Animation and expressiveness:** Personality is part of chemistry. Some people are attracted to someone animated and opinionated, while others look for calmness, strength, humor, or kindness. Personality and intellect are the key for some people's attraction to others, while for some, looks are so important that personality is relegated to a secondary role in deciding whether to be interested in someone.

Looking at the role of hormones in sexual chemistry

Anthropologist Helen Fisher discovered how human hormones are critically involved in people's attractions — and in people's physical response to someone they meet. She noticed that when animals and humans are attracted to each other, levels of the hormones dopamine and/or norepinephrine increase.

The brain on dopamine creates an almost obsessional focus on the person you're extremely attracted to. Dopamine is part of the reason you may be thinking about this person all the time, wondering whether she wants you

as much as you want her. If the person you're this attracted to doesn't give you the feeling that she's just as interested in you, the dopamine cells in your brain may produce even more of the chemical, making you even more consumed with this person and more committed to making her very interested in you.

Norepinephrine increases your love and sexual feelings. This hormone is associated with feeling on top of the world, being full of energy and desire, and needing connection.

- ✔ **Weight and body shape:** People vary on their weight and body shape preferences, but almost everyone has some kind of preference. Some people want someone slim; others want their dates to have "meat on their bones"; and still others like someone really big. Some women like the lumberjack look, and some men want a woman who looks fit or athletic. Some men care about breast size and leg length, and some women want a man with broad shoulders and a tapered waist. Some people are put off by a pot belly, while others think they're cute and expect them on older individuals. The variations are endless.

- ✔ **Complexion:** Skin color is weighted by social custom and social prejudice, and in some cultures, lighter skin is prized. That preference is changing as skin color becomes less identified with racial privileges, but there's no doubt that the range of complexion matters to many individuals.

- ✔ **Hair length, hair color, and eye color:** Some people have such a strong preference for hair and eye color that they really can't sexualize anyone who doesn't have that coloration. Men voice these preferences more strongly than women, and there's no denying that in American society, blond hair and blue eyes are preferred by many people of Anglo descent. Latinos, African Americans, and Asians are often drawn to darker hair and eyes, and sultry looks are widely admired. Some men seriously prefer long hair on women, and women may prefer everything from short to long hair on men.

- ✔ **Height:** Some women insist on a man who is taller than them, and some women don't care. Many men don't want to look up to a woman, while others don't think that height matters. Some men want a woman who is petite, and other men want a woman who is tall and leggy.

Pinpointing the origins of your love map

Your love map has been created from many sources, all of them powerful. You may consciously understand some of them, but other influences may have shaped your sexual tastes and drives way before you were aware of yourself as a sexual creature. Your love map is likely influenced by some or all of the following factors:

- ✔ **Your parents:** Some people's love map is largely defined by their parents. Their father or mother may have seemed the epitome of grace, charm, or sexiness, and so they expect to find a strong, silent guy like Dad or a soft-spoken, intellectually intriguing woman like Mom. But the opposite can be equally true. Parents can affect their child's love map by embodying exactly what their child doesn't want, whether it has to do with habits, personality, or appearance. For example, say a man is from a family of tall blondes, with everyone taller than 6 feet, including his mother and sister. He may never feel comfortable with tall women as dates and may never date anyone who isn't petite.

Don't cast your love map in stone

Although one's emotional tastes can vary widely over the years, sexual attractions can remain immovable. Yet the more rigid these preferences are, the harder it may be to find a partner who suits your tastes.

For example, Abe was a 53-year-old man who had never married, and he really wanted a relationship. He said he was looking for someone very special, so he hired a matchmaker to find him the person he was looking for. He should have been an easy customer: A tall, fit, attractive, and very successful businessman with a nice sense of humor. It was a wonder that he hadn't been married before. But then, as the matchmaker began to work with him, it became clear that Abe had very strict requirements about who he would even meet. She had to be medium height, have blond hair and a certain color of blue eyes, be economically independent, and never have had children, nor want them.

Don't be like Abe, whose love map was so exacting he couldn't be attracted to anyone who didn't fit each and every one of his many requirements. What attracts you to someone doesn't have to be a cut-and-dried affair. Try being even a little more open-minded and you may find yourself attracted to someone amazing — even if that person is the opposite of who your love map normally steers you toward.

✔ **Your early experiences:** Many people feel that their sexual tastes were formed by an early important relationship — sometimes as early as pre-school or middle school. For example, perhaps a schoolgirl's childhood crush on a classmate leads her later in life to date only men who look a lot like the boy she had a crush on.

✔ **Pop culture:** In the '50s, having ample hips, a tiny waist, and huge breasts was the epitome of female sexiness. These days, breast size doesn't seem to be a big deal, but being fit does, even though the idea of a woman with large muscles would have been repulsive in 19th-century America. Bodies go through fashion periods just like clothes do, and the culture and period you grew up in can shape what you find attractive.

Defining Your and Your Partner's Sexual Philosophy

When you're first dating someone, you may find yourself so caught up in watching your own feelings, gauging your partner's feelings, and trying to determine whether your date is as drawn to you as you are to him that you may not notice any difference in sexual desire or sexual style. If you do, you may be so excited about just being with this person that you shrug off any differences, feeling sure you can handle anything that needs tweaking. Most of the time you can, but sometimes, differences in sexual philosophy and sexual interest are too much to overcome. Thinking about your sexual philosophy and sexual interest *now* will do you a world of good in the near future.

Your *sexual philosophy* is the set of sexual values and behaviors that you find right for you at this time of your life, regardless of what sex used to be like for you. The next sections help you get in touch with your present-day sexual philosophy, start a dialogue with a potential sexual partner, and negotiate a sexual philosophy that's satisfying for both of you.

Creating your sexual philosophy

When you're ready to set aside some time to think about your sexual preferences and desires, I encourage you to ask yourself the following questions. You can answer them at your leisure, but you should eventually come up with answers that are comfortable for you.

- ✔ How early in a dating relationship do I feel that touching and kissing intimately are appropriate?

- ✔ Do I have different standards about oral sex and genital touching than I do about sexual intercourse? Would I be able to explain this to my partner?

- ✔ What kinds of feelings would I want to have with someone — and want that person to have about me — before I'd engage in any kind of genital sexuality?

- ✔ What kinds of communication would I have to have with my date before I'd consider having some kind of genital sex with the person?

- ✔ What kind of discussion about sexual health, including condoms, would I have to have before sex would occur?

- ✔ If I don't want to have sex before I know someone very well, and perhaps not until there's a serious or legal commitment, how do I talk about this with someone I care about?

The answers to these questions evolve from your recent history and values and may or may not line up with the way you were brought up. As they say, that was then, and this is now.

Whatever you decide, always bear these three rules of sex-related communications in mind:

✔ **Know what you're going to say before you say it.** Be ready for this conversation so you don't say anything you don't mean and you say what you do mean in a nice way.

✔ **Be clear.** This is an area where people often hear what they want to hear — not what you said. Don't leave room for misinterpretation.

✔ **Try to separate your sexual philosophy from how you feel about someone — and try to let the person know that.** In other words, you may have a huge crush on the person but may not want to engage in sexual intercourse until you feel like this relationship is more committed. You can say something like, "I'm crazy about you, but my own sense of security and my ability to enjoy sex require much more knowledge about who we are together. Sex is a big deal to me, and to enjoy it, I just have to be with you a much longer time."

Figuring out your partner's sexual philosophy

After you have a good idea of your own sexual philosophy, it's time to find out about your partner's. Without discussing what her values about sexual behavior are, how can you know whether you're on the same page in terms of the practicalities of a sexual relationship?

You face some interesting issues here, not the least of which is how much you both enjoy and want sexuality in your relationship. *Sexuality* is a broad term and includes kissing, touching, titillating talk, and various kinds of sexual options in bed. You don't want to give each other a checklist (how weird would that be?!), but you'll get a sense of your date's desires as the relationship progresses. And you really do want to be on the same page.

Broaching this subject with your date can be awkward, but you can take your cue from when the relationship starts to be physical. When you start to kiss passionately or soulfully, it may be a good idea to back off and say something flattering — but say additional words that set the stage for a deeper conversation. For example, after those first really great arousing kisses, you pull away and say something like, "That feels so good! So good, in fact, that I think I could get carried away with you. And while I want nothing more than that, my head tells me that we should talk about what we're doing here."

I know what you're thinking: This is a mood killer. Yes, it can be. But it's also a moment to catch your breath and talk about where the two of you are in your relationship and what (and what not) you're prepared to do. Here are some things you can say, depending on your values and your attraction to this person:

"I'd love to kiss you more, but I want you to know that until we know each other better, that's all I feel comfortable doing. Is that okay with you?"

"I'm so into you. I want to make love to you. Do you feel comfortable making love now?"

"I'd love to make love with you, but that can't include intercourse unless we're truly committed to each other. Is that okay with you?"

"I want you to touch me, but we have to stop there. I know that will be hard for me and maybe for you, but it's important to me that we stop there."

"You're amazing. I'm so turned on, but I really don't want to have sex until we know each other much better."

Granted, none of this is easy. But these sentences will open up a deeper conversation about sexual values and about the relationship. Sure, it would be easier in some ways to just go ahead or to never say anything and just push the other person away when things get too steamy for you. But wouldn't you really want to know what the other person is feeling or expecting? I think it's extremely important that no one is pressured into something that she regrets. Relationships get ruined early on if someone goes further than she wants to, and they can become more intimate when people talk about their sexual philosophy and why and when they have sexual intimacy. If sex "just happens," it could be romantic and wonderful, or it could put you in a situation where the other person feels you owe her more of a relationship than you're prepared to create. You may face anger and recriminations or — if the other person is cavalier about the whole thing and you're not — you may feel sad and rejected if it all turns out to be just a one-night stand.

Talking about what you're doing should be possible. Of course, talking about sex before you find yourself in the clinches is ideal. Then, undistracted by your own heavy breathing, you can discuss your values, whether you're ready for intercourse, what kind of sexual contact you like or want at this juncture of the relationship, and whether sex would signal a more serious or monogamous relationship. It would be great if you could discuss all this before you were aroused and hormonal. But in reality, sex is more likely to come up when sexual contact starts rather than as part of an intimate conversation. In either case, you should be prepared to know what you want to happen, find out what your date wants, and plan how you'll respond if you and your date aren't perfectly aligned on values or expectations.

Many people aren't honest with themselves, much less with you. It may help if you earnestly tell your date that you really want to know what she thinks and feels about sex, and sex in this relationship, but she may not actually know how she feels until some time later. You may not like my advice here, but I think your best strategy is to wait as long as you can before you have intercourse or oral sex with someone. The better you know someone, the more you'll know about what sex means to her — and maybe even how you feel about opening up that bond, and perhaps that responsibility, with her.

The single biggest sexual complaint of married and cohabiting couples is unmatched levels of sexual desire. It's hard to know how similar you are when things are hot and heavy, but keep this issue in mind.

Negotiating a mutually satisfying sexual philosophy

What to do if your sexual philosophies and behaviors don't immediately match those of your partner's? Don't give up on each other just yet! If you can communicate — and really share your feelings about how sex has affected you (when it's good and when it's not so good) — you may be able to work things out and even grow more intimate and respectful of each other by going through the process of discussion and adjustment.

If you can talk about how you feel, why you feel the way you feel, and how you want to proceed, you'll be way ahead as a couple and as two people who are really trying to understand each other.

Here are some examples of dialogue starters that you can modify as needed:

- "I'd like you to know why I feel shy about starting our sexual relationship."
- "I'm not as self-confident about sex as I used to be. I have some issues that it would help me to talk about."
- "I really enjoyed kissing you, and I'd like to just do that for a while until I know you better. My values are very important to me, and they affect how I express my affection."
- "My style is to dive right in sexually when I feel as close to someone as I do to you. Would you feel pressured? I want it to feel right for you too."
- "Last night was great, but I wasn't sure I was connecting with you emotionally the way I want to. Is there anything we need to talk about?"

Sexual philosophies can always be revised. Sometimes, you change over the course of dating and need time to think about whether the sexual philosophy you started out with suits your needs now.

Speaking of Monogamy . . .

If you're the kind of person who would never have sex with someone unless it meant a monogamous commitment, you may think that the fact the two of you had sex means you're now what people used to call "going steady," and that means no other sexual partners.

Not so fast! In today's sexual world, you have to negotiate rather than assume monogamy. Otherwise, you may find yourself truly upset because the two of you have really different values about sex. And if you didn't have a conversation about monogamy before you had intercourse together, you may be unhappy to find out that your partner thinks it was great fun, but that's all, while you were thinking wedding thoughts when you woke up the next morning. Modern dating requires talking about expectations, especially sexual expectations. The following sections offer advice on when and how to raise the topic of monogamy and what to do if the two of you have differing opinions on it.

When to have "the talk"

Monogamy is a big deal whether you're the person who isn't ready for monogamy and wants to date around or the person who can only have sex with one person at a time. Making sure your dating partner knows where you stand (or lie down) on the monogamy issue is critical.

You can have the monogamy talk at three different points in your relationship. One is way before you have sex together, while you're still exploring your sexual philosophies and talking about values. The second is when it's clear that you're going to have sex together that night or very soon. And the third is after you've had sex. (Guess which one of these is not highly recommended. . . .)

Having the talk early on

How early is too early to discuss monogamy? Definitely not at a first coffee date! You need to have a relationship before you start talking about your sexual rules. Bringing them up at hello is too presumptuous and controlling.

On the other hand, after you've dated a few times and you start to get more interested in each other, sexual philosophies almost always naturally come up. In this case, you don't owe each other big explanations (unless you want to give them), but you do need to make one of the following statements:

- ✔ "I'm a monogamous person."
- ✔ "I can be a monogamous person, but that's not the point of my life I'm at right now."
- ✔ "I'm not a monogamous person now."
- ✔ "I'm not a monogamous person in general. It just doesn't suit me."

After you've said your piece, the two of you can discuss the matter further — or just file it under "Now I know the answer to that question."

Having the talk when sex is right around the corner

If the two of you are so attracted to each other that you're already kissing and touching, then you need to have the talk sooner rather than later. You don't have to go into minute sexual preferences — that happens when you're actually having sex with each other — but it's time to say what getting sexually involved means to you.

Here are two examples to get you thinking about how to present your pro-monogamy or anti-monogamy stance:

Molly Monogamous

"I'm very attracted to you, and I'd love to go back to your place. But I need you to know what it would mean to me: It would mean that you and I are only going to see each other and that you can promise me that we're going to be monogamous. If you don't want to do that, I understand, but I'm a monogamous kind of lady."

Fred Oh-So-Friendly

"I'd love to spend the night with you; I think you're wonderful. But I need you to know that I can't make any promises that I'm going to see only you. Am I interested in knowing you better? Absolutely. But I want to date around for a while, and I'm not ready to be in a monogamous relationship. Can we go with that? If not, let's keep the relationship at a level that makes you feel comfortable and doesn't make me dishonest."

One guy's surprise

If you fail to have "the talk," you may be in for a surprise like this one:

I'm a traditional man. We had been going out for a while, and I invited her on a boat trip. We hadn't had an overnight yet, and this would necessitate one, so it was, I think, assumed that this would include our first sex. The trip was amazing, and we got along wonderfully, and the first night on the boat was really nice, you know, for a first time. When we got back, I just assumed that from then on, our weekends would be with each other. But you can imagine my surprise when I asked her if she wanted to go on another boat trip the next weekend, and she said she was busy with another guy she was dating. I said, as forcefully as I could, if she wanted to date other guys now, I was out. She said she wouldn't and she would cancel, so we've kept dating, but it made me doubt her character, and I feel much more cautious now.

Having the talk after you've had sex

Maybe you've already done the deed, and now you want to know what it means. Obviously, there's much more room here for misunderstandings about what happened than if you'd discussed the issue beforehand. But that's too late now. All you can do is move forward with either a pro-monogamy approach or an anti-monogamy approach:

Molly Monogamous

"That was a wonderful evening. I thought we were wonderful together, but I'm not sure what it meant to you. To me, it meant that if we continue to have sex together, I have to be the only one in your life. Is that something you'd like too? If not, I think we need to move this relationship back a few steps and not have sex."

Fred Oh-So-Friendly

"Molly, that was a wonderful evening. I loved it. But we never really discussed what we were doing. For me, it was part of getting to know you and appreciating our relationship. But I don't want to mislead you. I want to get to know you better and grow the relationship, but I'm not ready to be committed or faithful to anyone yet. I hope that's okay with you, but if it's not, I understand, and I'm sorry if we did anything that you regret, knowing the place I'm in right now. Let me know how you want to proceed. Of course, for my part, I'd love to keep making love, but I understand if you want to cool this down."

Is that awkward? Sure. But it may be the best you can do if you have sex without discussing what it means first.

What it means if you can't agree

If the two of you can't agree on the monogamy issue, the relationship prognosis isn't good. You absolutely need to agree on this one. Otherwise, one of you will keep feeling hurt, and maybe used, while the other person may feel so guilty that he won't want to stay in the relationship.

Of course, this all presumes you want a budding relationship. Maybe you don't! Maybe you just want a playmate or you want monogamy for a while, but you realize this isn't going to be the guy or gal of your dreams. You may rethink your sexual philosophy on monogamy, depending on what it is you're looking for or what you think this relationship can provide. Of course, either way, you must take health precautions, like the ones I address in Chapter 12.

You can change your sexual philosophy, but don't let yourself get talked into accepting something that you know will make you unhappy.

Chapter 12

Sex Together: Potential Issues of Middle Age and Beyond

. . . .

In This Chapter

▶ Identifying your and your partner's sexual insecurities

▶ Guaranteeing you both feel comfortable and safe the first time you have sex

▶ Letting your partner know what you like during lovemaking

▶ Coping with health challenges that can affect sex

▶ Using toys to add excitement to your sex life

. . . .

*G*etting back into sex is touchy, particularly if a very long time has gone by since you've taken off your clothes in front of anything but a mirror. It's also true that even if you had a good sex life with your previous partner, being with someone new always raises new issues. Plus there's the age thing. Only movie stars and the ridiculously blessed (or people who work out several hours a day) have a body that remotely resembles the one they had in their 20s or 30s.

In a perfect world, everyone would feel comfortable voicing sexual desires and concerns instead of just doing it and hoping for the best. In reality, most people are insecure about what to say and whether their words will hurt or help a budding relationship. Often people don't say anything — and that's when the odds of mutual health and pleasure aren't in anyone's favor.

This chapter helps you pinpoint concerns to talk about with your partner and concerns your partner may not talk about but may need to. It also highlights the physical issues that may be present that require sensitivity and perhaps a little adjustment of what you do and how you do it.

The idea above all is that your sex life may have a few more challenges than it did when you were younger, but it can still be playful, exciting, passionate, fulfilling, and loving.

Divulging the Top Five Male Concerns

Even the most confident-seeming man may have one or more of the following common concerns, especially after passing age 50:

- Being desired
- Making a sexual move that is *not* offensive and *is* accepted
- Pleasing his partner with his hands
- Arousing his partner and giving his partner an orgasm (gay men generally assume they can do this)
- Getting hard at the appropriate time and sustaining an erection long enough to please his partner

Men also worry about how their bodies are perceived, although perhaps not as much as women do. If a man has some figure flaws, find something you like about his body and give him extra praise for it. For example, you can say, "I love how tall and big you are" or "You have powerful shoulders."

Being desired

Men generally see themselves as the pursuer rather than the pursued, so they have to proceed with coming on to someone without really knowing whether the object of their desire is as turned on as they are. The person who makes the first move is always at a slight disadvantage — even if the other person accepts, the pursuer may be unsure whether he's desired as much as he wants to be desired. Given the possibility of being rejected or even of getting a reaction that shows your date is offended at the mere suggestion of sex, it's natural to want to know as much as you can about whether your date is sexually interested in you before you make that great leap of faith and bring up the topic.

You can tell whether a woman desires you if she does one (or all!) of the following:

- She sits close to you and touches you with a leg or a hand or presses against you — and does so multiple times. If she's being unmistakable, she'll touch your face, hair, or neck.
- She keeps eye contact with you and is serious, and her eyes are soft and seductive (as opposed to just being friendly).
- She kisses you spontaneously, and the kiss is long and not just light. And she keeps it going!

✔ She kisses you, and her breath (and yours, one hopes) is more like panting than relaxed air flow.

✔ She says seductive things to you, like, "I dreamt about you last night — you were wonderful!"

Some women are seductive all the time and act so sexy that you're sure they want you, but they just like acting sexy and have no intention of having it taken as an invitation. If you're with a woman who's pouring it on (tight, low-cut clothes, slit skirt, and so on), don't assume that's permission to go further. Start slow with kissing and let her direct the action just to make sure.

Gay men generally assume sex will occur relatively early in the relationship (although sometimes that assumption is wrong), and their signals to one another are much clearer. Because straight men are allowed so little intimate touch between one another, even the slightest lingering of a focused stare can make it clear between two gay men that they're both gay and that there's an erotic connection. Gay men will cross the "touch divide," so even just touching a hand for a bit will telegraph sexual interest. If a man is interested, he may just feel free to say so, or he may state his erotic style to make sure they share compatible sexual tastes. It's generally a lot more straightforward than with straight people.

Making a move that is not offensive and is accepted

Today's world has gotten a lot more timid about sexual overtures. People are generally more sophisticated about the rights of anyone to not only refuse a sexual offer but also not to have to even listen to one if there has been no indication that a sexual come-on would be welcome. There's a heightened sensitivity about sexual rights and personal space and no tolerance for what is perceived to be sexual harassment. Proceeding carefully in sexually charged situations is not only wise but necessary.

So how can you tell whether the other person wants more — whether that's additional kissing, more intense touching, or full-fledged intercourse? The answer is simple: Start a conversation. You may ask, "Can we go further?" or "I want to make love with you . . . is that something you want too?" Or you may choose to say something like, "I want to be touched, but I'm not ready for intercourse."

If there's consent and a mutual agenda (meaning you've both verbally said you want to make love, or touch, or whatever), make sure that you have a condom ready to use. I offer suggestions for bringing up condoms in the later "Rediscovering condoms" section.

As much as life has changed between men and women, it's still more common for women to wait until men make a sexual move than making it themselves. If men make it right away, they may be treating the relationship lightly (like a friend with benefits) or it just may be their style. But in more cases than not, this first move is up to you, guys. If you wait too long, she may not feel desired. If you're too quick, she may be insulted, so best to broach the subject if you don't know where you stand.

Here's a reasonable scenario:

> He: "I think you're so special. I would like us to go away for a weekend."
>
> She: "I think that would be wonderful, but what would it mean?"
>
> He: "I don't know yet. But I think it's the next step in getting to know each other better. I do feel strongly about you."
>
> She: "Well, is this a trip with two bedrooms or one?"
>
> He: "I'm hoping for one, but I'd organize it any way you like."
>
> She: "Let me think about it. It's been 30 years since I went away for a weekend with someone I hadn't known for quite a long time."
>
> He: "I understand. I would love to have this time with you. I would love to share a night with you. But if you're not ready, it's okay. I want this to be what you want too, and I'll wait until it is."

This is just a model, of course. There are many ways to have this conversation, but the elements in it are:

- ✔ Respect
- ✔ Wanting it to be mutual
- ✔ Not threatening that the relationship will end if there's no sex right now
- ✔ Listening closely and responding kindly and lovingly
- ✔ Not saying more than you really mean

Pleasing his partner with his hands

Men also worry about their touch. Lovemaking involves gentle and sexy touching of the body and the genitals, and it's hard to know whether you're doing it right for a new partner. This is especially true if you haven't had sex a lot before this or the only person you've had a long relationship with was your spouse. It can be particularly worrisome if your sexual relationship in a marriage or in a long-term relationship wasn't particularly great.

Understanding why some women fake orgasm

If you've ever suspected a woman of faking it, consider that there may well be a valid reason why, as this next story reveals.

Freda had only one man in her life besides her husband, a man she was engaged to but who died in an accident before they married. She had sex with this man before his tragic accident, but she didn't have an orgasm. When she married Sid, they had sex before they married, but again, she wasn't orgasmic. In fact, they were married quite a few years before she figured out how to climax. When Sid died after almost 40 years of marriage, Freda was terrified about the sexual aspects of dating again. She was worried about everything, but especially worried that a man would think she wasn't sexy if she didn't have an orgasm.

So when she started dating again and having sex with new men, she didn't even try to have an orgasm; she just faked it. When she got serious with Benjamin, he told her he knew she was pretending and he wanted to help her have a real orgasm. After her initial embarrassment, she felt grateful to him; faking it just wasn't the way of life she really wanted to continue.

The only way to know whether you're truly pleasing a woman is to ask her. And keep asking her, because the touch that was wonderfully soft on one day may feel too soft on another day. Bodies change, moods change, and when you're with a new person, there's really no way to know whether you're touching the right places with the right pressure unless she tells you that you're on the right track or to change a position or pressure. Many women, however, are afraid a man will get offended if they give too many directions, so if you really want to be an effective lover, you have to reassure her that you need and want her feedback.

This is, of course, also true when a man has a male partner. If you've only recently discovered your gay identity or you've been in a sexual relationship with only one man up to this point, you may not be aware of what new acts may please you or someone else. You need to be open and clear about what you like and not assume your new partner likes the same thing. Besides the obvious differences in whether someone likes penetration, you may need to talk about even simple things like kissing or cuddling for sex to be fulfilling and comfortable.

Being able to give his partner an orgasm

Though of course women love having orgasms, most women would agree that they can enjoy lovemaking and intercourse without having an orgasm every time. Men, however, generally feel very worried or feel they've failed if their partner doesn't have an orgasm.

This is difficult because many women have trouble reaching an orgasm when they're young, but as they get older, orgasms can get increasingly difficult — and it has nothing to do with how turned on they are or how much they desire their partner. Hormones change, the vagina becomes a bit more thin-skinned, and if there's not additional lubrication, intercourse can be painful.

But even if a woman's body is fine, the fact is that there's a certain amount of awkwardness and inhibition the first time some women make love to a new person, so an orgasm may just not be possible.

Unfortunately, it's highly likely that the man will take this personally, which really is a lot of suffering over something that will eventually smooth out and generally work much better as the relationship deepens and more conversation and mutual education take place.

The best thing for a man to do is to ask a woman what she needs to have an orgasm and for the woman to tell him. If you're the woman who knows that the first time you have sex with this man you'll be too nervous or self-conscious to have an orgasm, tell him that and see whether you can create a mood of just enjoyment rather than being totally goal-directed. Many men, nervous about being able to please a woman, appreciate having lovemaking be more about arousal, touch, and excitement than a single goal.

Getting hard at the right time

Sometimes, the hydraulics of a penis simply don't work or don't work well enough for intercourse. This is more likely to happen as men hit middle age and quite likely to happen the farther up the age cycle they go. Even if it doesn't happen regularly, it's quite likely to happen some of the time, and both men and women should expect it — and plan for how to react to it.

Men over 50 may just be entering into perilous performance territory when it comes to erectile function, and their sexual esteem, sexual interest, and even sexual assertiveness can be affected as a result. Many men feel less virile when they can no longer meet those strict standards of performance and struggle with self doubts about their masculinity and sexual worthiness. Sometimes men even avoid sex with a partner because it's no longer the same as it used to be. Men with these performance anxieties need some reassurance and encouragement from partners or they may back away from the whole relationship.

I explain how to deal with erectile dysfunction in the later related section. For now, it's simply worth recognizing that

> ✔ If you're a man, you're not the only one with this concern.

> ✔ If you're a woman, it's best to be considerate of this concern.

Men shouldn't assume that all women will be disappointed if intercourse isn't possible as often as it used to be. Some older women say they're actually pleased when circumstances take the focus off penetrative sex and encourage more fondling, stroking, and extended foreplay.

Revealing the Top Five Female Concerns

It's a safe bet that the average woman over the age of 50 has at least one of the following concerns regarding sexual relations — even if she won't own up to it.

✔ Taking off her clothes and still being desired

✔ Pleasing her partner

✔ Getting aroused and having comfortable sex

✔ Having an orgasm

✔ Practicing safe sex

Taking her clothes off and still being desired

Most women have been self-conscious about their bodies since their youth, even though that's when their bodies looked amazing. Women have been taught that their breasts are too small, too large, or not the right shape. They've been told that they aren't skinny enough or don't have a butt that's shaped just right. In fact, in the last ten years or so, there has even been an assault on how a vulva should look: hairless (except maybe for a "racing stripe") and with tight lips (which physicians offer to surgically alter if the lips are longer or uneven!).

Given how much grief women get about their bodies when they're young, imagine the self-image problem many women have when their breasts have lost their resilience, their chest is scarred from breast removal, their tummies are larger, or their skin isn't tight. Many women — even those who are aging beautifully — are so ashamed of what their bodies look like that they don't have sex at all, don't have sex except for in a darkened room, or have sex but can't relax and enjoy it because they can't believe they're sexy, even if their partner says they are and means it.

One way for women to get over this concern is to put a new frame around the idea of what a "good" body is. It may seem hard to imagine if you still have a body that looks younger and you cleave to that vision of yourself, but as you get older, a good body is a healthy one, a strong one, and one that can still feel pleasure. Nonetheless, people want to be desired in traditional ways, and so men and lesbians should compliment their partner often. When your partner looks nice in a specific outfit, lavish her with praise. When you touch a body part and find it smooth, remark about it. When your partner's breasts are in your hands, give her feedback about how much you like them. At first, a partner who is ambivalent about her body may not accept your compliments, but over time, the comments will surely influence and reassure her and make it easier for her to enjoy sex with you.

Pleasing her partner

A woman who has had a lot of partners may not be so worried about how to please someone. But if she's more conservative and her only lover has been her husband, the prospect of knowing what to do with someone new is truly daunting. Women want to please their partner but they're not sure how bold to be, what acts are expected, and whether they'll be good at them.

The best way to figure out what pleases your partner is to ask. Figuring out your partner's sexual philosophy — and whether that philosophy jibes with your own — helps you know how to proceed with intimate actions. For help gauging (and defining) a sexual philosophy, see Chapter 11.

Is oral sex expected?

Getting each other's expectations out in the open *before* things get heated can help prevent situations like this one:

Rita had been married since she was 20 and had never had another lover. When Ernesto left her after 33 years of marriage for the wife of a friend, she was devastated and didn't think about dating for almost 5 years. But then she got lonely and asked several friends to fix her up. She became very interested in Jacob, who had actually been her children's dentist, and after dating for three months, they decided they were ready to have sex. But he expected oral sex during lovemaking, something that had never happened in her marriage to Ernesto. Rita was insulted and frightened, and she froze. The relationship ended that night, and now she's confused about what will be expected of her and how she can reconcile what she has always thought about oral sex versus how other people seem to regard it now.

Getting aroused and having comfortable sex

Often women over 50 haven't had sex in so long that they're no longer sure they have the ability to become aroused and actually enjoy sex. If they've been divorced or widowed for a long time, their vagina may have constricted and may need some attention: adding lubrication or maybe estrogen to plump up the tissues and revitalize the area so that penetration isn't painful.

This may not be a problem if a woman masturbates frequently, uses sex toys, and in general, keeps her sexual life lively, even without a partner. But if she hasn't had sex of any kind in a very long time, her body needs to be reconditioned, and her mind won't be at ease. This is even truer if she was in a dysfunctional relationship or failed marriage and sex had ceased to be arousing or fulfilling.

The good news is that bodies can bounce back, and if a woman receives localized estrogen (topical creams, a vaginal plumper like Replens, or an intrauterine ring that secrets estrogen), vaginal tissues can feel great and resilient again. Using sex toys such as a dildo or vibrator can bring back sensation and fantasies, and a strong sexual appetite can come back as pleasure increases and orgasms become more common. Couples can use the toys as part of intimate play that eroticizes the relationship even more and makes both people more pleased and confident about what they can do together to create a vibrant sex life.

Having an orgasm

A woman may have been easily orgasmic when she was younger, but as she gets older, diminished estrogen, more sluggish blood delivery, and less muscle tone and energy may be making orgasm more difficult for her. Why is this a problem? Aside from the fact that sex is better when both participants enjoy it to the fullest, women know that men feel better and sexier if they can help deliver an intense orgasm to their partner. If women worry about their need for much more foreplay than they used to need or their unpredictable ability to have an orgasm even under the best of circumstances, relationship issues may well occur.

Probably the best way to overcome this problem is to become less goal-oriented and more focused on enjoying the journey. There's no prize for getting aroused quickly, and so accepting the need for longer, more luxurious foreplay isn't a sacrifice! Yes, it may take longer to have an orgasm, and sometimes orgasms are elusive, but if you show extreme pleasure with all the fondling you receive, you'll encourage your partner to take more time with you, which ultimately will produce the extreme pleasure that partners relish. It's important, however, to make sure a woman's partner knows that she can experience erotic peaks without an orgasm, and so lovemaking that doesn't result in an orgasm is still worthwhile for her. Unless a woman tells her partner, in a convincing way, that she doesn't need an orgasm every single session of lovemaking, the partner may not understand that she can really be satisfied and happy if an orgasm doesn't always occur. If she's concerned that he's unhappy or confused when she doesn't climax, the two should talk about it so that he doesn't feel rejected or inept.

If you do have an orgasm or experience pleasure from something your partner does, let him know it. A recent study showed that one of the top three things men want during sex is to hear their partner make noises of excitement and pleasure!

Practicing safe sex

Neither men nor women want to catch a sexually transmitted disease (STD), but women seem to be more worried about STDs than men are. If you're at all worried about catching an STD from a new partner, speak up for yourself and insist on using protection.

If a man refuses to wear a condom, you may be better off walking away from the relationship because if he behaves this way with you, odds are he has behaved the same way with other partners — which puts you both at greater risk. Many men, especially older men, don't like using a condom, and in fact, some will out and out refuse to use one. This is no longer a pregnancy issue for most (but not all) women over 50 but it is a health issue for everyone.

I offer advice for bringing up protection in the later "Rediscovering condoms" section.

Ensuring a Comfortable and Safe "First Time"

Given the number of fears that are likely for both men and women, it seems provident to suggest a certain amount of honest and straightforward discussion, particularly regarding comfort levels and safe intercourse — if you want your first time together to be the first of many as opposed to an angst-ridden misunderstanding and disappointment. You need to be clear with each other, but that doesn't mean the discussion should feel like an interview by your doctor! There are ways to talk about these intimate matters that bring you closer and don't cause resentment or additional worry, as the following sections reveal.

If you're insecure about something, chances are your partner is as well. Just saying you feel a bit insecure or unsure of how to proceed can take some of the pressure off the other person.

Discussing having sex prior to your first time together

When it becomes apparent that you and your date are hot for each other, the bravest and best thing to do is acknowledge that sex seems imminent and talk about how to enjoy sex together safely before taking your passions further. Of course, if things are moving fast, talking about sex isn't what you're going to want to do. So why not make this discussion part of a seductive dinner conversation? As you see the relationship heading in that direction, you can say something like, "I'd love to make love with you, but I want to talk about it first so we do this right." This may set your date back on her heels a bit (after all, most people have sex more easily than they talk about it), but it's actually so much more respectful and serious a beginning that it will profit most budding relationships.

If your date consents to discussing sex ahead of time (and be careful about someone who refuses), you can first talk about your feelings (fears, uneasiness, desire to please, shyness, not having done this in a long time, and so on) and then talk about things you need to proceed (a romantic place, no children or phones around, a weekend away) and even what it means (everything from your need for a monogamy agreement for this to happen to quite the contrary). I offer advice for having the monogamy conversation in Chapter 11.

It would be great to do this several days in advance of the actual event so that anticipation can build and you can obtain any products (lubrication, an erectile dysfunction drug, nice underwear) you may need. But if it just precedes the actual event, that's okay, too, if you're both psychologically ready and have condoms. Sure, this isn't the scene in the movies where he comes in her apartment, tears her clothes off, and they have wild, abandoned sex all night with nary a condom in sight — but that works better in the movies than in real life.

Signs of a sexually secure individual

A sexually secure person would agree with each of the following statements:

- If I were in a situation where sex started to be part of the conversation, I'd enjoy it (with the right person).

- If I were thinking about having sex with someone, I might make the first move.

- If I were getting to a point where sex seemed imminent, I'd discuss the topic with my date and make sure I had a condom handy.

- If I had a disability or scars of any sort, I'd discuss this with my partner.

- If I had herpes, HPV, or some other viral sexually transmitted disease, I'd tell my partner before having sex.

- If I were going to undress with someone, I'd do it without worrying about how I looked to my partner.

- If I needed to take an erectile dysfunction pill or use an artificial lubricant, I'd make sure I took the necessary steps.

- If I were making love with someone for the first time, I'd help the person by saying how I like to be touched.

- If I were enjoying sex with this person, I'd feel free to make noises of pleasure or talk to the person while making love to express how good things feel.

The best of plans for safer sex can go out the window if the two of you are drinking a lot. It's not so wise to have sex together when you're drunk; doing so may make it harder for either of you to perform well, and it certainly makes it less likely you'll use a condom. If you're tempted to drink a lot because you're nervous, try just to talk about it rather than use liquid courage.

Rediscovering condoms

According to AARP, only one in five single and dating people over the age of 50 use a condom. For most people over 50, pregnancy is no longer a concern, but sexually transmitted diseases still are. In fact, STDs of various kinds (think chlamydia, herpes, HPV, and so on) have been increasing among the plus-50 population. And the Centers for Disease Control and Prevention estimate that by 2015, half of the million or so Americans infected with HIV will be over 50.

One of the best ways to ensure safe intercourse with someone new is by using a condom. Using protection gives you a higher chance of having a safe sexual experience each and every time. Not to mention that by using protection, you may feel more comfortable having sex and therefore enjoy yourself more.

Condoms today are so much different from what they used to be that you and your partner may be wrong about how much they may interfere with sensation. The last time either of you used a condom, it may have been much thicker and genuinely uncomfortable. But now, there are micro thin (but still strong) condoms, ribbed ones for fun, and ones that have hot and cold lubes that are a major turn-on.

They're also very reliable. For many years, I served on the advisory board for Trojan (a condom maker), and I saw how impressive the tests for safety in the factories really are. Actually, every single condom is tested! Most of the stories about condoms breaking are told and retold with utter exaggeration about their fragility. Condoms can be abused (used way past their use date, punctured with a sharp object, and so on), but used correctly, they're dependable (not 100 percent effective in preventing STDs and HIV, but very dependable). Additionally, some condoms, such as Ecstasy and BareSkin, have innovative designs and could easily be categorized as sex toys. You should have no trouble finding a type of condom that you not only should use but want to use!

But what if your partner balks at the idea of using a condom? Table 12-1 lists possible reactions you may encounter, along with responses for each one. Pick the response that appeals to you and suits the situation, and *do* either use a condom or hold off on having sex until two thing occur: You both take a blood test and get the results showing that you're STD- and HIV-free, and you agree to be monogamous (and you know the person well enough to believe he really will be monogamous).

Table 12-1	Bringing Up Condoms
Reaction	*Response*
"So, do you think I just sleep with anybody?"	"I don't judge anyone's background, but it's just a rule I use because I need to be safe, even over my emotions. I want to have sex with you, but I have to be true to my own principles."
"How many people are you sleeping with anyhow?"	"I need to use condoms, but if you don't want to, there are so many other ways to please each other. Let's discover some of those!"
"I'm not worried about myself, and I know you wouldn't have sex with me if you had a disease, so why do we need to do this?"	"I never checked to see what, if anything, my ex-spouse brought home because I thought he was monogamous. As far as I know I'm fine, but I don't really know. So let's be safe and use condoms until we both get tested."

(continued)

Table 12-1 *(continued)*

Reaction	Response
"I lose my erection if I use a condom. I've tried."	"Condoms have changed. We can get some that are like sex toys and have fun with them. They'll be sexy — I promise!"
"I just am not going to do this if I use a condom. What's the point?"	"If I don't use a condom, I'll be so nervous I won't enjoy it. Can we do this for me so I can feel protected?"

Explaining How You Want to Be Made Love To

Most people just settle for what they get, at least in the beginning of a sexual relationship. Now that you're a mature person, why not get what you need right from the start by asking for what you want? Asking for what you need or want seems to be hard for both sexes, but it doesn't have to be if you follow the advice in the next sections.

Even though it's hard to do, it's better to be honest about what you need early on in your sexual relationship, before you develop a lovemaking pattern that's hard to change.

Giving instructions

When providing your new sexual partner with feedback and direction, make sure to use a conversational tone rather than a corrective one. After all, no one wants a lover who feels like a traffic cop directing each move. The secret to giving instructions without sounding overly dictatorial is talking about it first out of bed.

Perhaps you're sitting together, each with a glass of wine, and you lean over and suggestively say, "You know what I'd really like?" Your partner perks up. And you say, "I'd love you to [whatever it is]." If things are going well, your partner will generally say, "I can do that!" and then you give some exact information. For example, "I know you want to give me as much pleasure as possible, and I love that about you. But once I have an orgasm, I'm really through and don't want another one. It's best not to touch me in a sensitive spot after I climax."

After sharing your preferences, be sure to ask your partner what she would like. If your partner is shy and says, "Nothing — everything is perfect," then it's up to you to say something like, "Oh, I can always do better. Give me an assignment!" to get a true dialogue flowing.

Rediscovering one's sexual confidence

Your previous sexual experience doesn't have to define your current one, particularly if the former was less than stellar.

Barry and Sara were married for 38 years. The first 5 or so years were fine, but after they had three children, their family seemed to work better than their love life. The relationship went from warm to cool to cold to finally just making do. One particularly painful area was their sexual incompatibility. Sara constantly told Barry that he was heavy-handed, a sloppy

kisser, and came too quickly. After the divorce, Barry was terrified that every woman he made love to would find him similarly inept.

But it was quite the contrary. Barry started dating and had several relationships that became sexual, and the women seemed to truly appreciate his tenderness, his touch, and his ability to put them at ease and feel appreciated. Barry wasn't sure if they were really being honest with him at first, but over time, he gained confidence and a lot more sexual self-esteem.

After your partner tries to please you the way you've suggested, go out of your way to thank her for her effort and thoughtfulness.

Focusing on the present for more passionate lovemaking

It's important to remember that each relationship has to create its own style of lovemaking. Maybe your ex-wife didn't like doing it doggie style, but that doesn't mean your new partner feels the same way. Or maybe you had a ritual when you were married of getting into bed without showering together, but you could start a new ritual that included it. Or forget the bed entirely — maybe the two of you want to start out on the living room couch, or for that matter, the living room floor!

The important thing is to be open to new things, create something between the two of you that builds passion, and stay present in this relationship and not confuse it with any other one.

Remembering that it doesn't have to be all about intercourse

At each stage of the aging cycle, people often find that new accommodations are required. Some of these changes may simply be related to less energy, physical endurance, or a less-intense sexual appetite. Other issues may be health-related, such as vaginal tissue that's more sensitive and needs more care so that penetration doesn't hurt or a penis that needs days to recover from an ejaculation or simply isn't that hard anymore.

An important transition for some older adults is to stop treating intercourse as the main, much less the only, sexual event. Touching, kissing, fondling, and stroking don't require penetration and can be just as intimate and mind-blowing when executed well. In fact, men can have orgasms without having an erection, and women can be stroked to climax without being entered. If these sexy things can be seen as the centerpiece of lovemaking rather than as foreplay, various sexual issues become less important. (If, however, you still have concerns about common sexual

Seducing yourself into feeling secure and sexy

Seduction is a surefire way to overcome the fears and insecurities you may have regarding sex. I'm not talking about seducing your new love — that comes later. I want you to spend some time seducing yourself into believing that you're sexy, desirable, sexually competent, and capable of pleasing a partner and being pleased by your partner in return. If you can do this, the reward is pure pleasure, deep connection, love, and loyalty.

Here are some exercises to help you seduce yourself:

✔ Look into the mirror in flattering light. Admire your features. Think of your good points for the age you are, not the ages you were.

✔ If you're a woman, go get professionally made up. Take pictures.

✔ If you're a man, get a new haircut, shirt, or sport coat.

✔ Get new underwear, something sexier than you'd normally get. If you're a woman, get some lingerie, a teddy — something lacy. It's amazing what some sexy lingerie can do for a mood.

✔ Get reacquainted with your own body. Explore the world of sex toys and reacquaint yourself with turning yourself on if you haven't already. Try vocalizing your pleasure.

✔ If you haven't already, join a gym. Feel stronger and fitter and you'll feel sexier, guaranteed. Don't like gyms? Join a dance class and learn to like your body more that way.

✔ If you're overweight, try a weight-loss program and see whether you can get a friend to join you; the buddy system really works. Don't worry about losing a huge amount of weight. Any weight loss will make you feel sexier, even if you're still bigger than you want to be.

✔ Flirt with people you meet. Most will respond. You're not coming on to them; you're just engaging them, focusing, and learning eye contact. You'll feel more empowered when you can do this.

✔ Read some sexy books or magazines.

✔ Get a full-body massage.

✔ Soap yourself up in the shower and fantasize that someone else is doing it!

problems due to aging, you can check out the next section.) The goal is to give each other pleasure, and you can achieve this goal easily without intercourse.

It's not overly optimistic to say that the majority of partners can build a great sexual relationship by carving out new territory. If couples treat the changes in how they make love in later life as a mutual exploration of new ways to be satisfied, they often feel their sex life is better than ever.

Surveying the Sexual Issues That Can Arise as You Age

Yes, this stage of your life often comes with a specific set of sexual issues that you likely didn't encounter in your youth, but that doesn't mean you can't still enjoy sexual activity. Every age-related sexual problem has its solution. The following sections delve into some of the issues that you may need to contend with in your sexual relationships after 50 and the strategies for overcoming them.

Erectile dysfunction

Erectile dysfunction isn't just the failure to have an erection. It can also appear as the failure to

- ✔ Have an erection as quickly or as long as desired
- ✔ Have as hard an erection as desired
- ✔ Ejaculate or have an orgasm when desired

As men age, the odds of experiencing erectile dysfunction grow from 19 percent in their 50s to 38 percent in their 60s to 56 percent in their 70s (and older).

With those numbers, it's a good thing scientific progress on erectile problems took a gigantic step forward with the invention of Viagra, quickly followed by Cialis and Levitra (drugs that work in a similar fashion but aren't exactly the same). Popping a pill may be all you need to do to solve your problem.

If, however, you have heart problems or take blood pressure medicines, you're better off skipping the pills in favor of other methods of holding an erection. These methods include

✔ **Inserting a vacuum erection device, or "pump," that requires active squeezing of the pump to create the erection and decrease it:** This is a big step, but a majority of men (though not all) who have the operation are satisfied with it because it allows penetration to continue, and they can still have an orgasm, although not ejaculation.

✔ **Receiving a Caverject injection in the penis right before sexual intercourse to fill up the hollow tubes that create stiffness:** A shot in the penis sounds painful, but men who opt for the injections say they don't hurt at all. This sounds impossible, but if you've had a flu shot lately, you can understand that some of these new needles simply can't be felt unless the composition of the shot itself has a painful aspect to it.

Never order erectile dysfunction medications off the Internet. At the very least, you could be out the cash you spent on fake drugs; at worst, you could experience a serious health problem. If you want to treat your erectile dysfunction, contact a urologist to discuss erectile dysfunction treatments given your personal health and complications with other medications you may be taking.

Vaginal dryness and pain

Vaginal dryness can happen at any point in a woman's life cycle but is most commonly experienced in the perimenopausal period before the cessation of menstruation and directly afterward. Dryness may increase as time goes on and estrogen levels dip lower until menopause is "officially" over. Dryness can also result from birth control, but for those over 50, it's more likely a side effect of other kinds of medicines such as antihistamines (it's not just your nose that dries up!) and other prescription medications.

In many cases, vaginal dryness is easily fixed. Water- and especially silicone-based lubricants can make vaginal penetration (penis or finger) much less painful. However, not all vaginal pain is related to dryness.

Vaginal pain is generally a more complex problem than vaginal dryness. Two categories of vaginal pain exist:

✔ **Vulvodynia:** This term describes various kinds of pain in the vulvar area that may exist without intercourse or touch or may be present when any kind of penetration (penis or finger) is attempted. The causes of it are not generally understood. Sometimes there may have been some injury to the genitals or perhaps an infection. Other times, there is real pain but no traceable cause. At one time medical personnel shrugged off this kind of genital pain as a woman's psychological issue originating in some kind of problem with her feelings about sexuality, but that cavalier attitude has been dropped, and now sufferers can track down the source of their problem and receive specialized treatments for reducing pain.

✔ **Dyspareunia:** This term refers to other kinds of pain that happen only during intercourse or penetration. The causes of dyspareunia aren't entirely understood. Women may have problems with the pelvic floor, which means that the muscles that support the vagina and other internal organs no longer function properly.

Most types of vaginal pain can be rectified with medication, but some need surgical intervention (for example, a prolapsed uterus). The cause of some pain, however, isn't so easy to identify, so some medical professionals have told sufferers that it may be psychological. Today, however, the great weight of medical opinion is that the pain women feel is real, and if their own doctor isn't looking for medical causes, they should find a specialist who understands the issue and can usually find a way to end the pain. This is truly important because otherwise, the pain not only infringes on a woman's ability to have a sexual life but also affects quality of life in general.

You can go online and get great advice from several vulvodynia associations and some specialists in women's pelvic problems. You can also seek out therapists who specialize in helping women cope with the pain and the impact it can have on their relationships.

Bad knees and bad backs

Knee problems and back problems can be present someone's whole life, but they become more common at every decade of life from early adulthood on. What does this have to do with sex? Well, as you get older, your back may hurt more during the act, and your knees may fail to support you if you stick to positions you used in your younger days (such as doggie style and man on top). The following sex positions are kinder than others to backs and knees:

✔ Spoon position (male in back of female, both lying on their side)

✔ L positions (woman lying on her back with one leg over the man, who is on his side facing her; woman tipped toward the male with a leg up over him, allowing him to penetrate her at an angle)

✔ Scissors position on the side

✔ Bending over a bed, man standing behind

Medicines that lower or eliminate desire

If you're really attracted to the person you're dating but you're not feeling any desire, the medications you're taking could be to blame. The following kinds of medications can all cause a decreased — or nonexistent — sex drive:

- ✔ Blood pressure medications
- ✔ Depression medications
- ✔ Diabetes medications
- ✔ Heart medications

Lack of ability to be aroused isn't normal, nor is it an inevitable outcome of age. So if this is your situation, go see a doctor, and if you can, find one that specializes in sexual medicine. The doctor may be able to change your medications or the strength of your medication. Don't assume that you have to live with lack of desire.

Life-threatening diseases of the past or present

After you decide to engage in sex with your partner, you need to discuss any serious conditions or diseases you've had. A woman who has had a mastectomy may be worried that her partner can't handle her unreconstructed or reconstructed chest. Men who've had prostate cancer may need to talk about the accommodations they've had to make, including partial or total impotence. People who have had cancer but are now cancer-free may still be shell-shocked from the experiences they had with chemotherapy or radiation. These are real challenges in a person's biography, and at some point, they need to be discussed, and both partners have to think about what they need to share and whether they can deal with the other person's body changes or even continuing trauma.

If you fall in love with someone who's coping with the aftermath of cancer (and even the fear that it could return), you need some patience and kindness as you both work through the emotional issues and tend to the special care that person needs to be sexually active again. Regaining a sex life, however, is a wonderful gift, not just to the relationship but to embracing life after it has been threatened.

Adding Sex Toys to the Mix

One great assist to 21st-century sex lives are all the wonderful toys that help people get even more aroused and sexually satisfied. Vibrators were actually introduced in the 19th century, so they've been around for a long time. But it's taken more than a hundred years for toys to be seen as perfectly legitimate couple's sex play or aids to keep your sexual life alive when you don't have a partner.

You may be shy about suggesting toys when you're with someone in a relationship that isn't committed yet. But if you can muster up the courage to do so, vibrators and other toys may help create an even more vivid sex life between the two of you — and usually make it a lot easier for a woman to have an orgasm. Some men are rather anti-toy because they think that all arousal should come from attraction and body-to-body lovemaking, but more men than ever realize that the toy isn't their competition — it's their colleague!

Numerous toys are on the market, and companies are always inventing new ones, but here are a few that may help when orgasm is difficult or erections are sometimes a problem:

- **For him:** Probably the most interesting device for men who have erection problems or softer erections is a ring (made of metal or leather, with snaps that make it into a circle) that goes over the flaccid penis and scrotum and helps trap the blood in the penile shaft when a man becomes aroused. Many men with perfectly good erections like the feeling of fullness the ring presents.

- **For her:** Vibrators are the toy of choice for older women. You have a variety of options (internal, external, remote control!), and you can use them to shorten the time from arousal to readiness or just as an adjunct to excitement and play.

- **For both of you:** Wonderful things for sex play include reading a sexy book together, watching an explicit film, or using fun lubricants. Condoms can be playful too. Besides the different textures and ribbing, you can get them in colors, and some of them even glow in the dark.

You don't have to go to a sex shop anymore to find great sex toys. Many reputable stores are online, and many of them are women-owned. A few reliable ones that offer a lot of information and high-quality products are www.evesgarden.com, www.goodvibes.com, www.loverspackage.com, and www.yourfascinations.com.

Chapter 13

Considering Money Matters

In This Chapter

▶ Analyzing your financial philosophy and expectations

▶ Navigating the money question at the beginning of a relationship

▶ Deciding how to talk about and share expenses with your date

Chances are that when you first started dating in your teens or 20s, both of you assumed that the guy always paid. You wouldn't talk about money except for a thank-you for dinner or a particularly nice time. How simple it was (and how expensive for men!).

Today, things aren't so straightforward and clear. There's no single template on how to handle money in a dating situation, unless both of you are very traditional, and the old way is the only way you both feel comfortable with.

But what if you have different philosophies about money? Then some discussion, and perhaps negotiation, is necessary. Money is a big deal. You do need to find someone who shares your values about lifestyle, spending, and the importance of money in everyday life. If you don't share these values in the beginning of a dating relationship or you can't come to an easy understanding about how you'll spend and share money, those values won't likely change over time.

Exploring Your Feelings about Money and Dating

Men and women may have different philosophies about how to handle money matters while dating, depending on their general approach to money and their financial situation. And even though men and women over 50 may have grown up with a traditional point of view, they've seen gender relations change, perhaps even in their own marriage or cohabiting relationships.

Some women who never expected to be the sole financial support of their families or the higher earner of a couple shucked off the old expectations a long time ago.

Whatever your economic traditions are, from your marriage or from how you managed your finances over time as a single person, you may have to rearrange them when you start dating. You may need to rethink your financial philosophy and see whether a revision is necessary for dating.

Getting to the root of your thoughts on money

Your feelings about money may come from a number of sources that no longer exist but still have some power over you if you don't reexamine them:

- ✔ **The way your parents handled money:** A lot of mature women think that because their dad was the primary wage earner and paid for stuff, they need a man to do the same thing for them. Men feel that if their dad was the head of the household and created the family economy, they too need to preserve that role. Even if you didn't grow up in a home with a male wage earner who acted as the head of the household, the cultural expectation that there should be a primary wage earner may affect your vision of who you're looking for or who you intend to be in your relationship.

   You may idealize your father's role in the family. Many men who looked like the main wage earner were not (or were not all the time). Also, the dependence on your father's income may have influenced other aspects of family life, like his control of decision making or family lifestyle, and as a result, it's possible that no one had the power to resist or even question his decrees. If you're looking for someone else to be the main wage earner or provider of all good things that cost money, remember that there may be a different kind of price to pay. If you're totally dependent on someone else for your economic maintenance, then the odds of that person taking the lead as the primary decision maker are quite high. Some people do resist the equation of money equals power, but more often than not, they want veto power or even everyday power in exchange for their economic superiority. If *you* are the person who has all the economic wherewithal and responsibility, you may want to dial down your authority over decision making if you can so that the relationship stays romantic and emotionally generous. There is much to be said for keeping a feeling of equal influence in a partnership, and a heavy hand regarding money can make that impossible.

✔ **The way money was handled in your marriage:** Money may have been an area of conflict in your marriage. High earners sometimes use money to control a low earner or non-earner, and money can be the source of bitter conflicts on a number of levels. If there was a shortage of money, you may have frequently debated spending patterns, and even if there was no shortage, you may still have had disagreements. In fact, in *The Normal Bar,* a national and international study on what relationship patterns are most likely to create extreme happiness in couples, my coauthors and I found that people who earned more than $250,000 a year argued more about money than people who earned less than $20,000.

✔ **The way money was handled in your cohabitation:** People who live together (including those in same-sex couples, particularly women) tend to keep everything separate. There's something about not having an agreement for a shared future, at least not a legal future, that tends to make people want to keep their finances and financial contributions separate and equal. This can be very egalitarian. On the other hand, it can be really tough if a low earner has to match a high earner's contribution. The partner with fewer resources can become anxious about living above his means. This kind of anxiety isn't good for a relationship.

✔ **The way money was handled in your last dating relationship:** The way money was handled in your last relationship may have set a standard for you — or it may be exactly what you want to avoid the next time around. If you carried someone financially who took advantage of you or if you were used to being taken care of, you may rebel at the thought of replicating a bad experience or finding yourself more responsible for the financial maintenance of the relationship. Of course, that was then and this is now, but the residual memory of what used to be may influence who you're looking for or what you're willing to do.

Learn from past relationships but don't project the last one on the next one. Don't assume that everyone you meet is either dishonest or controlling about money just because you've been with someone who was one or both.

The economics of living together

A lot of men and women cohabited starting in the late 1960s and 1970s. Now more than half of all people who marry have lived together first. Cohabiters are notoriously egalitarian, so about half of all people over 50 have experienced a situation where both men and women were expected to pay for things separately, and no one person paid for everything unless it was an unusual cohabiting relationship. These people may have had less traditional marriages or retained a different philosophy about who should pay for what.

Considering new thoughts about who pays

Whatever the past was, the present is different. You're different, your partner is different, and you both need to discuss, from the beginning, your expectations about money — at least for the near future. That arrangement may change as the relationship gets more stable and more desirable, but in the beginning, who pays is an awkward but necessary discussion.

Think about some of the reasons people do or don't want to pay, and examine your own money philosophy and practices in light of what benefits paying your way and paying someone else's way creates.

✔ **Reasons men may want to pay:**

- **It pleases many women.** Some women like generosity and like the feeling of being taken care of. If you have the ability to treat dates to dinners or experiences that they enjoy or may not otherwise afford, you get a lot of positive reactions.

- **It's a tradition that many women expect.** A lot of women over 50 expect the man to pay. This is the way they were raised or what they experienced in prior relationships. They may or may not offer to pay their way for something like an expensive dinner or a trip somewhere, but if you don't pick up the coffee tab or the movie ticket, they'll think that you're cheap.

- **It makes it easier to call the shots.** If you want to do something that costs a lot of money, you don't have to confer as much or change what you want to do because your date can't afford it. Though paying for things shouldn't transfer all power to the person who pays (people don't like to think they're being bought), it definitely gives the payer an advantage over decision making.

✔ **Reasons men may not want to pay:**

- **Women may want to contribute.** By this time many women have been on their own, and they like the idea of carrying their own weight. They may think it's nice that the man buys the coffees or dinners part of the time, but they don't want to feel obligated by too many dinners, especially too many expensive ones.

- **They don't want to feel like a woman is attracted primarily to their money.** Some men get downright aggravated about the idea that they're always expected to bear the expenses of dating. They reason that women want other kinds of liberation — equal pay, equal clout in decision making, and help with chores — so why shouldn't they chip in on equal financial responsibility? Some men feel that the primary motive of some women they've dated was financial help. Whether or not that was true, it soured their feelings for women, and sometimes, dating in general.

- **They can't afford it.** Not every man can afford paying for dates every week. A boutique cup of coffee these days costs $4 or $5 in many parts of the country, and a man who is going out with several people could find himself spending $20 or $30 a week just on coffees, much less dinner and a movie. At some point, these men wonder why they always have to pay for an introductory meeting that benefits both parties.

Though coffee dates are traditional, there are other enjoyable ways to meet people that don't cost anything: walk your dogs, go on a free gallery walk night, or attend a free concert in the park. (For more ideas of what to do on your dates, turn to Chapter 9.)

✔ **Reasons women may want to pay:**

- **They don't want to feel obligated.** Do many men feel entitled to more decision making, even more sex, when they take a woman out to a fancy dinner? Yes, says the research on the subject. As a result, many women, having experience with this kind of reaction, insist on paying at least their half of the bill, just to make sure that they don't incur any emotional or sexual debts.

- **They want to reassure the guy that this isn't about money.** Some women, especially women with jobs or means of their own, are sympathetic to men's burden of always having to pay. They don't mind paying their own way, and they know that some men are suspicious of women's motives if they always defer the check to the guy. They'd rather pay their half or occasionally treat their date than have him think that dating has anything to do with getting freebies.

- **They're used to paying their own way, and they want their date to know that.** Some women have shared financial responsibility their whole life, even with their husband or other committed partner. They've kept everything separate — it's just the way they do things — and they don't feel a need to do anything different now.

✔ **Reasons women may not want to pay:**

- **At least in the beginning of a relationship, it may offend their date.** Some men are a bit put off or at least uncomfortable if a woman insists on paying her way on the first coffee or even the first date. They may see it as overly aggressive or controlling, or even an indication that the woman doesn't want a second date. Women are unsure of what a man's reaction will be, so on a first or second meeting, they may not even offer to pay and just say thank-you, hoping that this is honoring a man's traditional role.

- **They're looking for someone who wants to pay for things.** Some women are very clear that they want someone who will support them or at least do the financial heavy lifting in the relationship. They don't want to split bills, and they resent a man who asks them to. They wouldn't want to set the wrong precedent by offering to split anything. This can be particularly true for women who had to support someone in the past and don't want to replicate that situation.

- **They can't afford it.** Some women have to watch their pennies very carefully, and they can't afford $10 just for coffee every first meeting. Women who are helping support adult children or grandchildren, who don't make a lot of money, or who are on a minimal fixed income welcome a man who likes to take a woman out or expects to pay for the bill on the initial meetings.

Handling Money in the Early Stages

Who pays what is particularly awkward in the beginning of a relationship, especially at the first meeting. You don't know each other at all and you don't even know whether there's a spark between you, so most people don't talk about money, and the guy usually foots the bill. But if the meeting might progress into a relationship, you have to figure out the money plan pretty quickly. Otherwise, misunderstandings may end the date before it has a chance to grow into something else.

The first meeting

It's almost axiomatic: The man pays for the first coffee or casual get-together. If you want to change that tradition, you have to do it in the most gracious way possible. You have a few choices, and all of them are risky. For example, if you're a man who doesn't want to pay for all these first meetings, you can just say to your date, "I'm all for men's and women's equality, so I like to split all bills. Is that okay with you?" A traditional woman may write you off, but a more modern one may chip in without a second thought. But be warned: Even feminists like to see a little gallantry at the beginning. Perhaps you only want to make this move if you're not totally enchanted with your date!

On the other hand, if you're the woman in this situation, the offer to split the bill will give you plenty of points with some men. But if he insists on paying, let him. Otherwise, he may let you help pay but feel like you're too defensive or strident to pursue further.

Don't let your first coffee be your last

If you aren't careful, your first meeting for coffee with a prospective date could be your last. Consider this example from Barney and Leigh:

Barney felt strongly that if women wanted to be treated as equals, they should pay as equals. His first coffee with Leigh was going so well that they had a second and then a third coffee, and then the coffee date lengthened into the early evening, so they ordered some appetizers. At the conclusion of this promising beginning, Barney said, "How about we split this?" Leigh, a professional woman, felt rather stung that her date wasn't going to cover what was ultimately, in her opinion, a fairly inexpensive bill. She was obviously hesitant about it, and so Barney challenged her on her feminism. Saying something like, "I presume from our conversation about your career that you believe in women's rights, and I'm very supportive of that — and so I assumed you would

be comfortable with splitting 50/50." Leigh was surprised at how she felt, but she felt he was being cheap and provocative. She forked over her credit card with obvious disgust, saying, "No problem," but her body language and tone made it clear she wasn't happy with the way things had turned out. Both of them walked away from the table irritated and pretty sure that they wouldn't be seeing each other again. But perhaps they were fated to have a second chance. They met again at a gathering for a local political candidate, and after a chilly beginning they relaxed, talked again, and with much good humor recounted their initial feelings about the "check fiasco." They started going out again after that and are still together. Perhaps "all's well that ends well," but most people don't get second chances. Point to be taken: Don't complicate the first coffee by letting money become an issue right away.

 The issue of paying more equally is a lot easier for both men and women on a second meeting for coffee or the like. You're not on a date quite yet, but you've both signaled the desire to know each other better. Offering to split or take care of the second coffee is more likely to be seen as just a nice or fair thing to propose.

The first dates

Sometimes it's a bit hard to distinguish between the last coffee and the first date, but you'll probably call it a date when you go out on a weekend and do something (such as see a performance or have a nice meal) that costs money. Again, the man usually pays for the first one, but women should be prepared to split the tab. It's quite unusual for a woman to pay for the whole thing unless she sets up the date and picks the event.

Your early dates set the tone for how finances are handled. In most cases, it's worth talking about how to pay for things at the onset of dating. If you can't live with someone else's financial philosophy, you probably won't be a match on other issues either.

Times are changing when it comes to money issues — but more so for men than for women. Research by Dr. Janet Lever and Dr. Rosanna Hertz shows that even in 2013, most women preferred to be paid for on a date, but an increasing number of men wanted women to offer to pay the bill at least some of the time.

Figuring Out Your Shared Financial Responsibility

If you're interested in someone enough that you want to address how the two of you will handle finances, you have three major ways of going about this: picking up on clues as you get to know each other, leading by example, and having a direct conversation.

Picking up on clues during initial conversations

During your first meetings, you can learn a lot about their work, values, and experience. Those insights can give you an idea of their position on sharing financial responsibility while dating. Here are some clues to watch for:

- ✔ **Clues that a woman is willing or able to split the bill:** Feminist ideology, liberal politics, a period of independent living, or pride in her professional (as opposed to family) accomplishments.

- ✔ **Clues that a woman isn't able or willing to split the bill:** A more conservative set of values about male and female roles and a desire for men to display conventional manners (hold the door open, guide the woman to her seat and push in her chair, clearly ask for the bill). She may also never have worked outside the home, or even if she did, she may drop hints about how she likes to be treated by a man when she's out of the professional environment.

- ✔ **Clues about a man's desire to split the bill:** Liberal politics, feminist ideology, was married to a professional woman or a woman who worked full time, or drops hints about wanting a woman who has her own hobbies, passions, and independent means.

> ✔ **Clues that the man wants to handle all the bills himself:** Traditional politics and values about male and female roles, traditional manners, and a previous marriage to a woman who didn't work outside the home or who stopped professional work to raise children and didn't resume it until after the children were out of school.

Though these aren't absolute giveaways of how people want to operate financially today, they're pretty reliable clues as to what you can expect. If you don't want to have a talk about finances right away, you can use these profiles to guess about how the economics of dating may proceed with this person.

Leading by example

Leading by example is a smooth way to send a signal without having to have a big conversation about money. (See the example of Louise in the nearby sidebar, "Navigating financial responsibilities is different for everyone.") Having a date on your own turf (for example, using theater tickets you already have or inviting someone to a benefit dinner you already intended to go to) sets the stage for women willing to share bills. Men can do the same thing, of course, but because many women expect them to pay for things, the effect isn't the same. A man who wants to set an example of bill-splitting might say something like, "How about I get this one, and you get the next one?" This isn't a full-scale conversation; that may follow, but it may not be necessary because the model of sharing has been put forward. (Whether the woman is happy with it is another story . . . .)

Navigating financial responsibilities is different for everyone

Every relationship is unique, and there's a wide range of approaches to how to share financial responsibilities. Consider these two examples:

Louise, a 58-year-old accountant, liked setting a precedent where she paid for some of the activities from the beginning. "I'm a sports fanatic and have season tickets to the Kings. When I was dating [she's now in a relationship with someone she met online], I would ask the guy whether he wanted to go to a Kings game and say that I had tickets. Usually, the guy was

game, so he would come and pay for the soft drinks and junk food at the game — or we'd go out somewhere afterward for dinner and he'd pay for that. It set up a model I could live with: splitting things."

Tito, on the other hand, wanted to set up an entirely different expectation. "I'm not comfortable with having a woman pay or even contribute. I treat women like ladies, and if they don't respect themselves enough for me to treat them right, then they aren't the lady for me."

Talking about it directly

Perhaps the financial aspects of dating are so critical to you that you really don't want to go forward without a firm understanding of what the financial roles will be on your first or next date. If this is the case, a conversation has to take place. This section discusses ways to introduce this sticky issue with as little difficulty as possible.

A 50/50 arrangement

A conversation to establish sharing costs equally is a bit daunting, but it can be easy if both people are on the same page. Unfortunately, you may not be on the same page — and that's best to know sooner rather than later if this is an important consideration for you.

Timing is everything here. Waiting until you've had at least a few coffees together may make the conversation much more pleasant. As I explain in this chapter, insisting on sharing every bill on "hello" may seem boorish, even to a woman who eventually wants to share but doesn't want to feel like sharing the finances is the most important thing in the world to her date.

If you're a man who wants to split costs 50/50, you can start a conversation like this (after you've paid for the first couple of coffees):

> "You know, I've enjoyed these dates, and it's been my pleasure to treat you to a couple of coffees, but my philosophy about having a relationship [or dating] at this stage of my life is to share the cost. Would it be okay with you if we alternate who pays for what? I'd be glad to get the next one and you could get the date after that."

Good news here: You're intimating that you two will have more dates, and you've graciously taken on an extra cost by picking up the next bill. The bad news may be that your date doesn't want to stick around for any more dates if she has to pay. Best you know that sooner than later!

If you're a woman who wants to split the bill 50/50, you have an easier task: Most men will be happy to let you do it. You can bring this up on your second or third coffee or when discussing your first date:

> "You've been really generous, and I appreciate that you picked up these tabs, but I like to share the costs when I date. I like to think of myself as someone who carries my weight in a relationship, so would it be okay with you if we share this?"

As mentioned, men usually think that women splitting the dating expenses is just peachy, but occasionally someone traditional or wealthy won't want you to share (see the next section). Can you hack it or is it a deal breaker for you? If it is, you have to insist more forcefully and see whether it's a deal breaker for him.

A traditional arrangement

Some men and women grew up with, and like, the tradition of the male being the breadwinner and the female taking care of domestic tasks. The older a person is, the more likely the person is to expect a strict division of male and female roles. The man is happy to bear most or all of the expenses of a relationship, and in return, he wants a woman who will fit into his life and take care of him — emotionally and on the domestic front (home-cooked meals and so on).

If two people meet through online dating, these preferences are probably made clear in their profiles, so when they meet, they know they share those values. (If you're interested in online dating, turn to Chapter 6.) But if they meet in other ways or the profile doesn't mention traditional values, a mismatch can be awkward. A traditional man or woman may be insulted if someone messes with the traditional order of things and wants to split the bill.

What's the answer here? If you're a traditional type who comes across an untraditional man or woman, see whether the person interests you enough to experiment with a different economic model. Maybe pitching in on a bill is worth it with the right guy, or perhaps not taking care of the bill every time will introduce you to someone worth knowing. If straying from tradition really doesn't appeal to you at all, just be polite if a date handles a bill in a way you disagree with, and then e-mail or call the person after the date and politely state that you don't want to continue seeing each other.

A means arrangement

What if only one partner can afford to pay for your dating lifestyle? Sometimes it's impossible to share everything. One person, for example, may love to go to the theater, but the other person simply doesn't have the budget to go frequently, if at all. Whatever side of that situation you're on, such circumstances require an honest and open conversation.

Being upfront and honest

You may choose to be upfront and honest about any financial circumstances that may restrict your dating life. For example:

Len was a retired pilot who lost a lot of money because his pension plan was hugely diminished when the airlines he worked for declared bankruptcy and restructured debt. He decided to go back to school and learn some skills that would make him employable again in a new field. As a result of both his financial loss and his new student status, he had to be very careful with money. His approach was to tell women about his situation right away, and if they couldn't handle it, they couldn't handle him. His honesty proved to be the right approach: While some women commiserated with him but didn't want another date, others were perfectly happy to go on dates that didn't cost much money and to shoulder their share of the dates that did require some greater outlay of cash.

It's only money

The good news about money and dating is that many people grow more flexible about money as they age and are so happy to have a partner to do things with that they're willing to try a new approach to money matters. For example, Martha, a widow in her late 60s, explained why she didn't mind paying for almost everything while she was dating Xavier: "He was so much fun. Honestly, even though my husband paid for everything during our marriage, it didn't bother me to be the one who paid. Here was a man who loved to dance, loved to go out, dressed so well, and was so charming with my friends. So I paid for just about everything we did together, and we had such a great time. I don't regret it for a second. I knew that ultimately we weren't going to go into the sunset together, but so what? This is the time to live as well as you can."

If you're the person who can afford the dates but your partner can't, you have to decide how important it is to have a date or potential partner with the same or similar resources that you have.

For some people, this equality is critical. In particular, I've heard quite a few older women daters say, "I don't want to be a nurse or a purse." And I've heard more than a few men say that they don't want to be anybody's sugar daddy. If you feel this way, you may resent having to cover some, or many, of the things you like to do on a date, so this situation may not be one that you want to enter. On the other hand, you may have met someone who intrigues you and has many fine qualities but is on a tight budget. Life is full of exceptions, so if you want to have a relationship with this person and do the things that are fun but that cost money, you have to make a decision early on to cover these expenses.

One way of handling this situation that may suit your values is to do a *means contribution* — an arrangement in which you and your date contribute to expenses according to your means. For example, you can say, "I know you love the ballet. What if I contribute the tickets and dinner and you pay for the parking?" Or, "Tell you what, what if I take us out this weekend and you make dinner at your place the weekend after?"

There's usually a way for a date to contribute something. If you don't set the bar too high (for example, 50/50 on very expensive dates), your date may be able to do enough so that you don't feel taken advantage of and your date doesn't feel embarrassed.

Your date may be temporarily insolvent, and you may feel like it's okay to carry the person a bit until the person gets a new job, pays off a child's college bill, or whatever the case may be. But be careful: If you don't want to turn into "the purse," make a deal with yourself about how long you feel comfortable paying for everything, and stick to your own deadline.

Money isn't everything. You may decide that it's better to go on inexpensive dates and not have to deal with the money gap as you continue to learn more about each other. See Chapter 9 for some ideas for dates that cost little or nothing.

If you're the person who can't afford the dates that your partner suggests, you should speak up. Explain that you can't afford to split tickets or go to expensive dinners. There's no dishonor in that; sometimes, you meet someone who is simply used to a more expensive lifestyle than you can afford. You have three options:

- ✔ Suggest inexpensive or free activities that you can afford.
- ✔ Suggest that you pay what you can.
- ✔ Withdraw from the relationship if your date obviously wants you to share more of the costs than you can afford and isn't willing to pay for you or change to the kinds of dates that don't cost much.

Of course, it's also possible that your date will back off from sharing if she really likes you and will graciously pay for the dates that cost more money than you can spend. But if your date does pay and you sense discomfort about the situation, this may not be the person for you.

Part IV
Addressing Special Situations

Five Rules for Addressing Medical Issues with a Date

- ✔ Never talk about your or your date's health on the first meeting. You eventually need to bring up the health conversation if you and your partner start to get serious, but it's not appropriate or necessary to discuss at the beginning of a dating relationship.

- ✔ Try to put the discussion off until you get a feel for each other and you sense some real magic between you.

- ✔ When you first talk about your medical status, start with the good news. For example, "You'd never know from looking at me today that I had cancer five years ago. It was tough, but my report card is great. Still, I wanted you to know about it."

- ✔ If you don't have much good news to share health-wise, tell the truth but with an optimistic spin. "Yes, I have diabetes, but I'm pretty confident it's under control, and thank goodness I have minimal side effects."

- ✔ If your condition is something that changes what you can do (such as impotence after prostate cancer), bring it up only when necessary. For example, if the two of you are getting close to having sex, talk about it then. The discussion is unnecessary until that situation arises.

Dating after 50 brings with it some special considerations for health and medical conditions; get advice on dealing with conditions such as cancer, osteoporosis, and heart disease at www.dummies.com/extras/datingafter50.

In this part...

✔ Get familiar with the medical challenges you're likely to face yourself or with older partners. Find out when and how you should talk about any medical challenges you have or have had in the past.

✔ Be mindful about how any date will affect your friendships. Whether you're in a same-sex or opposite-sex relationship, being in a new relationship potentially rearranges the way you fit into your family or friendship group.

✔ Find out where to look for gay and lesbian dates over 50, especially if you're interested in a serious partner and relationship.

✔ Find out about the different issues that come up regarding monogamy and marriage. Though same-sex marriage isn't legal in all states, the questions about monogamy and committing to a life partner are universal. You need to know what you really want.

Chapter 14

Dealing with Medical Needs

. . . .

In This Chapter

▶ Introducing the issue of your personal health

▶ Considering what health issues you can and can't accept in a partner

▶ Dealing with illness in a dating relationship

. . . .

*F*ace it: Getting older is humbling. When you make a connection these days and make a commitment, "until death do you part" isn't such an unimaginable ending. Everybody is degrading a bit at a time. You probably didn't notice it in your 20s, but in your later years, you or someone you know (and perhaps love) is likely to have problems such as arthritis, heart issues, cancer, or other scary diseases and conditions. You need to be able to talk with your partner about these issues and know what you and your partner are signing up for as well. This chapter helps you do that.

Talking about Your Personal Health

If you had a chronic or life-threatening illness when you were younger, you've had experience talking about your health. Maybe you had to repeatedly tell the tale of your chest scar or leg brace or explain the handful of pills you had to take every day. It wasn't fun, and you probably had some scary moments, but it was part of who you were.

However, for many people, health issues only come with age. There are the small annoying ones, like suddenly needing glasses, and then the larger ones, some of which creep up slowly (like some kinds of arthritis) and others that are a sudden, unwelcome diagnosis, like cancer. People start to hear tragic stories about friends and relatives, perhaps as young as in their 30s and 40s, and then the stories grow more common. Illness and disability are no longer theoretical; you have to deal with yourself as you age, and the health issues become part of the equation of a relationship. Naturally, it's a downer to contemplate these issues with your date, but you can handle most of them well, and they often result in a closer, more honest, and more supportive relationship.

Bringing up the discussion

You may have heard the ungenerous saying, "I don't want to be a nurse or a purse." This saying refers to the twin fears of becoming tied down by someone dreadfully ill and becoming the primary earner. The issue of being a caregiver is a tough one. It brings great rewards, but it's also a challenging role that can demand time and energy and can take a toll on the caretaker's own physical and emotional well-being. So it's fair for people to think about whether they want to get weighed down by someone with a serious illness (or even potential illness) or move on to someone else who's healthier.

It's a natural fear, but it's often based on irrational information. Everybody is one diagnosis away from an awful prognosis. And most people would like to be loved for things other than whether they have the potential to become ill or fail to maintain a certain amount of wellness with the illness they already have. And just because someone suffers from an illness doesn't mean that you'll become a full-time caregiver or even take on a significant responsibility.

You may worry that an insurance company won't cover you or your partner because of a preexisting condition, or that you won't be able to manage the rising costs of healthcare, or that you'll miss special years with someone. If health is your number one gateway criterion, so be it. But you can ask yourself: should it be?

In any case, you eventually need to bring up the health conversation if you and your partner start to get serious. Be smart about it and choose your moment carefully. Here are some guidelines on how to start out slow and then later, how to be frank, but not frightening, so that you can have a good discussion:

- ✔ Never talk about your or your date's health on the first meeting.

- ✔ Try to put the discussion off until you get a feel for each other and you sense some real magic between you.

- ✔ When you first talk about it, start with the good news. For example, "You'd never know from looking at me today that I had cancer five years ago. It was tough, but my report card is great. Still, I wanted you to know about it."

- ✔ If the report card isn't so great, tell the truth but with an optimistic spin. "Yes, I have diabetes, but I'm pretty confident it's under control, and thank goodness I have minimal side effects."

- ✔ If your condition is something that changes what you can do (such as impotence after prostate cancer), bring it up only when necessary. For example, if the two of you are getting close to having sex, talk about it then. The discussion is unnecessary until that situation arises.

Weighing potential health costs

The healthcare debates that will probably go on and on are tenacious and serious because uncovered healthcare expenses and the sky-high costs of hospital treatment, surgery, and medications have bankrupted more than a few people. At a point when the relationship is starting to get serious, it's fair to exchange health information and how it affects your life. Your situation may range from stable (you have good coverage and you're healthy) to somewhat serious (you have a manageable condition, and your medications are expensive but covered) to worst-case (you have difficult health issues, and the expenses are worrisome). If your date is compassionate and financially secure, even the worst-case scenario may not be a problem. But if your date chooses to consider it a problem — or you consider it an insurmountable problem in your relationship — so be it. It's your life, and to have a real partnership, each person has to know what the other person's life is really like and accept it — or not.

Confronting a Personal Illness and How It Affects Your Relationship

Obviously, not all illnesses are the same. Diagnoses, outlooks, and the effects on a person's physical and emotional functioning vary widely. But some illnesses are more common in people over 50, and they carry some related issues that you may want to consider if you're in a dating relationship and you or your partner is affected.

Cancer

It's not uncommon for older people to have had some kind of cancer. According to the American Cancer Society, 1 in 8 women will get breast cancer during their lifetime, and according to the American College of Obstetricians and Gynecologists, approximately 3 out of every 100 women get uterine cancer. As men get older, their risk of getting prostate cancer increases; if they live long enough, 1 in 6 men will have the disease.

Many kinds of cancer are not only dangerous but also disfiguring or disabling. The treatments for prostate cancer can cause partial or complete impotence and urinary incontinence. Breast cancer surgery can require removal of the breast and other tissue, and uterine cancer can require removal of the ovaries, triggering menopause if it hasn't already occurred.

Other kinds of cancer, such as certain kinds of skin cancer, may require cuts into the face or lips, places that hurt people's vanity as well as their body.

These body changes can have psychological effects that go far beyond the health prognosis of recovery. The body has changed and it doesn't do what it used to or look like it used to, and some people are ashamed to date (or get near sex) because their body is damaged in some way.

It's possible that you don't want to take someone with cancer into your heart and home, and your date may feel the same. But as people become more comfortable with cancer being an often curable disease — or at least a controllable one — the choice to be with someone who has or had cancer is increasingly a positive one.

Heart conditions

As people age, heart conditions and bypass surgery become more common. The good news is that operations that were once so hit or miss now have huge success rates and give people back their energy and their health. Of course, it takes time for that to happen, and for a while you may feel terror or anxiety while you learn whether you can depend on this newly engineered organ.

Conquering cancer with love

Although cancer is obviously a very serious disease, it doesn't mean you can't have a relationship — even an intimate one. Consider this story:

Adele decided to date just for companionship and, in particular, to have someone to discuss movies with. However, her chosen companion wanted to be more than that, and she was growing very fond of him as well. But she never intended to have a serious relationship, and as he pressed her for more intimacy, she recoiled, not wanting to show a body that had had unreconstructed breast removal and that also had some scars from an earlier cancer problem. She referred to her body as a "battlefield" and didn't want to turn the relationship into

something more serious, precisely because she didn't want to have to face her own self-loathing.

But Dan, her suitor, knew about the operations, knew more or less what to expect, and still wanted a more intimate relationship. He knew she was scared; he faced his own fears of this sort when he was diagnosed with blood cancer, which thankfully responded well to treatment. He was in love with Adele, and he wanted to express it to her and cherish her. Eventually, he won her over with his loyalty and his obvious adoration. Finally, she took off her clothes and thought, "The fact that he desires me so is still a wonderment to me."

The rehabilitation period is long, and for some people, it's harrowing. Strength rebuilds slowly, and it may take time to feel sexual again. Sometimes, drugs that are used to safeguard the heart have compounds that complicate sexual arousal. Sometimes, your sex drive goes away for a long time and then resurfaces again on its own. Many people are distraught during the period when sexual interest disappears because they think they've lost something precious forever. But sexual interest does come back for most people. It may or may not be as strong as it was initially, but there's a lot of evidence of people forming satisfying emotional and sexual relationships after having surgeries or taking medications.

As with all conditions, talking about a heart condition is important so that, for example, a partner doesn't imagine things to be worse than they are, and issues like a lack of arousal aren't seen as personal but as a physical and psychological consequence of the disease or defect.

If you're taking drugs for a heart condition, tell the prescribing doctor that you're concerned about sexual and other side effects, and ask whether there's anything that can be done to minimize those effects without risking overall recovery.

Arthritis or osteoporosis

When you were younger and older people would mention aches and pains, it seemed somewhat irrelevant. Well, sadly, those aches and pains may now be relevant, and some of them may be degenerative.

Arthritis is often easy to spot by way of swollen fingers or enlarged knuckles. Can it be disabling? Yes, there are some vicious forms of it. But for the most part, degeneration to a painful and disabling extreme takes a very long time. It's also possible to reduce its effects by weight control, vitamin supplements, and exercise. (See the section "Taking Charge of Your Health and Your Date's Health" later in this chapter for more on these lifestyle improvements.)

Osteoporosis is a decrease in bone density, and it can get so bad that bones are more likely to break. That isn't the worst of it; by itself it causes further aging of the body. Still, most people can live with all but the most severe cases and not be restricted in what they do. Some medications can slow the process, but in many people, it's a progressive disease that's most common after age 65. If your date exercises and doesn't smoke, she can probably limit the disease. But people do get it who have a genetic predisposition to it, so it's not a person's "fault" if she has it. You can, however, help your partner live better with osteoporosis by engaging in healthy behaviors (such as exercising and taking in enough calcium) that help her reclaim all or a significant part of her ability to function.

Diabetes

Diabetes is characterized by high levels of glucose (sugar) in the blood. Problems are caused by a hormone called insulin that takes sugar out of the blood and stores it in body cells. There are two common types of the disease. Type 1 diabetes was previously called juvenile diabetes because it typically was first diagnosed in children and young adults. Most people with this kind of diabetes will need insulin shots for life. The majority of people who develop diabetes later in life will get the other common type, type 2 diabetes; these people often need medication to maintain the right amount of blood sugar. This type of diabetes generally develops after age 40 and may be connected to weight gain, obesity, or genetic predisposition.

Diabetes is a serious condition, and if left uncontrolled, it can be deadly. Diabetic people have higher risks for stroke, coronary artery disease, kidney failure, foot and hand nerve damage, and serious eye problems. Because the disease can impair nerve impulses and affect both the neuro- logical and vascular systems, approximately 50 percent of male diabetics will be impotent. The good news is that modern medicine can help people regulate their glucose levels, and many diabetics can control the disease through a healthy diet and exercise alone. However, it's also true that some of the medications that many diabetics have to take (such as medications to control blood pressure) can affect sexual drive and performance for both men and women. Women with diabetes who are postmenopausal may have more yeast infections and urinary tract infections than is ordinary for women their age.

Other illnesses that affect your sex life

Some issues come just as a part of aging; it happens to everyone. But it's also true that many of these effects happen to different people at different times. Some men stay potent, with strong erections and easy orgasms way into very old age; others start to have problems even when they're quite young. It's also true that any condition that causes a limited supply of blood to the geni- tals causes impaired function for both men and women, so it's possible that any of the health issues I discuss in this chapter could impair your sexual relationship.

Changes to hormones are natural, but they change at a different rate, with different effects on a highly individual basis. Men lose testosterone over time, and women lose estrogen. No one loses all these hormones (they're secreted through the gonads and ovaries and also from cells and the pituitary gland), but much lower testosterone and estrogen does affect your sexual interest and sometimes your orgasmic ability.

If a man used to have a "five o'clock shadow" but no longer does, it may be that he has a testosterone deficiency, which affects his sexual appetite and performance. If your date has trouble maintaining an erection, it may also indicate low testosterone (which sometimes can be boosted by testosterone replacement).

Women famously produce less estrogen as they age, and eventually, they have too little estrogen to menstruate. When that happens, they're in menopause. If your date is going through menopause and has uncomfortable or really difficult symptoms (like hot flashes, insomnia, or mood swings), she may have decreased sexual interest. But about a quarter of postmenopausal women have increased sexual interest!

But even if someone has physical issues that can interfere with her sex life, don't immediately count her out. Men and women can be very inventive in bed and don't necessarily need to be athletic or totally potent to have a great sex life. Sure, it's easier to have no physical problems to contend with, but the best lover may not be the one with the best health.

Still, here's a list of things that may get in your way and need your sensitivity, patience, and perhaps inventiveness so they don't undermine your sexual and sensual connection:

- **AIDS:** Both heterosexual and gay people can contract AIDS, no matter their age. In fact, some years ago, there was a scandal about some residents in nursing homes in Miami, Florida, testing positive for the disease — and few people were using condoms!

  People over 50 know that AIDS is a terrible disease. It was a scourge in the early 1980s and continued to be devastating until drug concoctions were developed to control it — although sadly, not cure it.

  Some lucky people now consider it a chronic disease rather than a deadly one, but the fact is, it still kills people. In any case, if you have a partner with the AIDS virus, you can easily catch it through oral, vaginal, or anal sex. Many people want their partner tested for the disease before having sex, and unless you do get tested together (and know you'll both be monogamous), health professionals recommend using condoms.

  For some people, of course, a partner with AIDS is a deal breaker, and they don't want to take the chance that it could be transmitted. But for others, it's not.

- **Bad backs:** Some people have trouble getting comfortable enough to have sex if they have serious back pain. This can be true also of hips and shoulders.

  Anti-inflammatory drugs like aspirin or commercial products like Aleve or Advil can sometimes make sex possible and painless.

- **Herpes:** Herpes, an incurable virus, made the rounds in the 1970s and on, and a great number of people have it — even if they don't know it. If you have an outbreak — a sore on your lips or on or near your genitals — it's easy to abstain until the outbreak is over. But there's evidence that the virus can be passed without an active outbreak, so people have to either use a condom or get tested together to see whether they have the herpes virus.

Oral herpes can be passed to genitals from oral sex, and genital herpes can be passed to the mouth. If either one of you has had herpes (or you don't know), you need to use barrier protection for oral, vaginal, or anal sex.

- **Human papillomavirus (HPV):** There's evidence that HPV is almost universal among people who have had more than one sex partner in their life (or their partner has had other sex partners) and they haven't always used a condom (and even then, it can be spread through skin contact). Most kinds of HPV aren't dangerous, but two of the many types do give genital warts (not attractive and hard to get rid of), and two types can even transmit cancer.

  Most people don't know whether they have HPV, so this is another thing to get tested for if you and your partner don't know your status or want the comfort of having scientific data to make sure. Condoms help here, but they can't completely protect you.

People with diseases like AIDS and herpes know that a very large number of people will reject them for that reason, so some lie about their condition. The vast majority are honest, but you can't take a chance on the exception. Until you know the character of someone very well, you need to assume that the barrier protection of condoms is warranted.

Taking Charge of Your Health and Your Date's Health

Many of the problems I talk about in this chapter can be moderated, and some of them can be entirely cured. You never know what phase a person is in unless you have a long discussion, but it's possible that together you may be able to make things better. This section outlines a few things that can make a difference.

Eating better

Many people who live alone stop eating healthy meals and, as a result, are undernourished or overweight — all because they eat the wrong things or eat out of boredom or loneliness. If you make a connection with someone, you can help her eat better, and of course she can do the same for you. A person who is fabulous but heavy or out of shape may be helped enormously by your partnership, and together you can correct a lot of conditions created by too much weight or the lack of the right healthy foods.

Lately, a lot of information points to the importance of eating tomatoes and tomato products for lower rates of prostate cancer. Reading nutrition newsletters like "Nutrition in Action" and the Harvard or Johns Hopkins or Mayo Clinic bulletins can keep both of you informed about such beneficial information regarding the right foods.

Taking supplements

Simple additions of supplements can make such a difference, but be sure to check with your doctor first. The addition of one or two baby aspirin a day can protect many people from heart attacks or a stroke. The addition of selenium and lycopene may support much great prostate health. Vitamin E increases the lubrication of the vagina (and applied, makes it more supple), vitamin C helps improve your immune system, vitamins C and D together increase bone health, and fish oil is now recommended for eyes and skin. There are even combinations of vitamins that are said to help delay macular degeneration in older people. The two of you can find out about what you need and then help each other stick to a regimen.

Not every credible medical source is pro-supplement. In fact, most of them will tell you to get these vitamins from food if you possibly can. With the exception of vitamins C and D, the Johns Hopkins newsletter "Health After 50" advises against over-supplementation and indicates that some supplementation using multivitamins increases risk of death for older women. It also says that vitamin E may increase the risk of prostate cancer for older men. And taking supplements when you're on multiple medications may cause dangerous interaction effects. Bottom line: The best bet is to talk to your healthcare provider about what's safe for you.

Exercising

The jury is in: Aerobic and weight-bearing exercise is necessary for good bone health, for rebuilding or keeping muscles, and for controlling or even getting rid of diabetes and other serious diseases and their consequences. You can support each other in exercising and create a great leap forward in overall health.

Getting second opinions

Sometimes people are intimidated (or, let's face it, just plain lazy) about getting more medical information about their problems. When there are two of you, you're more likely to do the detective work to find out what you need to know — and to double-check it. Some of the things your date has lived with or suffered from may actually have a better answer — but you may need to help your date find it.

Providing and receiving emotional support

The power of love is incredible. It can calm anxiety and depression or create the peace of mind and happiness that allows people to take care of themselves and stop destructive habits (like overdrinking and overeating). It's not a panacea; love can't transform every person into his best self, and if you think it can, you inherit a truckload of problems. But some people are actually different in a relationship than they are on their own.

Test the relationship as it deepens: Does the person you're dating use your support to take better care of his own health? Do you do the same? If so, it's a strength of the relationship and a sign to go forward. If the relationship sends you down unhealthy paths, then maybe backing away is a good idea. If you can't help someone take care of his most precious asset, his health, it doesn't bode well for the future.

Forging Ahead with Someone Who Has Physical Issues

It's an awesome responsibility to be a caregiver or to provide support for someone who comes with physical challenges. Sometimes people do it out of extraordinary love for a partner. Sometimes it's a total burden, and you take on the job because there's no one else who can or will.

It's understandable that you may not want to date someone with a progressive or disabling disease. But think of yourself, if you had some physical challenge. You'd still be worth knowing, still be fun to be with, and still be the same attractive person — just with some issues that require a sensitive and caring person.

Disabilities and physical challenges aren't the whole picture. The physically challenged person who is interesting, insightful, emotionally available, and honorable is worth far more than someone who is able-bodied but shallow and narcissistic. Think about it before you reject someone who comes with some physical issues. You never know when it will be your challenge, and perhaps having someone who has already faced these demons and conquered them is the best possible partner you can have.

You can find online dating and/or support sites for people with AIDS, herpes, HPV, diabetes, physical disabilities, and other conditions. Check out one of the following sites if you're looking for someone who will understand and accept you if you have one of these conditions:

- ✔ http://diabeticdate.com
- ✔ www.disabledsinglesdating.com
- ✔ http://hmates.com
- ✔ www.HSVsingles.com
- ✔ www.mpwh.net
- ✔ www.positivesingles.com

Chapter 15

Staying Connected with Your Friends While Dating

. . . .

In This Chapter

▶ Including your longtime friends in your dating life

▶ Understanding why your friends may reject your new partner

▶ Bringing your friends and your date together

. . . .

Y ou're not so different now from who you were in high school. Back then, you may have let some of your friendships wane while you focused all your attention on your boyfriend or girlfriend. The same thing can happen when you're dating later in life. When people fall in love, they tend to crave their lover's attention and time so much that they forget about the life they led before their relationship. When you fall in love, falling out of your routines is easy. But dropping your friends or starving them for time is never wise. Being mindful of the impact of a relationship on all aspects of your life is really important. In this chapter, I look at how your friends may affect your new relationship and how that relationship may affect your longtime friendships.

Protecting Your Friendships

Why do you need to maintain contact with your friends while dating? The people you know best are the people you've selected — and who have returned the favor — as your inner circle. This circle may be one or two people or many people spread across the country or the globe. But among them are people whom you've told secrets to, who have confided in you, and, most important, who have demonstrated their love and loyalty to you over the years.

That's not to say that you don't have awesome new friends. But while all friends are valuable, friends that you've had for many years have the long view of you, your choices, and your best interests. They may feel possessive, and they certainly want to be included in the news about your new dating life. Sometimes, their needs and reactions are hard to understand and even harder to attend to. That's why you need to think about how your dating life affects your deepest friendships — and how those reactions affect you.

Making sure your friends feel important

If you don't make your friends feel important, they may feel dumped by you while you're dating a lot or when you become especially interested in one person. They may start to get angry if they feel you've left them by the wayside. Friends know that love and sexual attraction are powerful feelings that deserve your attention, but they don't want to feel like they've just been placeholders when you had nothing better to do with your time. Here are three simple things you can do to reassure them they still matter — even if you're infatuated with and dedicating most of your time to someone you're dating.

- ✔ **Use media to keep them in the loop.** Texting, e-mailing, and social media are great ways to keep your friends close when you don't have a lot of face time available. You can tell them who you're seeing, where you've been going, and what you've been learning. They'll be flattered and feel like you're not forsaking them, even if they're seeing a whole lot less of you.

- ✔ **Share your feelings about your date.** If you're dating someone seriously, or even if you aren't, don't forsake the kind of conversation you used to have when you were checking in with your friends. Tell them a little bit about the person you're seeing and how that person makes you feel. Give them a sense of where your emotional life is so they understand if you're getting serious or if you're feeling down because you're not meeting anyone who truly moves you. Let them be supportive or happy for you, depending on what they know — and they won't know unless you take the time to tell them how you feel.

- ✔ **Ask their advice.** Part of being a friend is being helpful. If you've been a very private person up to now, changing your stripes would be hard and perhaps odd. But you may feel out of your depth and unable to read someone's character or you may need help interpreting what happened between you and a date at a specific moment. If so, don't deprive your friends of a chance to really be a friend and to participate by giving you advice. If they don't feel comfortable in that role, they'll let you know either directly or by changing the subject. But for many friends, just being asked a single question lets them know that you respect them and want their opinion.

Rewarding loyalty

Your closest friends have a history with you. They were there for you when your marriage or engagement broke up or when you lost your spouse to a terminal illness or accident. If people have given you a lot of support over the years and you want them to be there for you again, you can't shut them out now. Friends often don't ask for much in return, but they do ask for your friendship. How active your friendship is depends on what you've established up to now. You may have some close friends you only see every few years and other close friends you talk to every day — and their expectations will differ. You can reward friends with whom you interact a lot by making sure your date knows their names and the fact that they're special in your life. Make your date want to meet your closest friends and get together with them. If you can, plan ahead so that your date meets your closest friends before she meets the more peripheral people in your life.

Let your best friends know how anxious you are for them to meet your date so that they'll feel like you haven't forgotten them and that their opinion matters.

Using friends as a sounding board

You may never have needed friends as much as you need them now. Unless you're dating just for fun, you need the opinion of your friends about anyone you're really interested in. If you haven't dated in a long time, you may have trouble reading the people you're meeting, and you may need someone who has your back and can give you real insight into the person you're dating.

Here are several ways friends can be invaluable:

- **They can give you technical advice.** For example, they can tell you whether you're being too aggressive or too passive. It's hard to judge whether you're moving too fast or too slow if you haven't moved at all in a long time! If you tell your friends how things are proceeding, they can get a different vantage point than you have and see whether you're crowding this person or making the person feel like you're barely interested. They can provide insight about when to step up the amount of time you're seeing the person or even when things are ready to get sexual. They can give you the opposite advice, too: You may be suffocating a relationship by asking too much of it too soon. Friends can look at what's happening, analyze the dialogue you pass on, and give you valuable insight.

- **They can tell you if they see things in this person you should but don't.** Sometimes, people are so bedazzled by someone that they miss things that other people pick up right away. If you can't believe your luck, sometimes a friend can tell you that what you see as luck is really misfortune. You may find a person so attractive and sexy that you don't notice that he's bad with money and arrogant. Your friends may notice that he has never once asked them anything about themselves but that he tells story after story about his own successes and lifestyle. Perhaps you find it charming that your date is hapless about money or too intense to notice other people's contributions to the conversation, but if friend after friend tells you that you have a world-class narcissist on your hands, you might rethink your attachment, despite your head-over-heels attraction.

✔ **They can tell you whether you're making a mistake you've made before.** Your friends know you. The friends that have shared a lifetime with you know that you go for bad boys or wild girls, and that every single time you've done that, it has ended badly. When you say that education isn't everything, they can recall a past mate who had much less education than you and how you hated that he hadn't read the kind of books you had read or couldn't keep up with conversations around the dinner table. Your friends can remind you that the last time you dated someone 25 years younger, you were dumped and chastised for thinking you could hold the interest of someone the same age as your children. These aren't pleasant memories, and hearing about them again may sting, but if you've made similar mistakes over and over, you need a friend to at least try and dissuade you from making them again.

✔ **They can support you on things you know you should do but are having trouble actually doing.** If you're shy, friends who go to parties with you and introduce you to people are essential for dating success. Yes, you have plenty of things you know you should do (eat less, exercise more, find a good relationship, and so on), but sometimes, fears and habits stop you from doing what you know you want to do. A friend who says, "No excuses. I'm picking you up at 7, and we're going to that new singles group for people over 50" is of extraordinary value.

You may have a friend who's capable of being your dating guru but who may not think of it unless you ask him to take on this role. Most good friends are delighted to help you, but they may not consider doing so unless you make a direct request.

✔ **They can tell you things you don't want to hear but need to hear.** Onlookers may shake their heads about something you're doing but never say anything. Or some friends, when you ask them, "How do I look?" or "Do you think being overweight will bother anyone?" may not want to tell you what you need to hear because they don't want to hurt or anger you. That's understandable, but you need at least a few friends who tell you exactly what they think — even if it hurts — because they know what they need to tell you the truth about is getting in the way of achieving your goal. For example, suppose you have bad breath but you've never noticed it. Somebody has to tell you or you're going to offend every date you have. A friend may just bring over some breath spray and say, "Hey, use this to be more appealing," and you may be embarrassed, but you should really be grateful that someone cares enough about your future to let you know you have a problem and also how to fix it.

Your friend's honesty gets much trickier, though, if what he says concerns your date and not yourself. It takes a brave friend to tell you that he thinks someone you're infatuated with is wrong for you. Prize that person's honesty, even if you decide to disagree with him and proceed with the relationship.

Considering the Truth and Value of Friends' Opinions of Your Partner

Though most of your friends will do their best to give you honest and supportive feedback about the person you're dating, not all friends give advice worth listening to, and some friends start to project their needs and values on you in ways that are inappropriate for who you are. Furthermore, friends differ on their opinions, and you may need a variety of opinions to help you decide what to do. (If everyone you know well has the exact same opinion about your date, that ought to tell you something!) The tricky part happens when you're ambivalent yourself and your friends have conflicting advice. The following sections explore various reasons why your friends may not accept your new partner and what you can do about it.

Exploring valid reasons why your friends may reject your date

No one likes to tell a friend discouraging words about a romance the friend is excited about. But good friends have to tell you what they think if they believe they see something that you don't but that you need to know. This could irk or anger you, but there are good reasons a friend might have to intercede:

✓ **They don't like the way this person treats you.** You may be so infatuated that you don't notice that your date addresses you in a condescending tone, lectures you like you're a teenager, or picks at what you're wearing or what you say. You may miss these things or write them off as the behavior of a strong personality, but your friends aren't missing anything. Your friends love you, and the last thing they want to see is you being treated as if you aren't valuable. They want to hear your date rave about you or act protectively or admiringly. If they believe that your date isn't treating you well, they're going to say something — and you should listen.

✔ **They think you don't act like yourself around this person.** You've been around for a while, and your friends have gotten used to how you act. In fact, they like your sense of humor or your strong presentation of your opinions. If they notice that you're keeping your opinions to yourself or you're walking on eggshells, they're not going to be supportive of your relationship, and they're likely to say that "You're not the same person when you're with Maury." This is really a wake-up call that you need, because what you may see as just a relationship accommodation, your friends may see as a brain transplant.

✔ **They see signs that make them think your date is interested in other people.** Does your date's eye rove so much that other people notice? Does your date flirt with your friends? If either of these is true, your stalwart friends are going to feel protective and not amused by too much attention from your date. Of course, your friend telling you that your date was coming on to her is embarrassing, but if this friend is generally believable, you should take her observation under serious advisement. A date shouldn't make your friends uncomfortable and should make you feel that you — and no one else — are the center of his world, at least while he's with you.

Any date who's really flirtatious with your friends, even if that date has no intentions of becoming sexual or dating anyone but you, is an insensitive person at best. You should never have to worry about a date coming on to someone while he's with you.

✔ **They're good psychologists; they see some character flaw and let you know it.** Sometimes your friends have a conversation with your date that's very different from the ones you have, or they have a different perception because they get new information.

For example, suppose your friends have a conversation with your date and find out that she checks out the credit rating of everybody she sees more than a few times. Maybe your friends find out, as you did, that your date has had several marriages but that she feels utterly blameless about each situation. So your friends may get information in the discussion that leads them to a different conclusion than you have. If they feel your date always blows up relationships, is overly interested in the financial position of the people she's been involved with, or doesn't take any personal responsibility for commitments that didn't work out, they're going to report back to you. You may disagree, but these insights can make you think twice when you should think twice.

✔ **They see some major differences between you and your date that you're disregarding.** When you're infatuated, it's easy to dismiss things that you can't believe you dismissed when they come back and bite you later. Your friends may think your date is swell but notice that she's highly orthodox about her religion, and you've always been casual, to say the least, about yours. Or they may notice that your date believes that women and men have different biological and psychological roles to play in all aspects of a couple's life, and your whole philosophy is about men and women sharing roles. You know these facts, but you dismiss them because you just think your date is a wonderful, exciting, sexy person. But your friends are looking down the road and figuring that you really don't want to go to church three times a week or that you'll ultimately rebel if only one person has veto power in the relationship. Friends who have these insights may have to throw some cold water on hot relationships. That may be unwanted — but very much needed.

Recognizing unworthy reasons why your friends may reject your date

Not all advice from friends comes from good, caring sentiments, nor is all advice wise or even close to on-target. It's important to know some of the conditions that make it smart to disregard a friend's advice:

What it looks like when someone changes character for a date

Sarah is a top-flight manager in a headhunter firm. She's confident, cheery, funny, and talkative. She considers herself a feminist. But when she had a dinner party to introduce her friends to Martin, they were shocked. Sarah kept turning the conversation over to Martin, hardly talking herself. She waited on him, and he never rose to help her with anything. She bragged about all his accomplishments but talked about none of her own. When, near the end of the dinner, she finally told a funny story of an odd job candidate she had interviewed, her friends thought it was delightful, but Martin hissed at her, loud enough for everyone to hear, "Do you always have to be the center of attention?" They were appalled, and she was embarrassed. But the next day, when she called up all her friends to find out how they liked Martin, she seemed to have glossed over that moment. They all told her they thought she wasn't herself that night. She hadn't noticed, until they all gave the same opinion. Then she realized how shut down her normal personality was in this relationship.

✔ **They really want you all to themselves.** This is probably the number one reason that friends get anxious and upset when you start dating. Suddenly, you're busy, and they have a lot less time with you. More than that, you were always available at a moment's notice, you were an easy friend to travel with, and you were a frequent guest at the family dinner table. You were around, and now you're not. Worse yet, someone else is getting all your news, confidences, and phone calls. They feel the loss keenly; you had become part of the fabric and pace of their lives. Rationally, they know that dating is good for you, but emotionally, they resent the loss of your time and investment in their lives. If you don't make some time for them, they may have a tough time accepting your date because they feel resentment at having you "taken away" from them. Some of their demands are unreasonable, and you have to tell them that you need to take that time for love. But you can also soften their feelings of injury by making sure you give them some time so they don't feel forsaken. (The next section recommends ways to nourish your friendships while you're dating.)

✔ **They have different values than you do, and they don't respect yours.** You may think that it's time to change your life and that you've found the perfect person to do it with, but your friends may not feel the same way. If you meet someone and decide to move to a new town, start a new hobby, or stop working, that change may disrupt your friends' access to you or challenge their values — some of which you may not have shared in the first place. If you have friends who believe that work is the center of life, and you now plan to stop working, that challenges their sense of how people should live. If you find someone to love who is disabled, and your friends think that you'll end up being a caregiver and consider that demeaning rather than ennobling, they'll tell you not to do it. If you fall in love with someone whose biggest hobby is golf, and you decide to learn the game after a lifetime of making fun of golfers, your friends are going to wonder what happened to you and tell you to come to your senses. What you have to remember, however, is that it's your life, and you're more than old enough to make decisions, even if they're very different from ones you may have made even a short time ago.

Sometimes friends think they're doing you a favor by stopping you from changing your life. Remind them that it's your life, not theirs. The good news is that they'll make you think, but don't automatically let their fears become your fears.

✔ **They're still attached to your previous partner.** Your deceased wife may have been the most wonderful person in the world, and everyone who knew her loved her. And that attachment may make it very hard for your friends to accept any new person in your life. They may also expect you to pick a replica of your past partner, someone who can step into your new life without missing a beat. But perhaps that's not who you're dating, and your friends just can't accept the fact that you may now be seeing someone of a different race or background. Any deviation from your former life may make your friends wary of a newcomer, but they may also feel you're being disloyal by loving any new person or even including the person in your circle. They criticize everyone you introduce. If this is the case, you really can't use them as confidants and advisors; they're simply too biased against the idea of you falling in love again.

If you have close friends who were devoted to your ex or deceased spouse, meet one-on-one with them to ask for their support. Tell them that you understand their loyalty but that you need them to help ease your date into your world. Usually, an intimate talk like this makes the situation much better.

✔ **They're jealous or competitive people, and your date arouses these emotions.** Your date may be very attractive, accomplished, or have other traits that draw you to him. Sometimes friends are competitive people, and they immediately feel compelled to downgrade this person because they feel threatened. Of course, one person's great attributes shouldn't affect others this way, but they often do. If your date has a prestigious job, more money than most of your friends, or extremely successful kids, the knives can come out. If you know this about your friends, you have to discount what they say and disregard their lack of support for this relationship. In general, however, you can tell whether you're getting an honest assessment from friends by their past behavior. If they've been jealous or competitive in the past, their take on your date is probably tainted. If, however, they've always been emotionally generous and happy for the good things that have happened to you in your life, they probably can accept your date's fine qualities and give him a fair chance to show who he is in your life — and as an addition to your friendship circle.

Maintaining Your Friendships while Dating

Most people don't have enough time for everything they want to do. If you're retired, you may be able to draw on a wealth of open, unscheduled time. But if you're working, maintaining family relationships, and taking care of your home and health, time seems to evaporate. But your friends are one of your life supports; you lose them or let them get dusty at your peril. The good news is that maintaining these relationships, even while dating, isn't that hard if you consciously decide to do so and adopt one of the following strategies.

Scheduling some time, even if it's brief

Quality and quantity time tend to go together, but not always. A lot of friendships are refreshed with just an occasional hour spent getting each other up to date and sharing some feelings about how things are going. You don't need to have the same relationship you previously had with your friends; maybe Sunday night bowling is out for a while. But if it is, you have to find some alternative method of hanging out or sharing information. An hour for coffee at the end of the day, a quick sandwich at lunch, or a meeting at the gym is enough to keep most friendships pretty happy. If you make any time for your friends, even if it's only a little, they'll be reassured that you still value them. They'll be happier because they know that time is precious — and yet you're still making sure that you see them.

Apologizing if you've been neglectful

An apology goes a long way — for just about anything. If your new dating life has absorbed you, so be it. But at some point you'll notice that you haven't talked to or been with your friends in a long time. If you acknowledge that you've been neglectful and that you'll try and do better, most people will understand. If you say nothing, and a lot of time passes, some friends will get genuinely hurt, while others will just invest their time elsewhere.

Explaining your new relationship to your friends

You'll help both your friends and your date if your friends know something about your date before you introduce them. Some pointers:

- ✔ Tell your friends some of your date's background so they can think of suitable topics to bring up.

- ✔ Give them a sense of what your date means to you. If you're serious or could be serious about her, you want your friends to be very supportive of you and of her.

- ✔ Remind them not to grill your date. This isn't a job interview, and they're not the employers.

- ✔ Ask them not to do too much insider joking about things that happened before she was on the scene.

✔ Make sure they know that you don't welcome any references to your past romantic life or your ex husband or ex wife. There will be time enough for those stories, but they never belong in the beginning of a relationship.

If you're afraid of what your friends may say when they meet your date, give them strict instructions about exactly which stories are off-limits.

Bringing your date and your friends together

You may think it's too early to introduce a date to your friends, but if you're really worried about your friends' impact on your date, maybe you should reexamine your friendships. Of course, some friends are an acquired taste and may not be the first people your date should meet. But surely you have some friends who are trustworthy and fun whom you can easily go on a double date with. At the very least, let your best friends share a coffee or drink with your date, just to make them feel like they haven't lost touch with your life. Your date is likely to enjoy it, too; he wants to know more about who you are, and friends help flesh out the details.

Planning first meetings

This may be your date's first look at your life as you live it, as opposed to how you talk about it. Both literally and figuratively, your friends say a lot about who you are, so some planning is a good idea. Follow these steps:

1. **Introduce a few of your friends to your date, one at a time, for coffee.**

   Pick a quiet place, and don't let the coffee go on too long.

2. **If your friends suggest getting cocktails instead, stick with coffee.**

   People change how they act or what they say when alcohol is involved.

3. **After your date has met a few friends, you can try a double date or a dinner with friends.**

4. **Wait until you go through these steps before attempting a party.**

   Parties full of people who you know but who are strangers to your date aren't much fun for most dates who are newcomers to your inner circle.

In general, don't include previous partners in these gatherings, even if they're among your close friends. Including them allows for too much comparison and perhaps some jealousy or competitive feelings. Leave that for a lot later.

Deciding what to do if your date doesn't like some of your friends

Sometimes your date and your friends aren't a match. Maybe later on they'll find something to like about each other, but for whatever reason, they don't hit it off. This puts you in a tough position: You want to explore your relationship with your date, and you want to integrate her into your life, but she's offended or bored by, or just not drawn to, someone who's important to you.

You have to decide how important and permanent this situation is. I suggest that in the early stages of dating, you don't overestimate the importance of a lack of chemistry between your friends and your date. Not everyone is going to love who you love, or even like who you like. On the other hand, you can't ignore the situation. If this is an exception — that is, your date likes most of your friends but not every one of them, then it's no big problem. But if she has no interest in any of your best buddies, then this could be a big problem in the future. She'd want to minimize contact with the people she doesn't care for, and, at best, you'd have to see your friends without her. This isn't the worst problem in the world, but you need to consider these five questions:

- ✔ Is your date trying to isolate you?
- ✔ Is she flexible enough to get to know your friends better and like them more?
- ✔ Does her lack of interest in your friends portray some incompatibility between the two?
- ✔ Are your friends more like you than she is or vice versa?
- ✔ Are you willing to drop some friendships if need be?

You don't have to answer these questions right away. But if you get more deeply involved with your date, you'll have to figure out your answers, and those answers will dictate whether you want to get closer to or farther away from the person you're dating.

Meeting your date's friends

Meeting your date's friends is a big moment. Your date is saying something to you, and in general, it's all good. Your date is proud enough of his relationship with you to let his friends meet you. He's also proud enough of his friends that he wants you to meet them. And he's testing the waters: How well will you all get along? He may be head-over-heels taken with you, but he still wants his friends' opinions.

If you meet your date's friends and find that you don't like them very much, you need to handle the situation delicately. Those friends were there before you and represent a significant amount of history and emotional investment for your date. Here are some considerations that can help you decide how to act in this unwelcome situation:

- ✔ **Don't jump to conclusions.** Some people can be obnoxious on first meetings and be a lot better later on. They may have foot-in-mouth disease or be overly protective of their friend, but that doesn't mean they'll keep this up. If you like your date, and he has chosen them as special people in his life, they may offer something for you, too.

- ✔ **Don't let your date know how you really feel.** Control your emotions and opinions — first, because you may change them, and second, because you don't want your date to feel like he's in an either/or situation. If he has to choose who to drop, it may be you because you're the latecomer.

- ✔ **Don't let the friends know how you really feel.** Both you and your date's friends may know you're not each other's pick, but if you don't acknowledge the truth, changing how you feel about each other later may be easier. Furthermore, if you're in any way rude or dismissive to your date's friends, you may end the relationship, even if your date agrees with some of the criticisms. You really need to get along with your date's friends, even if they're not exactly the friends you'd pick for yourself.

One friend who you just don't jibe with is one thing, but if you don't like the majority of your date's friends, reevaluate the relationship. These are the people you'd be hanging with, at least some of the time. If you really don't like them, then you have to figure out why they're your date's closest buddies. They may be friends only because the friendships started as young children and stayed in place mostly because of proximity. But nonetheless, they're friends, and if you don't like them, you need to take that as a serious challenge to a continuing relationship.

Creating a new friendship circle together

I recommend that, as your new relationship progresses, a new joint friendship circle emerges — made up partly of your friends, partly of your date's friends, and, hopefully, partly of people you've met together. One of the things that builds a relationship is creating a group of people, or couples, that each person enjoys. This doesn't mean you dump everyone else, but it does mean that you see more of these people, perhaps even more than you did previously, because you both like and get along with them. This happens somewhat organically; you'll find that you and your date are particularly drawn to some of each other's friends more than others. It's a change that occurs when you create a continuing relationship with one special person.

Chapter 16

Unique Considerations for Gays and Lesbians

In This Chapter

▶ Figuring out where to meet potential dates and partners

▶ Exploring the top dating issues of older gay men and lesbians

▶ Talking about monogamy to see where you both stand

▶ Integrating your date into your friendship group and your family life

Much of the advice in this book is as appropriate for homosexual couples as it is for heterosexual couples — but not all of it is. That's why this chapter focuses on those unique issues people who want a same-sex partner are likely to have. It explains all the options you have for meeting potential same-sex dates, common dating concerns for both gays and lesbians, the importance of discussing monogamy, and the big "meet-the-friends-and-family" moment.

Meeting Potential Dates and Mates

Gone are the days when the only option for meeting a mate was in a dark bar in a bad neighborhood. Today there are online dating sites, affinity groups, political groups, singles clubs, upscale bars, events, and celebrations. Hooray for progress!

Online dating sites

Online dating is a great resource for anyone interested in a same-sex relationship, and the options seem to be growing and changing every week. Some online dating sites are for gay men or lesbians only, and others are the same-sex sections of heterosexual sites that also segment people according to hobbies (think www.chemistry.com, www.match.com, and www.perfectmatch.com).

You can meet according to sexual desires, intent (hookup, serious relationship, marriage), hobbies, and values — just like any other online dating site. Some sites, such as AARP's partnered site www.howaboutwe.com, even offer meet-ups and specifically encourage men and women 50-plus to use the site.

Gay organizations, events, and clubs

You now have innumerable gay organizations and volunteer possibilities to pick from, at least if you live in a large city. If you're politically conservative, there are the Log Cabin Republicans. If you're an activist, you may want to work for a group like Lambda, which is the legal arm of the gay movement. And if you're Catholic, you can join Dignity. You can find all kinds of outlets for gay fun, pride, and movement politics, and they offer wonderful possibilities for meeting someone who shares your values.

If you're not the joining kind, then go to celebrations and events that show support for the gay community, such as pride marches, Mardi Gras, opera fundraisers, and so on. Get out there and meet people; some of them are single and looking for you.

Mixed organizations and clubs

AARP has programs for gay people at the national and state level. Even if you just get involved as a volunteer, you have a chance of meeting someone interesting. California AARP has had an active program for gays and lesbians for quite a while and had a special meeting some years ago to help older gays and lesbians network and also to talk about issues of retirement, estate planning, and healthcare for same-sex couples. The AARP website (www.aarp.org) has special articles for gays and lesbians and a page in the "Home & Family" section where a number of community interactions are encouraged.

Some areas of the country are more conservative than others, but almost all professional organizations (such as the American Psychological Association and national nursing and social work groups) have specific sections for their gay and lesbian members. Likewise, some houses of worship openly welcome gay people. The Unitarian Church, in particular, is open and affirming, and many denominations now have gay or lesbian clergy. You can go to their events or volunteer and the chances of meeting other gays or lesbians are pretty good.

Same-sex bars

Some people still go to bars looking for a hookup, and there's always a chance that a hookup could turn into a longer-term relationship. Same-sex bars vary wildly in tone and type. Some are leather bars or grungy holes in the wall, but many are upscale and create an elegant ambience. Bars near gay-friendly resorts or second homes in places like Fire Island in New York can project a party rather than a predatory atmosphere. And gay-central parts of big cities, such as Manhattan's West Village or the Castro in San Francisco, offer places where gays and lesbians can meet potential mates.

Dating Concerns for Gay Men Over 50

For newly single gay men, reentering the marketplace can be daunting, especially because not everyone is completely open about his sexual orientation — a fact that can present real problems for coupling.

Research indicates that if one person isn't as open about his sexuality as the partner wants him to be, that lack of openness can cause problems and put the couple's happiness and longevity in jeopardy. Keeping your sexual orientation quiet is certainly understandable if you work in a job that's hostile to homosexuality, but when one partner is out and the other is not, the relationship is generally more difficult.

The following sections highlight other dating concerns that you may have at this point in your life.

Physical appearance

The ideal in the gay male community may be the Adonis-like figure with a six-pack chest, bulging muscles, and a handsome face suitable for the covers of gay magazines (or really, any men's magazine), but you don't have to live up to that pressure for so-called perfection. You _can_ find someone who will love you for you.

Consider Henry, who describes himself as "packing a few extra pounds." As a newly single gay male, Henry was intimidated because he had heard all the noise about how important it is to be trim and muscular, and he thought he'd be rejected by everyone. But that wasn't his experience. "I pretty quickly found Jim, and we fell in love while writing to each other. He was bald, like I am, about 20 pounds overweight, like I am, and very attractive. More than that, he was an old soul, and I immediately felt comfortable and loving with him. When we met, we were both in our early 50s, and I had no idea life could become so passionate, so romantic. Separating from my wife was hell, but my relationship with Jim was easy from the start — and it still is. We're having our tenth anniversary next week."

The other physical concern for gay males centers around the penis. There's a certain amount of lore among gay men about the importance of a large or good-looking penis. Among younger men, penis size is almost a fetish, in the same way that many straight men care about a woman's breast size. Some men will reject others as serious dating candidates if they don't feel that the sexual connection is great, and that may include everything from how big the penis is to preferences about where to put it. Whether you're a "top" or a "bottom" (or flexible about how you like to have sex) is important in some dating situations and not very important in others.

Penis size and looks are generally more of a concern if you're just interested in a hookup. If you're looking for interactions based more on love than lust, try visiting the gay sections of some of the mainstream dating sites such as www.chemistry.com, www.howaboutwe.com, www.match.com, www.perfectmatch.com, www.seniorpeoplemeet.com, and www.zoosk.com.

Age preferences

Though older gay men have plenty of dating opportunities, in the same way that many older heterosexual men express a preference for younger women, there's a well-known preference for younger partners in the gay male community at large, and sometimes age gaps are quite pronounced. This creates some angst among gay males who are older than 50, and it's especially upsetting if you haven't dated for a while because you've lost a longtime partner.

If you're worried about your "marketability" as an older man, don't be. The idea that all gay men want only younger partners is exaggerated. Many older gay men seek the wisdom and attractiveness of someone their own age, and quite a few young men fall in love with older men. Besides, no one stays looking like they're in their 20s or 30s forever. So even if getting older is tough on everyone's self-image, there's a sexy world out there. You just have to re-up and go online, where people who want an older partner say so, or do activities that put you in the company of people in your peer group.

Older gentleman seeks (way!) younger partner

If you're an older guy who really is looking for a younger partner, you'll be pleased to know that there are younger men looking for you. Websites such as www.daddyhunt.com and www.silverdaddies.com match younger men who are seeking older men. The cynical among you may think this is all about money, but that's not so. It just happens to be a preference for some younger men.

Consider 65-year-old Edward, newly single after ending his 30-year partnership. Early on in his newly single days, Edward attended a dinner party where he met Chip — a man 30 years his junior — who fell madly in love with him. Edward loved the attention and thought Chip was gorgeous and had a good heart. But Chip wasn't socially adept, entirely "out," or in the same league intellectually as Edward. They stayed together on and off for years, but ultimately, Edward couldn't see Chip as his life partner, and they finally broke up. Three months later, Edward met another man at a gay political event, and this time the age difference was less dramatic — just seven years between them. Edward says of his new partner, Gaston, "He's what I need. Just a little younger than me, but as much energy and curiosity as I have. He loves to travel, and he's very smart. I'm very proud of him, and I have to admit, I found Chip a bit embarrassing at times."

The bottom line: Age is only as big a deal as you make it. Plenty of men out there are looking for a serious partner, and though they may prefer to look at younger men, they want to fall in love with someone who's an age-mate.

HIV status

Having lived through the AIDS crisis, you may well have lost friends, lovers, or even a partner to the disease before the advent of the drug "cocktails" that have started to make AIDS a chronic disease rather than a terminal disease for most sufferers (in developed nations, anyway). You're therefore more conscious of the extreme threat of AIDS and less likely than younger men to think it's just another controllable virus.

For you, it's almost inevitable that your first discussions with an attractive man will involve divulging your HIV status and asking about his. Not everyone will divulge the truth, but most (not all) HIV-positive men at least want to use a condom. If either of you has HIV, having safer sex together and preserving your health and the health of your partner becomes the priority, which means you need to use condoms no matter what. It's also worth discussing which acts you can do safely so that both passion and health are uncompromised.

If you're the one who's HIV-positive, don't fear that you'll be an outcast. Many men are sympathetic and feel safe engaging only in sex acts that aren't dangerous. If you can't face a possible rejection for being HIV-positive, however, go to one of the Internet sites that help people with the same virus find one another.

Emotional availability

Gay men have more recreational sex than any other kinds of daters, but not everyone wants each date to be a hookup, and some men want to be upfront about their looking for a partner. You don't want to corner people about their intentions, but if you're looking for a serious partner, you're better off putting that statement out there sooner rather than later. Otherwise, you could easily be in a relationship with someone who really doesn't want it to progress to a living-together partnership, much less marriage. Chapter 11 has advice on discussing sexual philosophies.

Dating Concerns for Lesbians Over 50

Like women everywhere, lesbians face coming to terms with an aging body and appearance in a culture that venerates youth. Yet for many lesbians, being in the company of other women who are going through the same bodily changes takes some of the sting out of aging. If their friends are strongly united against cultural standards of slimness or anti-aging surgeries, lesbians can be more at ease with whatever their bodies look like.

Those friendship groups actually pose one of the main dating issues for lesbians. Unlike gay men, lesbians are likely to fall head over heels for someone within their circle of friends or someone who's the partner of a friend. Why? Because friendship and sexual attraction don't work independently for lesbians. In fact, even heterosexual women may fall in love with a lesbian or have a lesbian relationship because of the slope of love leading to sexual attraction.

If you find yourself falling in love with a friend's partner, bring it out in the open sooner rather than later. If someone has to break up to be with you, it's hard on the other friendships and certainly on the partner. If you notice these attractions early on, you may be able to stop the chemistry before it gets too powerful. If you don't want to avoid this situation, the two of you need to discuss how to save as many friends, and feelings, as possible.

The following sections highlight the other main dating concerns for lesbians over age 50.

Politics

If you're an activist in gay politics or women's studies or you're involved in some way in the political life of lesbians, finding someone with values similar to your own may be important. Some women are apolitical and just want to concentrate on the relationship; other women are used to being involved in women's equity or women's sexual rights and want a partner who shares that commitment and passion.

Getting into a political discussion early on when first meeting someone could get a fledgling relationship off to a rocky start unless you're both on the same page, meaning either involved or uninvolved in the political scene. If politics really are a big part of your life, however, it's probably best to get that issue on the table early on to see whether the two of you are compatible on such a fundamental point.

Sexualities and sex preferences

Lesbians face some interesting complications about sex and attraction to take into account. Some women are attracted to androgynous types, others to lipstick lesbians, while others like a highly differentiated vibe between them, so you have a butch looking for a femme and vice versa. It gets even more complicated when some women are kind of butch but actually transitioning into a more classically masculine approach to themselves and perhaps even to a sex change. This can happen later in life as well as earlier.

Talking about gender identity is pretty important if you want to see how comfortable you both are with each other's definition of the spectrum of masculine and feminine identity.

Sex is complicated too. Some lesbians want to jump into bed on a first date, but many more take sex cautiously. Additionally, sexual desire and sexual style vary greatly among lesbians, and it's important to find out, as you date, what your partner's sexual philosophy and history are. For example, does she desire sex only when love is present or is she up for a romp? Does she feel good about a wide variety of sexual acts or does she have rigid rules about what acts she will and won't do? You may have been in a relationship where sex was one of your strong points and assume that's the way it will be again, but there are no guarantees unless you find out relatively early on how important sex is to your date and how active a sex life she had in her previous relationship.

When one partner falls for a man

It's not unheard of for a lesbian to realize she has heterosexual interest, even after spending years in a loving, committed relationship.

June and Miki were together 22 years when June went back to school after their daughter Ginny entered college. June got involved in a study group and fell in love with one of her study partners. Miki would have been devastated if it had been another woman but was totally blindsided by the fact that it was a man. June had

never been involved with a man before, not even once. But as she put it, "I was vulnerable, more vulnerable than I admitted to myself. Miki and I had increasingly little in common, and Carl and I were intellectually so well matched, it just drew me in further and further. And when it got sexual I knew I had to tell Miki that we were over. It was so hard, not just because I hated to hurt Miki but also because so many friends thought I was doing this because I had a screwed-up identity."

A significant percentage of lesbians have been in rather sexless relationships and now feel that sex isn't that important. That's fine if you're not too interested in sex either. But if it's really important to you, make sure you're with someone who has a big sexual appetite and has had one throughout her life. If you want to make sure your date is enthusiastic about sex, check out her bedroom. If she has a lot of sex toys in her bedroom, her sexual appetite probably matches yours.

Commitment

The commitment issue has two sides: Sometimes a too-quick commitment is the problem, and other times a too-slow commitment is the cause of relationship troubles.

Sometimes in lesbian relationships the partners get in too deep, too fast thanks to grand romantic gestures that occur early on, such as thoughtful gifts, special dinners, or marvelous getaways. When this happens and the two people aren't on the same page, one of them may start to feel crowded and get squeamish about the relationship. Most lesbians have read about the dreaded lesbian "fusion," where people get so close that their sense of a separate identity gets threatened, so you want to avoid that if you can.

If you're not someone who likes committing quickly to a partner, make it clear that you need some space if the relationship is to thrive. On the flip side, if you're the person who's causing the claustrophobia, find a way to get busier elsewhere so you can let the relationship develop at a more mutually satisfying pace.

Occasionally, a relationship can develop too slowly for one partner's tastes. Often, though, this delay has nothing to do with how attracted or interested the other person is. Here are a few of the complications that can slow down a budding lesbian relationship:

- **Children:** Research indicates that biological lesbian mothers protect their primacy in their child's life and don't want to share their child early in the game. This is even true when some serious pairing has occurred. If you're dating a mother, you need to give her the time and emotional and physical space to parent as she sees fit. Don't push for a role with the kids or get too cozy with the kids until she indicates that's what she wants.

    If you're the mother, and if the relationship turns quite serious and you really want to encourage the other woman, give her some access to your children. Doing so is certainly a sign that you have a significant interest in building something profound. But don't do so too quickly because that access will raise the level of intimacy radically, and you don't want to get in too deep too early, only to change your mind and disappoint your children if they've started to see your partner as their new parent or friend figure in the household.

    Above all, if children (or grandchildren) are involved, time isn't going to be predictable; it will be parsed out according to the children's needs. Dates have to understand the time and emotional energy that children exert on their mother — and therefore on a budding relationship.

- **Work:** A woman you meet at this time of life may be intensely dedicated to her job or getting ready to retire. If you're in sync with how much time you have available, that's great. But one reason for a person drawing away from a relationship is that she still needs the time for her job and the other person doesn't.

- **Past experience:** If a woman has come out of a relationship that lasted a long time or was difficult to extricate from, the idea of reattaching may be really difficult. Much of the desire to draw away (or at least not draw close right away) depends on the psychological effects of the last relationship.

If you're in love with someone who has one or more of these complications, you can't push too hard for more time — at least not in the beginning. Your best strategy is to be understanding and to see how you can support your lover's needs and still have time together. That may mean spending more time with the kids as a couple or helping her with errands that involve the kids so that she has more free time. Likewise, being supportive of each other's work may just mean sharing time together while one person finishes up a task or meeting quite late, after one person has had time to catch up on things that have to be done right away.

Of course, your patience may wane if you really aren't getting enough time or affection. If you have a partner who has been scarred by a previous relationship and that's making it extremely difficult for her to connect to you in a meaningful, open, and vulnerable way, you may want to suggest going to a counselor together to get some help to develop the relationship.

Who pays for what

Money can be an issue among lesbians who are dating. Who should pay for what isn't exactly clear, but it's usually understood that if neither partner gallantly offers to pay, you'll split everything right down the middle.

Sometimes a woman who likes to cook will offer dinner, which is fine, but the right etiquette is to respond in kind, or, if you don't cook, to take your date out to dinner. There seems to be a high expectation of financial participation and equity among lesbians, so if you don't participate financially in some way, it's likely to be a problem.

Straight and bisexual women: Dates or disaster?

Sexual orientation labels can be very misleading. Queer theory says that every kind of sexuality is, by definition, individual, so sometimes, labels like *heterosexual* or *bisexual* don't do justice to a person's sexual complexity. A woman's behavior and experience can be different from her fantasies, people she loves, or even what kind of sexuality really excites her the most.

Furthermore, people change not only labels but also attachments over the course of life. Some women fall in love with the person, not the gender, and so even if their last relationship was with a man, their next one could be with a woman.

All that said, falling in love with someone who doesn't call herself a lesbian when you meet her is risky. She may be up for adventure but not a loving relationship. Or she may have more participation in the straight dating world than you imagine. Still, love is love, and if you fall in love with someone straight or bisexual, you already know that you could have some difficult times ahead.

Many women are honestly bisexual; that is, they don't have a clear preference by gender but rather choose by the person. Other women have been lesbian some part of their life and heterosexual at other times and have concluded that they're bisexual.

Moving from friendship to relationship

Sexual identity is complex and individuated, and you never know what may spark a relationship. Take this story, for example.

Jackie, who had been a lesbian and out since she was 15, met Margarita on a university committee. Jackie had admired Margarita's work but had never met her. When they did meet, Jackie was taken by Margarita's beauty and animation, but she knew Margarita was divorced and dating a man, so she didn't allow herself to get too interested.

But Margarita asked Jackie out for a drink after a meeting, and the two started a friendship. They began spending a lot of time together, and at one point, Jackie told Margarita she dreamed about her — and hoped that didn't offed her. Margarita said that the thought actually thrilled her. They ended up in bed that night and were together for the next seven years. Even though the relationship didn't go the distance, their eventual breakup was not about Margarita's bisexuality.

If you're interested in someone bisexual for more than a hookup, you want to ask her these kinds of questions:

- ✔ Have you ever loved a lesbian?
- ✔ Have you ever lived with a lesbian?
- ✔ What are you looking for in a woman?

Someone who is truly bisexual should have had a serious relationship with another woman, especially by age 50. Otherwise, she may simply be bi-curious, which is fine unless you're looking for a life partner and don't want to have to worry about someone who isn't ready to make a commitment to another woman. Still, if you take no risks, you may miss out on someone wonderful.

Discussing Monogamy Rather Than Assuming It

I can't say this strongly enough: Never presume monogamy in a homosexual relationship. Many women are into an open sexuality that may encompass several partners, and a large number of gay men have agreements about how to have some sexual freedom without ending or hurting the relationship. Research seems to indicate that the majority of gay men who have an agreement that has rules about how to include non-monogamous behavior in their relationship don't break up or get embittered over their open relationship. (The research does indicate, however, that absent that agreement, a relationship can suffer some ill effects if it includes sex outside the relationship.)

Deciding whether marriage is the ultimate goal

In 2013, the U.S. Supreme Court threw out the Defense of Marriage Act, a law that had previously made gay marriage unrecognized at the federal level. Gay marriage has also been gaining legitimacy in a significant number of states. So for the first time, gay men and lesbians looking for a serious relationship have to ask these questions: What is the goal of my dating? Do I want a relationship that would ultimately be a marriage?

If your state has yet to legalize gay marriage, these questions are still valid on a values level. Ask yourself whether you're undecided on marriage, open to it, or categorically opposed to it for personal or political reasons.

Knowing how you feel about marriage may guide your choice of whom to date. And if you change your mind down the road, that's your choice.

If you think you want to find someone who wants a sexually open relationship, you should give clues to your date in the beginning of the relationship. It's only fair to let a potential partner know who he's dealing with. In contrast, if you're monogamous and feel strongly about that, you should make that clear when you go online or start dating someone. Everyone is entitled to his own sexual style, but given the wide spectrum in gay dating (and somewhat less so among lesbians), it's kind and fair to give your dating partner a good sense of how sex and emotion are (or are not) linked for you. Generally, this takes a serious conversation in which one partner says what his preference is and whether it's just a preference or a total deal breaker.

Whether the preference is for or against monogamy is less important than that you both feel the same way about the issue.

Introducing Your Date to Friends and Family

Happily, most gay and lesbian relationships are public and proud these days, which makes dating easier and is even more important when you get a serious partner. Eventually, the question arises of when to introduce your date to friends and family.

Friends may be a much easier decision. You may have met in the same friendship circle or the two of you may go to places where friends are present and (hopefully) receptive.

Family is another thing entirely. Even if your family members wholeheart-edly accept your sexual orientation, they, like families everywhere, can be judgmental about the specific person you're involved with. It's probably wise not to introduce your date to your family (or vice versa) unless you have a pretty good idea that they'll like your date and your date will find your family endearing (or at least bearable). Too early of an introduction, such as after a few dates, may cause your family members to be unclear as to who this person is to you — a casual date, someone you're dating fairly seriously, or someone you're thinking about marrying. You'll be besieged by questions seeking clarification of your intent and future.

If you want to head those questions off at the pass, advise your family about the person you're bringing over. You can say something like, "Welcome him as your new brother, because that's what I hope he will be one day" or "This is a great guy, but he's not the one, so don't invite him on the family vacation."

Obviously, if your family members aren't completely comfortable with you being gay, you may want to skip introductions altogether.

People can make strong assumptions about you based on your family. If you think your family shows you in a flattering light, by all means introduce some-one you're interested in to your family early on in the relationship. If, however, your family or siblings are an "acquired taste" (translation: could be seen as off-putting to strangers), you may want to wait until your relationship is solid before you introduce them to your partner.

Part V
The Part of Tens

Self-esteem is at the core of your dating experience. Visit www.dummies.com/extras/datingafter50 for ten tips on how to feel sexier and build your self-confidence if it's a bit shaky.

In this part...

- ✔ No one ever said dating was easy! Prepare yourself for bumps in the road by getting the lowdown on common dating challenges and how to deal with them.

- ✔ Make sure the relationship you're forming is worthy of you. Learn signs that tell you flattering (or unflattering) things about the person you're seeing. Don't dismiss small things that can tell you a lot about a person.

- ✔ Consider the most important elements of character and test your date for mood, generosity of spirit, sexual chemistry, independence, and ability to trust and be trusted.

- ✔ Pick up great ideas for impressive dates — adventurous, luxurious, or just innovative — that will leave your partner awe-struck, grateful, and in love.

Chapter 17

Ten Common Dating Challenges to Overcome

In This Chapter

▶ Figuring out why you can't sustain relationships

▶ Dealing with manipulative or abusive dates

▶ Being on the same page with your date

The road to true love can be bumpy. Sometimes it's hard to figure out why things went sideways if the person you were interested in just disappears and you have no chance for feedback. Other times you're the one who wants out, but you want to do it in a nice way, and that isn't easy. The pitfalls are everywhere, and though most people are nice and will treat you politely, there are exceptions to the rule. This chapter reviews some of the more unpleasant situations you may face and offers suggestions on how to interpret them, avoid them, handle them, or disregard them.

You Have a Great Online Presence, but No One Responds

There are several possible explanations for why your stellar online dating profile isn't prompting responses from potential dates, but the bottom line is that no matter how good your profile is, how attractive your picture is, and how exciting the people are that you contacted, if you don't get responses, you have to change everything.

It's impossible to know which part of your personal presentation isn't working, so you need to revise it all. It may be the picture, no matter how attractive your friend says it is. It may be the profile; perhaps it contains something that you thought was an unimportant humorous remark that's turning off everyone who sees it! Or it may be the way you approach people, like just giving a generic "I found you attractive and I'd like to meet you" rather than a thoughtful paragraph about why you think the two of you should meet.

You Have Many Coffees but No Second Dates

If you have no shortage of first meetings over coffee but your relationships end there, you may feel like quitting, but you shouldn't. Here are three places to look for clues:

- **Did you misrepresent yourself in a photo or profile?** Is your photo from five years ago, when you were 20 pounds lighter? Are you significantly older than you said you were? These misrepresentations set you up for the wrong person (your date was looking for someone else), and even if your date likes you, she doesn't like being lied to.

- **Did you say the wrong things?** Did you only talk but not listen? Did you just talk about downers? Do you come on too strong or too shy? Reenact your dates with a close friend and get her honest reactions — even if it's painful to hear. This is the best way to figure out what to change and stop sabotaging your chances to find someone.

- **Did you pick the wrong person?** Do you always pick the most attractive and accomplished person on the web? Guess what: Such people have a zillion choices, so the odds are against you. They can afford to make snap decisions, discard your profile, and forget about you. So look a little off the grid — quirky but cute, self-sufficient but not the CEO. Most important, go after the person who describes you when she says who she's looking for.

You Have Great Chemistry with Someone Who Doesn't Want to See You Again

You were smiling, flirting, and getting along like people who were totally into each other, and then he doesn't call or he writes you an "I'm sorry, you're very nice but you're not the one" e-mail. You're having a crisis of confidence:

Were you wrong about the signs and chemistry between you? What could have happened?

You weren't wrong: Usually people recognize chemistry when they experience it. But chemistry isn't everything; someone may be drawn to you and still not want to move forward with you. Here are some reasons you may have chemistry but no second date:

- ✔ The person is on a serious hunt for "the one." He doesn't think that's you, and he doesn't want to waste time, no matter how great you are.
- ✔ The person is still emotionally attached to someone else.
- ✔ The person is just charming. *Everyone* feels chemistry with him. He's used to the sexual connection, but he's actually very picky about who to get involved with.
- ✔ Some crisis intervenes, and the person is no longer in the mood for dating.

Don't take it personally; move on and don't worry about it. Look for a true connection.

Someone Shares Something Unflattering about You with Your Date

Some people are loose-lipped and nasty. They tell tales that should be left alone and forgotten, because if they surface, the stories can hurt your feelings. For example, say your friend happens to go out with someone whom you dated. And the person you dated says something unkind about you, such as, "Oh, I met her, she's too heavy for me," or, "I went out with her once, and she was a terrible kisser." If your friend passes this stuff on to you, it can be devastating.

There's a lot of gossip that people don't hear, so it doesn't hurt them. But it does go on. People can be cavalier behind a person's back and indulge in nasty gossip because they just feel like being critical that day or that moment. Many people don't really think about the potential effects of dissing someone; they're just getting some licks in for fun. They may not even really mean what they say or the level at which they say it. Don't take it too much to heart, and just remember that most people have been dissed at some time in their life.

A Date You Care about Lies about Something Major

When you're really interested in someone, it's easy to make excuses for his behavior because you don't want to believe bad things about someone you thought might be "the one."

Here are some examples of lies that may be understandable and therefore potentially forgivable:

- **Lying about age:** This is so understandable, particularly online. If the website's algorithm divides people into groups by age (and most do), it's understandable that some people who feel they look and act younger (or older) may put themselves in another category. It's not smart or brave, but it's understandable. I'd keep the person.

- **Lying about health:** As long as the person isn't dying, it seems reasonable to withhold tough information about one's health until the relationship looks like it's going to be important. Depending on how bad it is, I'd keep the person.

- **Lying about being single instead of separated:** This one is iffy, but sometimes the person really wants to be divorced and can't hurry it along. A difficult divorce may keep him pinned down for years. So, depending on the rest of the facts, I'd keep him.

Here are some examples of lies that should tell you to slow down — and maybe change tracks:

- **Lying about financial stability:** If someone has no money, has gone through bankruptcy, or has been in deep financial trouble, you need to know because it may affect you, big time. Furthermore, this isn't a time of your life when you can afford for someone to drag you down and ruin whatever nest egg or savings you have or your ability to help your children. Motivations for being with you may also be unclear — I'd say, in general, run. (The facts may be so hazy and complicated that you may never know what you're dealing with.)

- **Lying about addictions:** If someone has been clean and sober for many years, more power to him. He may make a great partner. But if you find out that he still has a problem, whether it's with alcohol, a sex addiction, or prescription or illegal drugs, get packing. If he couldn't handle his addiction before he met you, the chances of him conquering it afterward are slim. The fix here is to leave.

- **Lying about accomplishments, education, or the past in general:** A person is who he says he is or he isn't. If you start finding inconsistencies in his biography, he may be a totally invented person, and you deserve someone real. If you find out that he doesn't have the degree he said he had from the place he said he went or in the profession he said he studied, get on your pony and gallop out of town. You can come back for your clothes later.

A Date Acts like You're a Piece of Meat or a Meal Ticket

You have to stick up for yourself, maintain good boundaries, and either nip bad treatment in the bud or just leave the situation. By age 50 and beyond, you should have clear enough boundaries to know when to stay and when to go, but you may be a victim of "nice-itis" and try to work with someone who displays any of the following behaviors:

- Every second word is a sexual innuendo.
- She never saw a bill she'd pay for or help pay for.
- She wants to move into your place right away, without helping pay for anything.
- She's always late or she cancels at the last minute. She never calls to say she's held up.

Don't let someone stay over at your place too early in the relationship. If she's a fortune hunter or abusive in any way, it could be hard to get her out.

A Date Likes You but Still Wants Someone Younger

Let's face it: There are prejudices about age. Most people over 50 who are healthy and fit think they look and feel younger than their chronological age. And if you're a 70-year-old who looks 60, you certainly have an advantage in the over-50 dating world.

However, even if you look ten years younger, you're still the age you are. You have to fess up to it — and for your sake, fess up as soon as possible. It may be a buzz kill for the person you're seeing, but what's worse is to have to maintain a lie that's bound to be exposed.

This one has no easy fix. If your date meant that he wanted someone 15 years younger than you are, so be it. Sure, he may break the rule for someone with modeling good looks or for a billionaire, but that probably isn't you. Some great love matches have happened between people of disparate ages, but they're the exception, not the rule. If you like the odds on your side, stay within a reasonable age range of your dates.

You're not the only one who's fit and looks younger than you are. You can find someone your own age who climbs mountains or dances all night if that's what you're looking for.

A Date You Like Is Dating Someone Else You Know

It turns out you can know too much. If you're really interested in the person you're dating, it's painful to know that your friend is seeing her too. In a perfect dating world, your date would forget about the other person and only see you. You can insist on that, but it's a high-risk maneuver, and your date may stop seeing you as a result.

What you can do that's less precipitous is to put her other dating life out of your mind and concentrate on having a lot of fun together. Promise yourself that you won't talk about this with your friend, unless you want to endanger that friendship. You don't want to say anything that may, and probably will, get back to the person you're dating.

It may be hard on you, but there's always a chance when you start dating someone that she's dating someone else, even if you don't know about it. Unless this is a question about monogamy, it's best to ignore the rest of his dating life and just concentrate on what's happening between you. Putting pressure on someone rarely helps anything.

A Date Doesn't Want to Be Monogamous

If the person you're dating doesn't want to be monogamous and you do, you have some decisions to make: What health risks do you want to take? What emotional risks do you want to take? If monogamy is important to you, you have to bring it up when it becomes clear that the relationship is going to become sexual. If the thought of whether this relationship is going to be monogamous occurs to you after you've already had sex, ask whether your partner is currently having sex with anyone else. It's not a fun question, but you need to know the answer. If he's not, your follow-up question should be, "Are we going to be monogamous now?"

Many people who are dating steadily and plan to be monogamous get a health checkup together or in sequence to make sure they won't pass anything on or get any sexually transmitted disease from their new partner. But if one or both of you doesn't want to promise or practice monogamy and you're not on the same page on this issue, then you have to decide what you want to do.

For some people, it's a deal breaker — no monogamy, no relationship. Or no monogamy, no sex. Whether you're the one who wants freedom or the one who wants monogamy, there can be consequences going forward, unless you agree and are on the same time schedule. For example, some people agree to monogamy but not in the beginning of a relationship. Unless they're the monogamous type, wanting to explore only one relationship at a time, they may feel that it's presumptuous to put monogamy up as a precondition for continuing the relationship or having a sexual relationship when the relationship is just starting.

You may feel strongly about this issue and hold firm: No monogamy, no relationship. But some people are surprised what they'll put up with when they're really interested in someone. You have to decide what compromises you're willing to make.

A person may be very into you and not want to lose you but also not want to lose his sexual freedom. So he may lie. Use condoms, even if you both swear fidelity. It may be too early to know whether your date is totally trustworthy. Plus, even if he's monogamous now, he may still be carrying an STD from many years ago.

A Date Is Crazy about You, but You Don't Feel the Same

Think about how it feels when you're the person who is more in love, and the other person thinks you're just swell — but to a point. It's a difficult situation. People love who they love, and just because a date thinks of you as a friend doesn't automatically cool the flames of attraction and desire.

If you're the person who likes someone only as a friend, and she wants more, you have to be very firm. You can't leave any gray area, any glimmer of hope, because if you do, she'll find it and hold it like a precious jewel. You need to be utterly frank and say something like, "You've been a great addition to my life as a friend, and I hope I'm a great addition to your life. But I only think of you as a great friend, not a lover, and this isn't going to ever change. If this makes our friendship impossible, I'll be sad, but in all fairness, you need to know what my limits are."

This is hard, but it's the responsibility of the person who loves least not to lead on the person who loves most. It's actually kind to break the romantic illusion; otherwise, the other person is always hoping and unhappy.

Remember this advice when you're the person who wants more, too. It's not like in the movies when people look at their best friend and finally realize they're madly in love with the person. Friendships don't usually turn romantic or erotic unless both parties feel a tension from the start.

Chapter 18

Ten Signs of a Solid and Worthy Relationship

- -

In This Chapter

▶ Evaluating whether your relationship is on solid footing

▶ Heeding the warning signs of a potentially unworthy partnership

- -

*O*ne of the biggest worries new or reentering daters have is that they'll pick the wrong person to get involved with. This may not be an unwarranted concern. You may have been married to or in a committed relationship with someone who was very wrong for you, or perhaps other initial tries at dating have been disappointing or even disastrous. You may only see the best in people, or perhaps your hormones make decisions for you more often than your brain does. If someone is selfish or dishonest, hints about his real character start to surface. The important thing, however, is that you recognize them when they do.

But you're not just looking for evidence of fatal flaws. You're also looking at whether the person you're dating treats you the way you should be treated — with affection, respect, interest, and sensitivity. In simple terms, does this person have sound character and good partnership skills? To help you figure this out, this chapter presents ten major characteristics and cues to observe that will help you see who you're dealing with and what your relationship is really like. If your date fulfills the qualities on the following list, he's probably worthy of your time and your affection.

Your Date Is Always or Almost Always on Time

It seems like a small thing, but not being on time really says quite a bit about a person. Punctuality shows respect for you and your time. People who are almost always on time generally have their act together in a

A case of being too late, too often

Punctuality is important to most people. Consider Marcie, who was always late for dates. She had acquired the habit of showing up at least a half-hour late while she was married and living in Georgia. Her late husband complained, but she didn't think it had caused them many problems. She laughed it off when dates were irritated, saying people just had to expect "southern time." However, she was truly hurt when Kent, a man she was seeing for almost six months, told her that one of the reasons he was calling it quits was "her selfish disregard for his time and his plans." She thought her habitual lateness was just "a little thing" and that it was part of her "southern charm," but after the loss of Kent, she conceded that being on time might be more important than she had thought it was.

number of areas. Always or usually being late is often a sign of one of the following:

- ✔ **A disregard for others:** Their time is much more important than your time, and it may get worse as time goes on and they care less about pleasing you.

- ✔ **A feeling of being overwhelmed with life:** Some people are so overwhelmed that they can't prioritize, get organized, or accomplish the things that matter to them.

- ✔ **A deep neurosis:** Something continually distracts tardy people and stops them from accomplishing what they set out to do.

Of course, the degree of lateness matters. Giving someone 10 or 15 minutes leeway is fair; there are day-to-day complicating factors for almost everyone. But if your date is continually a half-hour or more late, take this issue seriously.

Your Date's Relationships with Family and Friends Are Warm and Intact

Sure, some people get a raw deal, and their family includes people to stay away from rather than embrace. Sadly, many people bear scars from a disastrous upbringing and damaged family. Be cautious about someone who doesn't talk to her siblings, parents, or any extended family. If she's cool and distant, take that as a warning, but if she's in tumultuous conflict, take that as a sign that you may be in that same kind of situation with her someday.

This is also true for friends. A person who's over 50 and has no close friends is kind of an odd duck. There's really no positive explanation for that. If the person has old, true friends, that's a good sign, but alas, it's not a definitive one. Even Bernie Madoff had longtime friends . . . whom he betrayed, along with everyone else. So the quality of your date's family relationships and close friendships is important to evaluate and take into account.

Your Date Tells You How Much You Mean to Him

You should feel adored. It may be too early to ask for love; indeed, be wary of someone who immediately says he loves you. People who do that tend to fall in love with being in love and fall out of love just as easily. A relationship that's progressing well, on the other hand, should be full of compliments, affection, and maybe a "I think I could love you," but with some caution on those words — especially if they come in the aftermath of a great day or great sex, where blissful feelings are elevated but not necessarily permanent.

You want to feel truly appreciated, and if you're not, this isn't a promising relationship. But if your date expresses too much adoration or professions of love too early on, then step back and think hard about whether the amount of affection you're getting is proportional to the time you've spent together and how well you know each other.

Your Date Notices When You're Unhappy and Wants to Help

Marriage is *for better or for worse*. No one wants a lot of the worse, but the agreement is that you're there for each other, even if one person gets sick, loses a job, or needs therapy.

If you're with someone who disappears when you're having a rough day or who can't handle you venting about your problems occasionally, you're with the wrong person. (Unless all you do is talk about the downsides of life and your own unhappy existence, in which case your date has a right to run.) It's important to have a partner who's compassionate. You have the right to expect a partner whom you can count on for support and comfort when you have a run of bad luck, screw something up, or face a difficult health situation. Perhaps you had an unsupportive partner in the past, and that's what you're used to in an intimate relationship. But you can break that cycle now and only invest in someone who has the capacity to love you in both the good and bad times.

Your Date Doesn't Get Jealous

Healthy, reasonable people don't tend to get jealous. They're secure in their relationship, and they don't wonder about where you are every second of the day. They don't jump to conclusions about your opposite-sex friendships, and they certainly don't forbid you to have them. If they do, you're dealing with an insecure person, and insecure people can get angry and even physically or verbally abusive when they think they may be losing the person they're with.

The remarks may start out in a joking manner, but a jealous person always ends up checking out where you've been, who you were with, and what you were doing. She may even ask questions to try and catch you in a lie. Later on, the behavior can get obsessive and often dangerous.

Most people attribute stalking behavior and jealous fits to males rather than females. Don't make this mistake. Though the statistics may be in favor of men (because they're more likely to do something violent), women can exhibit this kind of behavior as well — and also be dangerous.

Dangerous dating

Watch out for those jealous types! Consider this story: Billy never made promises of monogamy when he was dating. He dated two or three women at once because he hadn't been divorced for very long and really wanted to delay creating a committed relationship. He made this very clear to dates, and though many women opted out, some were willing to share him and happy to have the freedom to date other people. But Billy, against his better judgment, had a one-night stand with a woman he met through a friend, and this woman was furious when he said this wasn't going to be a monogamous — much less a committed — relationship. When

he broke it off with her, she would park her car in front of his apartment building, and one time, she even etched a long, deep scratch on his car doors. She called and harassed him on the phone for months and talked about contacting everyone they knew in common to tell them what a jerk he was. Ultimately, she quit her surveillance and calls, but Billy took a lesson from this experience. He was much more careful about getting immediately sexual with someone, and he took more time to vet partners for their values and mental stability. He did everything he could to reduce the likelihood of being with a jealous, possessive, and angry person.

Your Date Thinks of Ways to Please You

People want someone who loves them enough to think about how to make them happy. You want the guy who passes a flower shop and remembers that you love fresh-cut daffodils or the woman who knows you've been stressed and sets the bedroom with candles and a massage table. Even the little things, like squeezing your hand when you've just had a tough phone conversation with a child or boss, are important. You want the person who gets pleasure from your pleasure.

If your date is thoughtless now, the relationship is unlikely to get better. Why would you want to be with someone who doesn't have you in mind now and then? You need someone who adds to your life by being thoughtful and emotionally generous.

Your Date Has Good Boundaries and You Respect Them

Respect is the core foundation of all relationships. You can get angry with someone or disagree about something important and still stay very much in love. But love won't last if you don't respect your partner — and you won't respect a person who doesn't respect himself.

Having boundaries means that a person sticks up for himself when you cross lines and insult his adulthood, his dignity, his right to his own time, or the way he needs to be treated. No one should let you boss him around (and, of course, you don't want that kind of treatment, either) or allow demeaning or condescending conversation to be a part of the relationship. A good partner insists on being treated with respect and gives respect in return.

If your conversation or treatment of each other is less than respectful, the relationship is likely unworthy. If you think you have a good relationship but there are occasional ugly exchanges, a counselor may be able to help you learn new ways of treating each other before you irrevocably damage the relationship.

Your Date Has Active, Happy, Fulfilled Days

You're going to be spending a lot of time together, but you don't want it to be *too much* time. Even if you're the kind of person who wants to be with someone night and day, you want your date to have things to do, things she's interested in, and a happy disposition when she gets to do something she loves. You don't want to be totally responsible for someone else's happiness. She has to have the ability to entertain herself.

This is really important because a person who has no passions, serious hobbies, or curiosity may be pretty boring after the initial period of getting to know each other is over. This has nothing to do with whether the person is still working. It's not a job that makes people interesting; it's their ability to enjoy life, have something to talk about, and be generally enthusiastic about everyday things like going to a movie, watching or participating in a sport, or reading a good book. If your partner doesn't fit this description, you may be headed for trouble down the road.

Your Date Is Generally in a Good Mood

As my friend and colleague Dr. Lana Staheli says, "It takes two happy people to make one happy couple." Don't underestimate the importance of temperament and the ability to be happy. A good mood is contagious, and it creates a happy home.

Beware of partners with too much of a dark side. Everyone has bad days, of course, and everyone has events in life that are truly disappointing or depressing. But the important thing is to eventually put those sad feelings aside and be able to enjoy life. People want partners who help them do exactly that and who greet the day in a way that makes them happy to greet it too.

Find out whether your partner is on antidepressant medications. If he is and the meds have controlled his mood for a long time, continuing the relationship is probably worth the risk. But spend enough time with this person to make sure he's really okay when on medication.

Your Date Is Affectionate and Sexually Interested in You

Whether you're 50 or 80, affection and touching are critical for emotional and physical health. Sexuality and sensuality don't ever have to be in the past: You're capable of a lifelong attraction and sexual connection.

Be careful if your relationship is more fraternal than sexual. You need a person who helps nurture your sexual side and who likes to touch and kiss

A sexual connection is a good sign

Sure, compatibility and companionship are important when you're over 50, but that doesn't mean you don't want sex and affection! For example, Renata was worried about dating in her 60s, partially because she thought there would be pressure to get sexual, and she hadn't been sexual with anyone in quite a long time. Nonetheless, she decided to date again, and she met Oscar, a man who won her over with his gentlemanly manners and caring questions about her emotions and life issues. After a couple of months of going out together, Renata found that she was interested in a bit more than a goodnight kiss. But Oscar was making no moves in that direction. After about four months, Renata brought the matter up, and Oscar acted as if she'd lit a torch to his feet. He said he was an old-fashioned person and couldn't have an intimate relationship without the deepest of commitments. When Renata pressed him about what it would take to get to that point, he indicated that he didn't think they were right for each other, and the relationship ended that night. When Renata thought it over, she realized that he had avoided even holding hands or cuddling. After that, she was less afraid of too much sexual interest than none at all!

you. Sometimes people meet someone quite wonderful but the companionship quickly becomes sibling-like. If you're both pretty asexual and sex hasn't been important in a long time, well, it may work. But for the most part, people start to long for a physical connection if there isn't one in their relationship. This leaves the relationship vulnerable to another person or to bitterness and loneliness. You may be tempted to underestimate that sexual connection when you meet a great companion, but it's a compromise that gets harder, not easier, over time.

Chapter 19

Ten Over-the-Top Dates Designed to Impress

- -

In This Chapter

▶ Checking out some amazing views and scenery

▶ Arranging a special introduction or a uniquely memorable day

▶ Enjoying experiences you wouldn't normally have

- -

Sometimes you need to make a bigger impression than the average date provides. Maybe you have intense competition because your date is highly sought after, or perhaps you want to kick up the intensity of your relationship with a flourish. Or maybe you just have a fantasy date that you want to take because you think it will be another wonderful way to grow the relationship. Whatever your reasons for wanting a lavish, over-the-top date, the ideas in this chapter are so memorable that even if the relationship doesn't work out, your date will remember you forever. And you don't always need to spend a lot of money to do something truly impressive.

Take to the Skies

Few things are more romantic than observing the twinkling lights of the city as you fly overhead or chartering a helicopter or small sea plane to fly you to a secluded beach for a private picnic. Oddly enough, you can make both happen without spending a fortune, especially if you just need a plane for an hour or two. Most companies offering such services have sterling safety records, but do make sure they've been in business a long time and have strict standards for their pilots. You can also ask them for a list of their most romantic offerings.

Make sure your date isn't freaked out by flying in a small plane. Ask subtle questions to ensure that your special adventure is exciting and not torture.

Go Behind the Scenes at a Local Attraction

Going behind the scenes at a public place always feels special. Most zoos, ballet companies, opera companies, and marine shows offer that possibility. Call them up and find out what kinds of behind-the-scenes opportunities are available. Tours may be available only on special nights of the year — or v places may, for a price, be able to provide a tour just for you.

Occasionally, public entertainment venues offer behind-the-scenes opportunities (such as swimming with dolphins or watching dress rehearsals) at fund-raising auctions. Be prepared to pay a big chunk of change for your one-of-a-kind experience, though, especially if your bid can be considered tax-deductible as a donation.

Arrange a Romantic Serenade

Serenading a date is old-fashioned but oh-so-romantic. Get a guy with a guitar or maybe a whole mariachi band! Call your date when you know she will be in the right place for the serenade, or be with your date and give the signal to the band to start playing when the moment is right. You can make the music romantic or a replay of some of the great hits you both grew up on or enjoyed together. (Extra points if you can find a local band or musician that the two of you have gone to see together and really liked.) Just don't let the performance go on too long. It's hard to stay in rapt attention for more than three or four songs.

If you don't have the money to hire an established local artist or band, go to your local junior college, college, or university and talk to the head of the music program for a student recommendation. If you have an arts and music high school in your town, you may find someone great there too.

Introduce Your Date to His Hero

If you can introduce the person you're dating to someone he has always been in awe of, you'll be your date's hero too. Here are some ideas about people who may bring you some reflected glory:

- **A famous person at a local university:** Often, such people are happy to meet an admirer if you can schedule dropping by at a convenient time. If that's hard, find out when the person is giving a lecture and see whether he can spend 15 minutes afterward with you and your date.

✔ **A famous rocker, actor, or celebrity golfer:** If you let the celebrity or the celebrity's manager know that you're trying to impress the person you hope to be your one and only, you just may stir the celebrity's heart and get a few minutes and maybe an autograph.

✔ **A famous politician:** Politicians are likely to agree to meet you, even a senator or someone of that stature. You may have to go to the politician's office and be patted down for security, but if you're constituents, a visit, especially for such a romantic purpose, can often be arranged (no promises on the President, though).

✔ **A person in your date's profession whom he has always wanted to meet:** Find out who the person is and call him up. Usually there's a way to get a least a few moments with this person. Or, amazing but true, you could invite him to dinner, telling him of your admiration and need to wow your date, and he may just accommodate you.

How can you find out who your date has long dreamt of meeting? Play a game with your date about the five most interesting people he'd like to meet in his city, in his profession, in the entertainment world, and in the political sphere. That list should give you plenty to work with!

Experience Nature Together

Experiencing the sheer majesty of nature may put your date in a romantic mood. Here are a few ideas:

✔ **Head to the slopes.** The vistas at the top of mountains can be breathtaking. Ride a ski lift up to check them out in the winter or summer at the end of the day, when you're likely to have the slope more to yourself. (Save this idea for non-skiers — or at least someone who doesn't go skiing all the time — to maximize the wow factor.)

✔ **Journey underwater.** Go scuba diving or snorkeling to see the riot of color found below the waves. If your date isn't a strong swimmer, many marinas in resort areas now have small submarines that can show sea life at a whole new level. Just make sure your amour isn't claustrophobic.

✔ **Explore a national treasure.** Almost all the national parks have amazing views, but Redwood National Park, Arches National Park, and Monument Valley are particularly impressive.

✔ **Rent a cabin on a rugged coast.** Enjoy a crackling fire while the waves crash around you.

The more dramatic Mother Nature is, the more memorable your getaway will be. But don't go somewhere that requires a survivor mentality. Antarctica is gorgeous, but not everyone wants to handle that kind of weather or rough seas. Plenty of monumental places don't cause sea sickness, hypothermia, or heat exhaustion.

Create Something with Each Other

Here are some lower-cost ideas that use your time and talent more than your wallet:

- ✔ **Compile a book of love poems.** Browse the Internet or library for poems that mean something to both of you, and self-publish two copies so you each have one.

- ✔ **Design a picture book.** You can include pictures of places you've been together or a wish list of places you'd both like to go in the future.

  Websites such as www.shutterfly.com and www.snapfish.com allow you to create high-quality, low-cost photo books.

- ✔ **Take an art class.** Blow glass, create a woodcut, learn how to throw pots, or try your hand at painting oils or watercolors and creating your own set of cards from the pictures you create (or learning how to frame them).

- ✔ **Spend a day revitalizing something together.** Whether you're taming messy landscaping or replanting flowerpots in wonderful arrangements, your efforts — and the fact that you're doing them together — will mean a lot.

Rent a Planetarium and Enjoy the Stars

Okay, maybe you don't have to rent the whole planetarium (although it's a very nice gesture), but doing something in the dark, with the stars, is almost always super romantic. Even if you're not near a planetarium, a nearby university may offer star tours by astronomers or as part of a continuing education class on astronomy. If you search a bit, you'll find that a romantic couple of hours under the stars is available. You can combine it with a chilled bottle of champagne and hors d'oeuvres before, during, or after to create an amazing mood.

Plan a Weekend Getaway with Your Date's Best Friends

If you've met a lot of your date's good friends or created a group of people you enjoy together, organize a weekend with a number of them. You can find a house near the water or with a great view and plan a getaway weekend with friends that would be a lot of fun. Everyone can chip in, so it doesn't have to be expensive. Do plan carefully though, so that everyone is on the same page about group activities and is guaranteed to enjoy them. Have good alternatives for when the group is engaged in beach walking, watching classic movies, mushroom hunting, or what have you. And if your plans involve being outdoors, make sure you have rainy day plans, too, in case you wind up with bad weather.

Be sure to pick people whom your date likes a lot. Even though it's just a weekend, it can be way too long unless you have people who are easy and fun to be with. Your goal here is to impress your date with the warm and wonderful weekend you've created and also to surround your date with a group that makes you feel even more like a couple with a shared lifestyle.

Spend a Day Doing Something Your Date Loves

Doing something that you know your date loves (and feels is a luxurious treat) will score you a lot of points. Experiencing the activity together makes it even better. For example, a half day at a spa where you get individually pampered but also have couple time (during a two-person massage, perhaps) can relax you and put you in a sensual mood. If you're both golf fanatics, hire a pro to walk the course with you. Or go on a day outing to an outdoor concert and make it special by getting a picnic lunch catered or by ending with an overnight at a nearby romantic bed and breakfast.

Sometimes, just adding a few touches to a fun day can make the day an especially memorable one.

Dine Together at a "Chef's Table"

If the person you're trying to impress is a foodie, you can easily create a particularly memorable event by going to a restaurant with a great chef and sitting at the chef's table. This is usually a separate table you pay more for, often in the kitchen, where you dine off of a special menu and have up-close-and-personal interaction with a talented chef. Sometimes, the chef's table has other people at it; you can have fun interacting with others or see whether the restaurant will reserve a table just for you.

Index

• G •

About the Author

Pepper Schwartz is professor of sociology at the University of Washington in Seattle, Washington, and the AARP sex and relationship ambassador. She's the past president of the Society for the Scientific Study of Sexuality and the Pacific Sociological Association, and she's the chairperson of the advisory board for the PhD program in sexualities at the California Institute for Integral Studies. She created the matching algorithm for Perfectmatch. com, is a consultant to HisandHersvacations.com (and its subsidiaries for same-sex couples), is a fellow at the International Academy of Sex Research, and is on the board of the Council on Contemporary Families. She has received awards from the American Sociological Association for public understanding of sociology and for excellence in the study of sexualities. Among her other awards are a Distinguished Alumni award from Washington University in St. Louis and recognition in education from Mortar Board and the International Women's Forum. Pepper was also on the graduate alumni council for Yale University.

Author of 20 books and more than 50 academic articles, she co-authored (with Chrisanna Northrop and James Witte) the *New York Times* bestselling book, *The Normal Bar: The Surprising Secrets of Happy Couples and What They Reveal about Creating a New Normal in Your Relationship* (Harmony). Her recent books include *Prime: Adventures and Advice on Sex, Love, and the Sensual Years* (William Morrow), *Getaway Guide to the Great Sex Weekend* (with Janet Lever, published by Worldwide Romance Publications), and *Finding Your Perfect Match* (Perigee Trade). Pepper lives on a horse ranch outside of Seattle, Washington, with four dogs, many horses, and various elk, deer, coyotes, and eagles.

Dedication

To the supportive, smart, and handsome Fred Kaseburg, who culminated my midlife reentry into dating life with a marvelous marriage proposal, and to my two extraordinary children, Cooper and Ryder, who make me continuously grateful for their friendship and fine character.

Author's Acknowledgments

I am very grateful to the AARP and especially Jodi Lipson, who created the partnership between me, the AARP, and the *For Dummies* series that resulted in this book. Of the many people at the AARP who have supported me in so many ways, I want to mention in particular Wade Osborne, Beth Domingo, Mary Hickey, Patti Shea, Myrna Blyth, Karen Horrigan, Heidi Sternheim, Allan Fallow, and Barry Spencer. Also, thanks to Larry Gannon and Nicole Shea for video production on dating, romance, and relationship issues. Outside of the AARP, Eli Coleman gave me advice on gay dating sites, and Duane Dahl gave me an invaluable introduction to the online dating industry, first at Kiss.com and then at Perfectmatch.com. And the people at Wiley have been great. I certainly needed a lot of help understanding the *For Dummies* system (we are all dummies in the beginning!). These people include Erin Calligan Mooney, Elizabeth Rea, and Todd Lothery.

Publisher's Acknowledgments

Acquisitions Editor: Erin Calligan Mooney

Project Editor: Elizabeth Rea

Copy Editor: Todd Lothery

Technical Editor: Danielle Davis, MSN, ANP-BC

Project Coordinator: Erin Zeltner

Cover Image: © iStockphoto.com/aldomurillo